Observing the Erotic Imagination

OBSERVING THE
EROTIC
IMAGINATION

Robert J. Stoller, M.D.

Yale University Press
New Haven and London

Designed by Nancy Ovedovitz and set in VIP Palatino type by Huron Valley Graphics, Inc. Printed in the United States of America by Vail-Ballou Press, Binghamton, New York.

Library of Congress Cataloging in Publication Data

Stoller, Robert J.
　Observing the erotic imagination.
　Bibliography: p. 223
　Includes index.
　1. Sexual fantasies. 2. Sexual deviation. 3. Sexual excitement. 4. Sex differences (Psychology) I. Title. [DNLM: 1. Fantasy. 2. Identification (Psychology) 3. Paraphilias. 4. Sex Behavior. WM 610 S875o]
BF692.S785　1985　　　155.3′1　　　84-29923
ISBN 0-300-03424-5 (cloth)
　　　0-300-05473-4 (pbk.)

The paper in this book meets the guidelines for permanence and durability of the Committee on Production Guidelines for Book Longevity of the Council on Library Resources.

10　　9　　8　　7　　6　　5　　4

CONTENTS

PREFACE

This book is part of an ongoing project on gender identity—masculinity and femininity—and the related subject, erotic excitement. My interest in the first years of this work focused on gender identity, which led to the study of perversions. In time, that work brought me to try to understand the dynamics of anyone's erotic excitement, primarily its nonsomatic roots.

In the daydreams of perverse people, especially those stories concretized in pornography, I can make out the construction of a script, the principal purpose of which is to undo childhood traumas, conflicts, and frustrations by converting these earlier painful experiences to present (fantasized) triumphs. To build these daydreams, the patients also make use of mystery, secrets, risk running, revenge, and dehumanizing (fetishizing) of their objects. In all these qualities, hatred is a manifest or latent presence. But having found these factors in perversions and their pornographies, I realized that the same dynamics were present in the pornographies of everyday life and in the erotic excitement of the nonperverse patients I had treated for years. So I was now studying normative erotic excitement. I found that what makes excitement out of boredom for most people is the introducing of hostility into the fantasy.

What is the relationship between excitement in people who are obviously perverse and in those who are not? The hypotheses for answering this question are (1) the overall structure of erotic excitement—*not the content or the behavior*—is similar in most everyone; (2) erotic excitement, due more to distortion of affection and tenderness than to direct expression, often flags without scripts in which one wishes—consciously or unconsciously—to harm, *by means of humiliation,* one's erotic objects;

and (3) it is not these dynamics that differentiate perversions from the lesser perversions—those states that others call normal or normative behavior—but whether the erotic excitement brings one toward or away from sustained intimacy with another person. In time, a study of hostility in erotism could lead to a new phase, the search for the circumstances in which affection, tenderness, and other nonhostile components of love participate in, perhaps even dominate, the excitement. The difficulty will be to find suitable people to study.

I see the particular moment of erotic excitement as a tangled, compacted mass—a microdot—of scripts made up from impulses, desires, defenses, falsifications, truths avoided, and memories of past events, erotic and nonerotic, going back to infancy—a piece of theater whose story seems genuine because of the truth of the body's sensations. Though the moment feels spontaneous, it is, rather, the result of years of working over the scripts in order to make them function efficiently—that is, to ensure that they produce excitement, with its end product, gratification, rather than anxiety, depression, guilt, or boredom. Like humor, it has its aesthetics, especially the requirement that it seem to be spontaneous, spare, uncomplicated, unmotivated.

I have pointed to, and shall elaborate on, the importance of humiliation as a goad to creating the microdot and as a hidden presence in the erotic moment. By *humiliation*, I mean the mechanism, within the script that makes up the excitement, of revenge—humiliating another as payment for others' having humiliated one.

Since I am a psychoanalyst, my perspective will naturally be psychoanalytic. I shall therefore put aside the somatic aspects of excitement and the imaginative discussions of psychobiologists on the possible evolutionary forces that shape the fundaments of erotic excitement. Instead, I take up the story only from birth on and—in typical analyst fashion—am caught up especially by the contributions of infancy and childhood to this later marvelous/inept/totally human/creative neurosis: erotic excitement.

There can, however, hardly be a more controversial subject than this, and efforts to apply the scientific method so successful in the natural sciences fail here. And so, in order to remind the reader how vulnerable is a study of the dynamics of an emotion, I have weighted this book as heavily with a discussion of how we explore the subject as I have with the discussion of what I find. How do we collect our observations; how do we interpret them; how do we report them to others so that our audience will be convinced that we saw what we saw and that what we saw leads to our conclusions: are our conclusions simply prejudices, guesses, propositions, hypotheses (testable propositions), or laws of nature?

To keep you from grossly misunderstanding, let me say a bit on how to read this book.

1. I ask those familiar with other works of mine to forgive the repetitions supplied for strangers. For both the latter and the former, there are other repetitions: having long since learned that I sometimes get very little from a first reading, I appreciate being told something over and over, as long as the author's repeating is not due to a failure to edit properly.

2. Using myself to represent the typical reader, I know how one is unconvinced by arguments that only generalize or quote authorities. We need something stronger. So sharper authors turn to metaphor, vivid writing, captivating rhetoric, anecdotal scraps, and high-energy theory. Rarely can we analysts use observations, since, in our work, they cannot be reproduced nor can the living clinical moment be repeated.

For some of my ideas, however, we need not be put off by these problems. The facts can be presesnted. If I say that Smith wrote the sentence to be quoted, it is easy to quote. And if I say that analysts typically write sentences such as that one of Smith's, I can quote enough of them that you will recognize that the style is typical. Fine so far. Yet in some cases you will not be convinced without being given many examples, since you know that you could be had with a few well-chosen items that seem to stand for a large class when they really do not. But will you, reader, bear to read enough quotes to make it beyond dispute that, say, analysts repeat ad nauseam (that is, defensively) that they are scientists?

Will you let me nauseate you? Not likely. Still, I shall try.

3. I cannot stomach psychoanalytic jargon and rhetoric and so do not use it (except when quoting a colleague or when being sarcastic). I realize, however, that certain concepts all we analysts think are clinically accurate and either demonstrable or almost so, such as "conscious," "preconscious," "unconscious," "defense," "drive," "dynamics," may strike nonpsychoanalytic readers as being as unreal as the words that repel me.

4. I write in a more or less conventional tone so as to be clear. Some of you will know that is not easy, especially when we are obliged to use written rather than spoken language (with its inflections, facial and body clues, pauses, and so on). I am amused, however, to realize that my urge to be clear has hit a brick wall. I was innocent and therefore optimistic to think that clarity was possible (even if still beyond reach). Now I know that *there is no such thing as a clear sentence.* Someone will construe different meaning from any you could ever imagine, and that meaning may be as inherent in the sentence as what you tried to say. (The poet Raymond Rousel: "His prose is so clear it needs decoding" [Sante, 1985, p. 14].)

Still, yearning for clarity contains a pleasure of which I am only now fully aware. Sometimes, on paring a sentence down to its barest minimum, I find it transforms into a question, paradox, or joke (all three being different states of the same thing, like ice, water, and steam). That is a relief: clarity asks; it does not answer. Maybe then, in a hundred years, sitting on my haunches like a Zen master, I shall finally write a clear sentence. But it will have no words.

ACKNOWLEDGMENTS

Once again I thank three people who have strengthened my work: Gladys Topkis for her intelligent, steady editorial hand that holds me to the line of the argument; Professor Gilbert H. Herdt, whose ethnography has opened my perspectives so much; and my secretary, Mrs. Flora Degen, whose attentive, lively goodwilled wiseness helps shield me from reality.

I also want to thank the following for granting permission to include materials published in whole or in part by them:

La Perversion et le Désir de Faire Mal. *Nouv. Rev. Psychanal.* 29: 147–71, 1984.

Centerfold. *Arch. Gen. Psychiat.* 36:1019–24, 1979.

Problems with the Term "Homosexuality." *Hillside J. Clin. Psychiat.* 2:3–25, 1980.

Theories of Origins of Male Homosexuality: A Cross-Cultural Look. *Arch. Gen. Psychiat.* 42:399–404, 1985.

Transvestism in Women. *Arch. Sex. Behav.* 11:99–115, 1982.

Erotic Vomiting. *Arch. Sex. Behav.* 11:361–65, 1982.

Psychiatry's Mind-Brain Dialectic, or The *Mona Lisa* Has No Eyebrows. *Am. J. Psychiat.* 141:554–58, 1984.

and

Grover, S. 1980. The Bodice Busters. *Wall Street Journal,* 5 Nov., pp. 1, 14.

PART I
Dynamics of Erotic Behavior

CHAPTER 1

Perversion and the Desire to Harm

Having come on almost no one in the psychoanalytic, psychiatric, psychologic, or other literatures I read who agrees (or disagrees) with me, in this chapter I again take up suggestions made in earlier books (Stoller 1975, 1979). I feel that the main issue in these studies—the desire to humiliate as an essential theme in erotics—needs more airing. I can then use that argument to look, in the following chapter, at the more general subject of aesthetics.

GROUND RULES

1. This is a chapter with its conclusions—answers—encased in a question I cannot answer: what specific piece of any individual's erotic behavior is *not* a perversion? The answers within that question are bits and pieces—the hypotheses and findings I shall now present—of what a pervision *is*. I shall not dwell on the problem of what is not perversion but shall only ask, in that regard, that you subliminally hold this discussion within that embracing issue.

2. I shall ramble a bit, which will require your patience. If you get uneasy, you might not read in the loose way needed to soak up the argument I shall present in the form of hypotheses, clinical vignettes, and impressions you are to let float from inside you to the surface. My line of reasoning (as is the case throughout this book) requires encirclement, not head-on assault by firm, lean cognition.

Does Perversion Exist?

In some of the fields where I play—a university, the literature on erotics, nonpsychoanalytic psychiatry and psychology— even to use the word *perversion* puts one in jeopardy. *Perversion* is so pejorative. It reeks of sin, accusation, vindictiveness, and righteousness. It has its absoluteness. In it thunder God and his agents on earth. How, then, could anyone familiar with psychodynamics, cultural relativity, social inequities, the foibles of mankind at large, the cruelty of the law, and the hypocrisy of those in power continue to use the term? In the name of decency and science, *perversion,* with its nasty implications, has dropped out of modern psychiatric, psychologic, and sociologic (but not psychoanalytic) discourse. It has stood in the way of research into the origins of sexual behavior and denies social realities—the sexual frankness unfolding in the modern world. There is little to the word but insult: hostility that aims to humiliate and subjugate others. As a label, it has been a power tool used by society to transform those who are different into those who are bad. The criteria for the judgment have been in the hands of the authorities, such as psychiatrists or courts, and these judgments have been made not on the basis of what an individual did—what the act meant to the person— but on the basis of the anatomic parts used and the culture's mores.

And so, in reaction against such dictionary meanings as corrupt, wicked, debased, misdirected, stubborn, and so on, a gentler, enlightened position has emerged. As an example of this social progress, let me sketch that shift in attitude as it developed in official psychiatric circles in the past thirty years or so.

The American Psychiatric Association began its effort to consolidate diagnoses with the publication in 1952 of the *Diagnostic and Statistical Manual—Mental Disorder* (*DSM I*). Before that time, there was no official nomenclature for psychiatric disorders, or rather, each social institution (for example, the Veterans Administration) had its own. In that era, as *DSM I* notes, the diagnosis "Psychopathic Personality with pathologic sexuality" was available. Then, with *DSM I* came "Sociopathic Personality Disorders—Sexual Deviation (Specify Supplementary Term)," with the following elaboration: "types of pathologic behavior, such as homosexuality, transvestism, pedophilia, fetishism, and sexual sadism (including rape, sexual assault, mutilation)." Toward the back was the listing "Supplementary Term—Sexual Perversion."

A humanitarian movement was under way: "Psychopathic Personality," with its powerful defamatory sense, had been rendered more objective by the change to "Sociopathic Personality." But as happens when we try to change beliefs by changing labels, old meanings infect new words: "Sociopath" did not clean up "Psychopath"; it only added a syllable (that overused technique for gaining entrance to Science). Besides, the former "perversions" were still called "disorders," though the accusation was softened with the rather neutral "deviation." Even calling these conditions[1] "pathologic behavior" was a weighty judgment.

In our society's fateful year 1968, the effort to release the bonds proceeded with *DSM II*. The category was now "Personality Disorders and Certain Other Non-Psychotic Mental Disorders. Sexual Deviations: homosexuality, fetishism, pedophilia, transvestitism, exhibitionism, voyeurism, sadism, masochism, other sexual deviations [unspecified]." But still, there was that word *disorders*.

Then, following battles in which homosexuality per se was removed as a diagnosis, *DSM III*, published in 1980, listed under "Psychosexual Disorders" two categories of what, in ancient days, had been perversions: "Gender Identity Disorders" and "Paraphilias." "In other classifications these disorders are referred to as Sexual Deviations. The term *paraphilia* is preferable because it correctly emphasizes that the deviation (*para*) is in that to which the individual is attracted (*philia*)." *DSM III* lists fetishism, transvestism, zoophilia, pedophilia, exhibitionism, voyeurism, sexual masochism, sexual sadism,

---

1. Are they conditions? Or are they no more than states, or styles, or traits, or activities?

and atypical paraphilias—for example, "coprophilia (feces), frotteurism (rubbing), klismophilia (enema), mysophilia (filth), necrophilia (corpse), telephone scatalogia (lewdness), and urophilia (urine)."

Paraphilia: how clean, how neat, disinfected, sanitized, and tidy. Science triumphant. Change the sign on the door and the activities inside change.

Nonetheless, I want to retain the term *perversion* just *because* of its nasty connotations. *Perversion* is a sturdy word, throbbing with assumptions, while *paraphilia* is a wet noodle. In trying to say nothing, it says nothing. It is not only neutral; it is neutered, pithed. It does not contain the quality I believe the person we would call perverse finds essential. That quality is the sense of sin, of sinning.

Everyone knows that the concept of sin is at the center of the word *perversion*. In the objectivity of science, however, there is no place for such a concept. Please understand: I am not saying there is such a thing as sin. (Whether I do or do not believe in sin is a private, unscientific matter.) I am only saying that people (even psychoanalysts, at least in their personal lives) believe in it. It may be unscientific to believe in sin, but it is also unscientific to believe that people do not believe in sin. And I doubt that we shall rid people of their sense of sinning by telling them they are not perverse but only paraphilic.[2]

In removing *perversion,* the authorities were taking an objective stance. They recognized that it is unscientific, in fact corrupt, for an outside observer to proclaim that someone else is full of sin—that is, swollen with *willful* disobedience of accepted morality. If we are allowed to call people perverse because we carry society's might in our back pockets, the diagnostic process is corrupted from the start. *Paraphilia* is directed against that unfairness. I, of course, agree: when diagnoses are simply power plays, they must go.

But I advocate a different criterion for name-calling, even though in practice the criterion is difficult to apply (especially

---

2. Watch: as soon as we get to calling them paraphil*iacs*, they will again know they are bad.

because it requires, in most cases, getting to know someone): does the actor, at the time he acts, feel that he is sinning? Now let my definitions cut even a layer below that. *The activity is perverse*, I shall say, *if the erotic excitement depends on one's feeling that one is sinning*. If such a dynamic is present, then using deodorized terms such as *deviation, variant*, or *paraphilia* wipes out the most significant feature of the act.

I am insisting, then, that in perversion the *desire* to sin is essential for being turned on.

And what, exactly, is the sin? It is the same as for all sins: the desire to hurt, harm, be cruel to, degrade, *humiliate* someone (including, at levels of lesser awareness, the desire to harm oneself). In the case of perversion, the person to be harmed (besides oneself—but that is often unperceived) is one's sex object.

The psychoanalytic literature, from Freud on, has not used these criteria. Instead, whatever an analyst felt was aberrance was called perversion. That is too diffuse, for it assumes that all sexually[3] aberrant people share crucial common dynamics. Such an assumption is, for me, too much like the other methods of thinking used when someone was labeled perverse. The classifying process was effortless. We did not have to search out what was going on inside the person. Our theory of behavior or of diagnosis did the work, saving us the trouble of listening to patients.

I would like, therefore, to offer this different system for defining perversion, one that requires more effort but is based on psychic reality: *what is the person's intention?* I wrote these ideas down several years ago (Stoller 1975) and have since poked at them regularly to see if they hold up clinically, theoretically, logically. I think they do, but you should be warned that, as far as I know, they never have been used by anyone else. (The present definitions are slightly modified from the original statement).

> By *aberration* I mean an erotic technique or constellation of techniques that one uses as his or her complete sexual act and that

---

3. And, from Freud on, analysts have used *sexual* without distinguishing to which of its two main features—erotic and gender behavior—they are referring.

differs from his or her culture's traditional, avowed definition of normality. Sexual aberrations can be divided into two classes: variants (deviations) and perversions.

By *variant* I mean an aberration that is not primarily the staging of forbidden fantasies, especially fantasies of harming others. Examples would be behavior set off by prenatal hormones; abnormal brain activity, as with a tumor, experimental drug, or electrical impulse from an implanted electrode; or an aberrant act that one is driven to *faute de mieux;* or sexual experiments one does from curiosity and finds not exciting enough to repeat.

Perversion, the erotic form of hatred, is a fantasy, usually acted out but occasionally restricted to a daydream (either self-produced or packaged by others—that is, pornography). It is a habitual, preferred aberration necessary for one's full satisfaction, primarily motivated by hostility. By *hostility* I mean a state in which one wishes to harm an object; that differentiates it from *aggression,* which often implies only forcefulness. The hostility in perversion takes form in a fantasy of revenge hidden in the actions that make up the perversion and serves to convert childhood trauma to adult triumph. To create the greatest excitement, the perversion must also portray itself as an act of risk taking. (pp. 3–4)

In other words, perversion is an erotic neurosis.[4] It (but not all aberrations) is a response to—an attempt to cure the effects of—traumas, frustrations, conflicts, and other painful conditions that could not be handled without one's changing his or her development. The visible manifestation of the cure is the story line of the perversion—the cast of characters with their assigned parts, action, mise-en-scènes. The script is then played out as daydream, in pornography chosen, or in the real world.

Though I cannot answer adequately, I must, even this early in the argument, confront the question: is there an essential difference between the person who performs a perversion, one who keeps from doing it but needs to fantasize it (by day-

4. In emitting this sensible and unremarkable sentence, I disagree with Freud and the whole analytic literature, in which perversion is considered a form of behavior different from neurosis, powered by a different constellation of drives and defenses, and serving different purposes. However, note Gillespie 1956, p. 397.

dreams or pornography) in order to be well satisfied, and one who does not need or prefer that portrayal but who nonetheless, when chancing on it, gets excited? To say that the difference is a matter of degree is not too helpful until we know what factors determine those differences in degree. We are probably as far from being able to take that measure as for any other aesthetic decision (that is, any other matter of taste). We are a long way from knowing yet, for instance, to what extent inherited or other constitutional factors play their part directly in erotic choice. For example, are males biologically more prone to erotic looking? Is there an organic element to some homosexuality? Or indirectly, as when one infant can inherently withstand a noxious parental factor more easily than can another infant. Or what parts of a constellation of postnatal psychologic influences are more present in one person's history than another's? The best I can do is to unravel certain dynamics, such as the desire to do harm or the theater of risk, and caution that finding these dynamics in a person does not predict when the dynamics will push one beyond fantasizing and into action. These are judgments theory cannot make; they can be measured only in the clinical situation (where, as we know, we have all too few accurate forms of measurement): when does orange become red?

And so I see perversion as a "habitual, preferred aberration necessary for one's full satisfaction."

There are probably few people who do not recognize their favorite script once they meet it. (Gagnon and Simon provide an essential introduction to the study of erotic scripting [for example, 1973, 1984].) If my definitions confuse you because they imply that everyone is erotically aberrant and most people most of the time are at least a bit perverse, so be it.[5] Then you may prefer to retitle this chapter "Sexual Excitement and the Desire to Harm."

5. So I find all pornography to be little perversions and probably all erotic daydreams as well: a very narrow-minded view. This is not to say that I believe masturbation is harmful, only that it is spiced up by a touch of badness. Modern thinkers on sex say that the guilt in masturbation is induced by society (including parents). Though agreeing, I add that if we could ask people exactly what is their story line while masturbating or exactly what they do, we would get closer to why they feel guilty.

Perversion may be difficult to study in part because the gross cases blind us to underlying subtleties. If you are as I was, you are so struck by the absurdity or monstrousness of the behavior that you stop thinking, comfortable with *perversion* in its accusatory sense. You need no explanation: "He must be mad" or "That is unnatural." The complex dynamics of the neuroses do not seem to apply. An example:

> L., labourer, was arrested because he had cut a large piece of skin from his left forearm with a pair of scissors in a public park.
>
> He confessed that for a long time he had been craving to eat a piece of the *fine white skin of a maiden*, and that for this purpose he had been lying in wait for such a victim with a pair of scissors; but, as he had been unsuccessful, he desisted from his purpose and instead had cut his own skin.
>
> His father was an epileptic, and his sister was an imbecile. Up to his seventeenth year he suffered from *enuresis nocturna*, was dreaded by everybody on account of his rough and irascible nature, and dismissed from school because of his insubordination and viciousness.
>
> He began onanism at an early age, and read with preference pious books. His character showed traits of superstition, proneness to the mystic, and showy acts of devotion.
>
> When thirteen his lustful anomaly awoke at the sight of a beautiful young girl who had a fine white skin. The impulse to bite off a piece of that skin and eat it became paramount with him. No other parts of the female body excited him. He never had any desire for sexual intercourse, and never attempted such.
>
> He hoped to achieve his end easier with the aid of scissors than with his teeth, for which reason he always carried a pair with him for years. On several occasions his efforts were nearly successful. Since the previous year he found it most difficult to bear his failures any longer, when he decided upon a substitute—*viz.*, each time when he had unsuccessfully pursued a girl he would cut a piece of skin from his own arm, thigh, or abdomen and eat it. *Imagining that it was a piece of the skin of the girl whom he had pursued,* he would whilst masticating his own skin obtain orgasm and ejaculation.
>
> Many extensive and deep wounds and numerous scars were found on his body.
>
> During the act of self-mutilation, and for a long time after-

wards, he suffered severe pains, but they were over-compensated by the lustful feelings which he experienced whilst eating the raw flesh, especially if the latter dripped with blood, and when he succeeded in his illusion that it was *cutis virginis*. The mere sight of a knife or scissors sufficed to provoke this perverse impulse, which threw him into a state of anxiety, accompanied by profuse perspiration, vertigo, palpitation of the heart, craving for *cutis feminae*. He must, with scissors in hand, follow the woman that attracted him, but he did not lose consciousness or self-control, for at the acme of the crisis he took from his own what was denied him from the body of the girl. During the whole crisis he had erection and orgasm, and at the very moment when he began to chew the piece of his skin ejaculation set in. After that he felt greatly relieved and comforted. (Krafft-Ebing [1906] 1932, pp. 238—40)

So that you can sense the less bizarre—or, perhaps, sense that the bizarre is plentiful—scan these advertisements, pulled at random from pornography magazines. They stand for thousands of ads in hundreds of magazines published each year. We cannot know how many people practice each of these (these what? will you disallow "perversions" as their proper label?), but it is safe to say that, however many one counts, there are still more. I shall start by quoting a few in full and then, for brevity, simply list the ads' titles.

SKYE PUBLISHING

Fact and fiction about dominant women, everything illustrated. Panties, foot worship, smother, killer girls, mixed wrestling, bloomers, water sports and other humiliation. Over 100 publications. Skye also published the *Dominant Newletter*, news of what dominant women are doing, contacts, and the *Dungeon*, the world's leading listing of submissive men. New from Skye: Turn-on posters, with story lines and special cock sucks. Sample and full info, $1. [Late 1970s price.]

WANTED: PANTY POOPERS

W/M loves to poop in panties. Would love to have correspondence with young ladies for same interest. Will pay for any photos sent.

PICTURES of My LITTLE GIRLS

Momma needs to pick up some fast money selling naked pictures of her Three Little Girls . . . 8–16 . . . some innocent and nude, others hot and wicked! Different kind of pictures with boys or with Momma. $2 for each group.

TESTICLE TORTURE!

White male masochist wants to learn about all forms of testicle torture used in the past, and what might be used in the future.

SHITEATING!!! CATFIGHTS!!! TORTURE!!!

Ass rape! Amputation! Black domination! More! Explicit fiction catalog, $1.

TELE-SEX Get Off over the Phone

Call our sexy ladies, or have them call you. BOTH ways will satisfy you. CALL NOW

DISFIGURED GIRLS

Anyone out there. Into girls with scarred faces, birthmarks, eyepatches!

PIERCED PENISES

This fully illustrated mini-novel, the first photographic collection of its kind ever produced, showing the art of tattooing and piercing including text by that renowned expert Doug Malloy is available exclusively by mail order from . . . [The ad reproduces the cover—with illustration—of the mini-novel.]

FOOT FETISH AND PANTY LOVERS

Fantastic foot fetish tape, $9.00. Join our foot fetish club. Monthly news bulletin, 3-month membership, $9.00. Enjoy my juicy panties worn 7 days, $7.00. Very aromatic stockings, $7.00.

SECRETION PHOTOS!

Trade or buy urination, defecation, menstruation, lactation. Postage refunded.

200 FT. SPECIAL COLLECTION OF BABY FILMS
BOYS AND GIRLS IN ALL NEW JUVENILE STAGS
CHERRY LICKER
DONNA'S DOGIE
POTTIE PEEKER
MAMA'S LITTLE DICKIE
ALL FOUR PLUS SURPRISE GIFT

"Scissor Stories!" "Cigar-Smoking Females," "Barefoot Girls Who Never Wear Shoes," "White Male Slave," "Saddle Shoe Fetish," "Oral Service Given Free!" "Pussy Galore!" "Wrestling Goddess 6'3"," "Horses Mating," "Pregnant or Lactating?" "Rape," "Bizarre Fashions," "Forbidden Beastiality" [sic], "High Heels and Other Sensuous Delights," "Roots Toilette!" "Twenty-Two Inch Negro Penis Worn by 200 lb. Negress while disciplining young white boys," "The Most Beautiful Transsexuals in the World!" "Dominant Goddess Trains Generous Slaves in Private Dungeon," "Seeks French Slaves," "Lean and Mean Skilled Mistress!", "Forced Enemas," "Fun Loving & Dominant," "Couple Offers total discretion to generous people. Threesomes, bisexuality, cross-dressing, S&M," "Enchanting Chestnut Dominatrix," "Foot Loving Male in Delaware," "Fighting Mad About Gals With Sexy Looking Feet," "Need Tickling Victims," "Female Wrestler/Writer," "Dominant Black Stud," "Big Strong Ladies," "Bizarre Photos-Dirty Panties. Will Exchange Shit-Piss Photos. Also sell dirty panties," "Fighting Female Wanted," "Spit and Saliva," "Tattooed-Pierced Women," "Golden Showers & Cunnilingus," "Discrete [sic] Submissive Females," "[Finger] Nail Fans," "Hard-Core Party Tapes," "Licking My Bikini Panties," "Girls Beat Up Men!" "Beautiful Bare Feet!" "Three-Way Action," "French Ticklers Will Make Her Hot," "All Mouth Sex Movie," "Bondage and Leather Catalog," "Juiced Letters," "Female Muscle Club," "Academy for Discipline," "Wet Panties," "Female Pet Wanted!" "Garters Galore," "AMPFan," "Unbelievably Submissive Male," "Male Shit Photos Wanted," "High Heel Shoe Lover," "Submissive Male Lesbian," "Dress Me Up and Put

Me Down," "Might is Right," "Honky Slave," "Crippled Female," "Amputee Lovers."

Ads for magazines: *Best of Bondage* volumes 1, -2, -3, *Teenagers in Bondage* 2/1, *Bondage Kaptives* -4, -5, *Bondage Review* -4, -5, *Bondage in Rope and Leather* -1, *Helpless* -5, *Roped* -5, *Ropes, Garter and Gags* -4, -5, *Housewives in Bondage* -5, *Kaptive Kittens* -4, -5, *Kaptive Beauties* -4, -5, -6, *Bonda* -2, *Bondage Digest* -3, *Bondage in Rope & Rubber* -2, *Advanced Bondage* -4, *L.A. Bondage* -1, *Loveknots* -1, -2, *Hot Fox Bondage* -1, *Ropa* -1, *Bondage Asylum* -1, *Hose, Heels & Helpless* -1, *Leather Bondage, Red Patent* -2, *Sapporo Bondage* -1, *Osaka Bondage* -1, *Kyoto Bondage* -1, *Spanking Movie Review, Bondage Movie Review* -1, -2, -3, *Taskmaster* -2, -3, -4, *Tokyo Bondage* -1, *Exotique,* Vol. 6 No. 4, *Queens of Cruelty,* Vol. 2 No. 2, *Bitches in Heat,* Vol. 4 No. 4, *B & D,* Vol. 6 No. 3, *Kinky* No. 5, *The Subjugators,* Vol. 2 No. 2, *Bitches in Boots,* Vol. 6 No. 4, *Whip,* No. 5, *Leather Master,* Vol. 1 No. 2, *Nude 'N Naughty,* Vol 2, No. 2, *Bondage Quarterly,* Vol. 6 No. 4, *Discipline and Desire,* Vol. 2 No. 1, *Bound Teeny-Floppers,* Vol. 4, No. 4, *TVEXPOSE, Infantile Analysis.*

I hope this list gives you the impression, in lieu of better data—statistical studies that cannot be done—that perversion may be more commonplace than is generally believed and that there are more categories than are dreamed of in our manuals. Beyond that is an issue embedded in these ads and magazine titles: most of these needs, these perversions, are for men, not women. And almost all are heterosexual: for men and offering women as the sex objects.

Remember: if these sports do not turn you on, do not take that for granted. No-excitement is as much to be explained as is excitement. Neither you nor I nor the courts nor Kinsey is the criterion, the absolute, the fixed point in the universe against which all movement is measured to find variance, aberrance. Not even "the normal," that slickest device of all for enforcing bias. There is no absolute in the universe of mental life against which everything else can be judged. To think that there is a fundamental tenet in most psychoanalytic theories of sexuality, which decree "the heterosexual" as the standard for normality (as if there aren't as many heterosexualities as there are hetero-sexuals). Erotic choice, really, is a matter of opinions, taste, aesthetics.[6]

The business of relativity suggests a digression into vocabulary. Some of the ads offer pornography, yet they do not appeal to all sadomasochists, most women, or nonpoopsniffers, for instance; we should add other pornographies to snare a bigger crowd. But how can we conceptualize pornography that does not excite? I do so via the following obvious definitions. Pornography is that product manufactured with the *intent* to produce erotic excitement. Pornography is pornograph*ic* when it does excite. Not all pornography, then, is pornographic to all.

Now back to the proposition that perversions exist. I shall shortly present you with a collection of fetishes. There is something for almost everyone. After reading this list, you should have a sense that there are indeed conditions—lots of them, enthralling lots of people, mostly men—for which even you would be hard pressed to talk only of variants. You might want, then, as I do, a stronger term than "alternate life-style," one that would connote that the unusual is present—even if my hypothesis of perversion as the erotic form of hatred is too strong a dish to swallow. Yet others of these fetishes are so unbizarre that they are normative. (And who dares say that something millions of people do is perverse? Only someone who defines perversion by what goes on in the mind rather than by statistics.)

My technique of argument has been first to give you examples of erotic need so strange that you will agree the behavior is at least baroque, beyond the ordinary, beyond the reach of bleached-out words such as *paraphilia*. Having perceived that, you will see that less extreme behaviors are not so differ-

---

6. And if some of these advertisements made you chuckle, then you see another point that I shall take up in the next chapter: humor, which in its dynamics has much in common with erotics, is also a matter of aesthetics.

ent from the bizarre ones. Then I shall have enough of your attention to get on to a more interesting issue: what common features (for example, hostility) do the perversions share?

The first step is in place. You are either convinced by now or never will be that some erotic behaviors are propelled by desires one might call perverse. Now let us drop down a notch from those who crave to eat a piece of the fine white skin of a maiden, those who get an intense lustful feeling from seeing the servant girl cut her finger and bleed, and those who turn on by eviscerating prostitutes.

Fetishes

For those who think the psychic origins of excitement are obvious (for example, biologic), the following list of erotica, depending on one's tastes, sex, or previous experience, may restore their curiosity: boots, underwear (for example, crushed and torn women's white underwear), raincoats, leather, rubber, painted fingernails, steatopygous buttocks, penises, protruding veins on erect penises, vulvae, plucked eyebrows, dead bodies, uniforms, cigarette holders, pipes, collar studs, the hollow part of an artificial eye, fur, eyeglasses, hearing aids, urine (hot and cold, fresh and fermented), feces, whips, skin color, fatness, foreskins, nostrils, hands, gloves (cloth, fur, long, with many buttons—kid—dirty—with sweat saturated fingertips), baby pacifiers, men in a coughing paroxysm, stockings, aprons, handkerchiefs, nightcaps on ugly women's heads, feathers, velvet, silk, roses, virgins, toes, mouths, fetters, shadows, amputees, shoes (creaking, high-heeled, polished), "the leg from the knee downward and exquisitely clothed," trodden grass rising, prostitutes, women smoking cigarettes, sucked blood, soldiers, policemen, jodhpurs, short women, tall men, tall women, short men, other men's wives, other women's husbands, prepubescent children, the aged, eyes, mouths, ears, fifty-year-old women with a left-footed limp, a woman's right little toe crossed over the toe next to it, sunsets, Wagnerian sopranos in full cry, wedding gowns, men with breasts like women, strangers observed by means of peeping, a woman pulling a toilet chain, handcuffs, baby carriages, photographs of nude women, a woman's hands blackened with coal or soot and observed in a mirror, string, coral jewelry, money, anuses, copulating flies, pianos, new suits, new cars, cross-eyed women, sweating feet, dresses (mud-spattered, slashed, wet, tight, loose, red, black, on, off, blue and covered with a white apron), hair (body, pubic, facial, head, braided, flowing, dark, red, blond, cut, shaved, intact, none at all), wigs, mustaches, animals (pigs, dogs, cats, rabbits, cows, mares, sheep, donkeys, goats, reindeer, monkeys, whipped horses slipping, hens, ducks, geese, and—rumored—bears and crocodiles). Add aesthetic modifiers such as texture, smell, colors, motion or stillness, active or passive. What about complex actions: to shave the lathered face of a smooth-skinned girl?

SAD TALES

These fetishes are benign enough: no one is killed, mutilated, or raped. In fact, the action is played out with an object, not a whole person, and whatever is done to that object—the fetish—it is either inanimate or a body part not apt to feel devastated. Why, then, should society not respond benignly, "Do not call these acts mental diseases or disorders or perversions. Do not talk of sin"? The modern, enlightened stance aims at reducing the priggish, defensive, projecting, hypocritical rules that treat deviations, including the erotic, as fundamental attacks on the body politic (though some philosopher-practitioners of perversion have used perversion as a paradigm for subversion). Our present instance, fetishes, are only symbols, highly compacted stories that subliminally signal their fuller meanings; they do not stab, bite, poison, smother, crush, or demolish. Nonetheless, hidden in these symbols, as I suggest and shall soon discuss, are scripts that portray hostile acts. That fetishists really harm no one need not be confused with the fact that their behavior hides, among other things, this hostility dynamic. (A dynamic is not an action; you cannot even measure the intensity of a wish by knowing the script that carries the dynamic.)

Perhaps this is easier to see if we turn to another excitement: humor (jokes, the comic, wit, irony, caricature, sarcasm, to suggest a continuum of increasingly expressed hostility). I do not believe you can tell a story that is witty, comic, or humorous—they are similar but not identical in the way they tickle—without there being a quality, as in caricature, of an implied or visible victim who is being put down. Still, seeing a slapstick movie in which someone slips on a banana peel and breaks his leg is different from seeing the same event actually occur in the street. (I suppose that those who laugh in the street—or who consciously set out to create accidents—are the equal of the erotically perverse.)

We advance into the thesis that perversion is made from a story in which someone is harmed. That is easy to see in the madder excitements, but now we need examples, beyond fetishism, of perversion where hostility is present but invisible. Let three examples serve: exhibitionism, voyeurism, and transvestism.

Here is a typical[7] exhibitionist episode. If we use *exhibitionist* in the restricted meaning that refers to perversion (not in the broader meaning, where *exhibitionistic* is more or less synonymous with *histrionic* without implying erotic excitement), then we are talking about a man, heterosexual, married (if in his twenties or beyond), not effeminate, not consciously warding off homoerotic desires. He is likely to have been arrested before for exhibiting his genitals. (The highest rate of recidivism for illegal erotic behavior occurs with such men.) Someone disparages him—a superior at work, a stranger, his wife. He feels badly, and, though he cannot articulate the form of the bad feeling, your questioning would help him describe anxiety, anger, depression, and disgust that is not clearly focused on anyone, including himself. This tensely unpleasant state builds up until he decides—usually without seeing that his deciding is related to the bad feeling—to put his M.O. into effect. He goes to another part of town, to a place, a public area he knows is

---

7. I really have no right to say "typical." I know no one else who describes the subjective experience reported here and would have to work with many cases before truly knowing what is typical.

not his own territory, where he can silently draw the attention of women by exposing his genitals. The witnesses of his act must be strangers or at least women he hardly knows.

As he positions himself, he awaits the women's response. When they are angry or otherwise shocked he is not upset but is either turned on or unexpectedly calm. Though it may be obvious that the woman is going to call the authorities, he is unmoved, in the sense that he does not rush away. He may be as if in a state of suspended animation, not wanting to escape and not understanding why. When thus affected, he is likely to be arrested, this being the proximate reason for the high recidivist rate. Not only does he wait to be caught after the act, but the act itself has being caught built into it. As the strange woman watches, he feels that her watching consists of her catching him doing wrong. He needs to believe she is thinking that—that he is doing wrong—or the behavior fails.

The scene, however, may go a different way in these modern times with a modern woman. If she is not shocked, not offended, not outraged—if she knows that she is not violated and is simply amused or unconcerned—the man is left feeling puzzled, unfulfilled, uneasy, embarrassed, humiliated.

The explanations for the behavior are at hand; one need only talk, in a situation of trust, with an exhibitionist to see what he is up to. First, his going to a strange part of town and exposing his genitals to strange women is not *the* perversion but only the first part, the foreplay. The second part, which has never been recognized as part of the erotic activity, is the woman's shock, the ensuing fuss with the police and bystanders, the arrest, and the court appearance with its potential for ruining the man's life. You—rational you—ask the same question as the judge: "Why do you do this, who do you repeat this, why—when you know the possible terrible consequences—do you not refrain?" And the poor devil can only answer, "I do not know." That is: "I do not know what I know." (The last applies, of course, to almost everyone, anytime.)

"What I do not know I know is that I was humiliated earlier today; I have not quite taken in that I felt worthless. I felt that and then transformed it by detaching myself from my aware-

ness. I went from precise awareness of my pain to vague discomfort. In that way, I could forget that I was made to feel
unmanly and have always worried about that. I am nobody
worthwhile, and someone made me know it again. But I discovered a cure for this most awful of failures. I can restore my
sense of value, of self, of identity, of being, with that most
essential of all definers of maleness and masculinity: my penis.
Look what happens when I display my penis (at the right time,
in the right place, of course). People are shocked, the police
arrest me, society—through its agents, the courts—reaffirms
the terrible thing I have done, and the price that I pay is ruina-
tion. And I was able to do all that just by showing my penis.
By God, what a cock!"[8]

The perversions—all perverse acts (not all aberrations, just the
perversions; that is the purpose of the effort at precise definition)—are instant cures, magic bullets. That, even beyond body
pleasure, is reason enough for repeating them. The sad part is
that, without insight into what he does, the perverse person
must repeat his destructive acts endlessly—aspirin for a brain
tumor.

And why a stranger? Because a familiar, such as his wife,
could not possibly be shocked at the view of something so
domesticated. In our culture, a woman—and her husband
knows it—is not assaulted by the sight of his penis.

---

8. The classical analytic explanation follows Freud's: "Under analysis, these
perversions—and indeed most others—reveal a surprising variety of motives
and determinants. The compulsion to exhibit, for instance, is also closely dependent on the castration complex: it is a means of constantly insisting upon the
integrity of the subject's own (male) genitals and it reiterates his infantile satisfaction at the absence of a penis in those of women" (1905, p. 157n). My explanation—in fact, my explanation for male perversions in general—is similar. However, I see castration anxiety as a mild misnomer for a threat that is best put in
identity terms; for humiliation is about "existence anxiety," threat to core gender
identity. The second part of Freud's explanation—men's "satisfaction" at
women's not having a penis—does not, I believe, conform with reality. He had
an earlier theory about exhibitionism that he did not repudiate but supple-
mented in later years with the above quoted description: "exhibitionists . . .
exhibit their own genitals in order to obtain a reciprocal view of the genitals of
the other person." That is not true (though it is in children's sex play).

Now let us try this mode of explanation on the sort-of-opposite of exhibitionism: voyeurism. The voyeur, too, goes to a strange place and is excited only by strange women. If he is married to the most gorgeous woman in the world, he is elsewhere, passionate to glimpse a stranger secretly but bored with the view of his wife (who, in turn, is the passion of men who do not yet know her architectonics). The common factor, once again, is violation, hostility, the desire to harm. The voyeur imagines (accurately, probably, most of the time) that he is robbing the woman of her privacy, forcing her to give up what she wouldn't give *him* voluntarily (unless her pleasure is to stage a show in which she imagines that the view of her incites a man to violate her; certain aspects of fashion, for instance, arrange for that). When he cannot manage malice, boredom sets in. How can he, if married, abuse his wife by looking, when the marriage contract, in our society at any rate, gives him rather free access?

Transvestism is the third example of a perversion in which the hostility is not manifestly visible. By transvestism I mean dressing in or otherwise handling clothes of the opposite sex in order to be ,turned on. (Like exhibitionism and voyeurism, this is essentially a male activity, but see chapter 7.) Let us get into this one by a nonclinical route: pornography. Pornography is a published daydream. Perversion is a performed daydream. Pornography is a *forme fruste* of a perversion. When one is researching excitement, pornography has the advantage of being a dependable daydream; it is visible, can be examined over and over, and—because it is produced for sale—we are guaranteed that it represents a genre, that it is the preferred daydream for lots of people (or its producer would lose money).

EACH DETAIL COUNTS

Imagine before you the cover of a piece of transvestite pornography to be described shortly. (For the picture itself, see Stoller 1975, p. 64.) What does it say to the transvestite that tells him, in a flash,[9] that it is worth the high price charged? Why does it arouse him and leave nontransvestites untouched?

The first rule in daydreams is that each detail counts. Each has an effect—even if its assigned effect is that it be unimportant, empty space—or it is dropped. (The same is true for other creative work, such as musical compositions, paintings, poems. There too, we know, dead spaces and redundancies—such as rests and repeats in music—are needed in creating effects.)

Though the illustration says little to the nontransvestite, for the susceptible man, a lot is communicated. Let us start with the printed words and pick out some of the information, concealed from the nontransvestite but erotic to the transvestite. (I presume I have missed more, for each time I attend, more surface.)

The title is "Panty Raid." That will erotically signal to men, not women; it refers to an attack on women, for panties are intimate, genital-related, delicate, hidden garments with the potential to provoke men erotically. (You may wonder why I construct careful sentences on matters everyone knows.) In our culture, especially when this booklet was published—1963—the public was expected to believe that panty raids were simply manifestations of exuberance in masculine, middle-class, collegiate youths, silly but cute adventures in anticipation of more serious commitments to be later fulfilled. High spirits and good-natured frivolousness were excusable, for the young men were heterosexual, and they meant no real harm. To steal women's underwear was to promise society that its future men—fathers and citizens—would turn out just fine. No one was hurt. It was a good joke. And besides, the myth said, the

9. We experience a moment of excitement—any excitement, not just erotic—as spontaneously and instantaneously produced, as if *we* played no part in its creation. Therein are interesting questions, not to be considered further here, regarding aesthetics. Out of what bits and pieces of past experience, memories, fantasies, and so on, are aesthetic judgments made? How are they fit together to make an intact fabric? How are we able to experience this complex activity of construction as being spontaneous, uncomplex, unconstructed, unproblematic?

girls were undoubtedly pleased by the attention; a cheap thrill: only their panties were at risk.

There are in this title, then, built-in safety factors, information given to the transvestite that, though in reality he is masturbating, he has split away a part of himself who is the man in the story. And what *that* fellow is doing is socially approved, manly, cute, and perhaps even a bit lovable (naughty). Were the real man to feel anxious, guilty, or disgusted, he could not so easily buy the booklet.

Below the title are two boxes with clean, neat print. One tells of "other stories of transvestism and female impersonation" within. The other says, "No. C-18." This notice, without substantive meaning, puts the publication in the mainstream of orderly, accountable publishing, free from dirtiness. At the bottom, after the announcement "includes actual correspondence from transvestites" (which both fills the cornucopia and lets the transvestite know he is not alone), appear "A Connoisseur Publication" and "Limited Edition," again safety factors giving the illusion that this is high-class stuff.

What about the main feature, the drawing? Let me emphasize a few points only. It depicts three people, two women and a man. The women are clearly—extravagantly—female. There is no suggestion that they are male-like. They are, with all their femaleness and femininity, powerful, dangerous, cruel. They overpower, but not by brute strength. (The brunette's grasp is delicate; a healthy young man could easily break it.) They do have physical threat available to them beyond the nonphysical implied in their dangerous beauty: along with the other phallic elements in the drawing, whips are depicted. But, once again, the man could escape easily enough if the women's inner power did not hold him captive.

The young man is the center of the picture. A tear runs down his face. He is certainly unhappy in his lovely lingerie. The women have overpowered him and, I suspect—we become sure on reading the text—humiliated him. He is forced to do something he does not like. We cannot fill in all the details from the text, for it has no scene quite like that on the cover. Nonetheless, in all samples of this genre of transvestite pornography the fundamentals are the same: the heterosexual young man, unquestionably totally male, innocent, is captured by females who do so not by physical power but by the mysterious power inherent in femaleness and femininity. Humiliated, he is forced by them into women's clothes. That is the essential story, and that is what the cover promises the transvestite. For him the story is a winner. For the rest of us it is uninteresting. If we even wondered about it, we would only be puzzled about how this could be erotic.

TRAUMA AND HUMILIATION

How can humiliation excite? When the text shows that the women have forced the man to question the solidity of his masculinity and maleness, we are hardly enlightened. But the cover does not tell all; it only shows trauma. There is a happy ending: with the women's help, the man's humiliation is changed to a pleasurable, nonerotic state[10] when the women openly accept him as a man, a male who has remained a man and a male but who looks pretty and graceful in women's clothes. To the outsider, it hardly sounds like the stuff of excitement. Why is this so compelling that it is repeated over and over in transvestite pornography?

Let us look for clues in the story. On the title page the author's name appears: Carlson Wade (a pseudonym, I suppose). Refined, literary, masculine; he surely smokes a pipe. The story begins. Note the inordinate—to those not fetishistically attracted to women's clothes—naming and describing of garments, their colors and textures.

> As Bruce King made his way stealthily, under cloak of a velvet near-midnight darkness, toward the forbidden grounds of the sorority house, he began to feel apprehensive. Suppose he did not succeed in this panty raid? Suppose he failed to come back with the booty—a pair of lacy-fringed bloomers or skin-tight, peach panties, the silk-and-satin slip with red bows for straps, perhaps a panty-girdle or two, not to mention the thigh-length black mesh stage hose! It was his "initiation" task as a freshman

10. For the hero; the reading transvestite, however, is aroused.

to stage a one-man panty raid upon the sorority at the other end of the campus grounds of the university.

"If you don't bring back a complete girl's outfit," warned the frat prexy, while wielding a flat wooden paddle which would warm the taut flanks of helpless initiates during secret ceremonies, "you'll be paddled right out of this initiation . . . you won't be able to sit down for a week!" The others had laughed gleefully but Bruce King saw no humour. He desperately craved acceptance and if he had to steal feminine underclothes and lingerie, not to mention some silly bloomers, to gain their respect, he would do it!

A few comments at this point: Bruce King, in those days a hero's name—totally masculine, no breath of effeminacy. Note that he is further defined as a masucline male in that his raid is done as part of a male initiation rite. If he is to join the all-male organization, he must go on a dangerous mission and abuse the intimacy of females. He does this because he craves acceptance by the males, signifying a masculinity insecure enough to need bolstering from other men.

(The item about the paddle and the taut flanks of helpless initiates does not appeal to all transvestites. For some, it is too sadomasochistic. And does it not have just a flicker of homosexuality?)

Bruce approaches the hanging lingerie:

The lace front paneling matched the pleated Bikini pantie. Bruce grinned. It sure would be interesting to see a girl wear such a baby doll outfit! And to catch her by surprise would really make him a hero! [That is, to attack—degrade—a female will promote him to being the best of males.] . . . Suddenly there was a cry. Squeals and bubbling laughter suddenly enveloped him. He turned, whirled around to discover he was suddenly surrounded by no less than a half dozen sorority girls, some wearing satin slacks and halters, others wearing silk shorts. All were shrieking with joy. [That is, he suddenly—three times suddenly—is attacked himself.] . . .

"We'll give him a lesson he'll never forget!"

Bruce fought but they entwined his arms with silken robe belts. "Stop!" He tried to cry but suddenly found his mouth being filled with a silky-soft sheer stocking. The stocking was bound around his head and knotted tightly. His arms were bound behind the small of his back. Suddenly he found himself being carried, horizontally, by the chattering females. He was taken into the sorority building, up the steep stairs and into a bedroom! He tried to protest but his gag was too tight; he wiggled but only succeeded in getting the brunt of their sharp fingernails into the muscular flesh of his flanks and thighs. This brought much raucous laughter from the victorious vixens who thrilled at the helpless struggles of their male captive.

As the bedroom door locked, leaving Bruce King a helplessly bound victim of four fierce looking girls, he had a sinking feeling. What were they going to do to him? This was only a harmless little college prank. Didn't they have any sense of humour? [That is, the difference between raw hostility and humor is a matter of perspective, of aesthetics.]

In this section, then, we have seen Bruce, for all his maleness, captured by squealing women, with their chatter, bubbling laughter, and shrieks of joy. They ensnare him with silken belts, sharp fingernails, and a silky-soft sheer stocking. In brief (briefs), femininity's power brings him down, not the brute strength of males' paddles. We have here a story full of man's humiliation by woman.

Now we meet Lori, who possesses "a strange form of arrogance which demanded obedience and respect" (that is, his reading of woman's femininity). She commands the women to dress Bruce in female clothes. A few more quotes are enough:

Before Bruce could protest, he found himself descended upon by the girls, who ripped off his simple white business shirt, cotton khaki trousers (he was grateful he wore protective boxer shorts), off went his moccasins, wool socks. "It's cold . . ." he shivered, feeling more embarrassed and humiliated than the elements of the weather in early Spring. To be stripped, bound and in the captivity of four domineering types of females was certainly an experience that shattered his manhood. There was no telling what they could do to make good a threat that Lori not [sic] voiced: "We'll teach him that the female of the species are the *real* aggressive members of the human race!"

"Good boys shouldn't wear such sloppy things. We'll teach our Brucie how to dress."

With a sigh of relief, he remembered he wore his tiny athletic supporter which the girls ridiculed by giggling, "Look—he wears a G-string!"

"Brucie-boy."

"Behave yourself."

Bruce flushed and no sooner were his arms and legs freed than he tried to cover himself with his hands but his awkward knock-kneed position and round shouldered position of embarrassment only provoked more laughter. "Very funny! Very funny!" he gasped.

"See, Bruce," she dangled it [a brassiere] before him, as if threatening his manhood.

An illustration in the text shows Bruce pinned down by the four beauties, kicking and bawling as they apply makeup to him and dress him in their shoes and undergarments."[11]

The man who gave me this booklet, a transvestite, has been described elsewhere (Stoller 1975). Suffice to say here that the pornography tells the same story as his traumatic experience of being cross-dressed at age four by women: a defenseless male, who knows and values being a male (it is his core gender identity) but who, at this early age, is not so sure his sense of maleness can withstand assault, is put into girls' clothes; his gender identity is threatened. Then, years later, the perversion surfaces, and now Bruce repeatedly gets excited in women's clothes. But, rather than being traumatized, today he is triumphant when cross-dressing—excited, potent, on his way to maximal pleasure.

In review, study this ad for another transvestite booklet. Now you should be able to see below the surface.

PANTY RAIDERS
by———Gilbert

. . . has as its theme a "sport" quite popular in most co-educational institutions. It deals with a group of under-

---

11. I also have found a drawing, aimed at normal folk, of four totally lovely Gibson Girls gently observing through a magnifying glass a minute, cowering man whom one of the girls is about to dissect with (I think) a hat pin. It is entitled "The Weaker Sex."

graduated [sic] students who undertake a panty raid on a girl's [sic] dormitory. Unfortunately, for them, they are caught red-handed by three of the co-eds and their House Mother. By way of atonement, the boys are subjected to various forms of humiliation. They are even compelled to don the very panties they tried to steal as well as other bits of feminine apparel they never dreamed of wearing in public.

The tale is told in 48 exciting chapters. Each chapter is vividly illustrated and contains over four-hundred words. The chapters are reproduced on a heavy vellum stock (approx. 5 ½ × 8 ½ inches).

The first unit of 8 chapters is now ready.

Send $1.00 for our current illustrated bulletin listing over 35 assorted and interesting items. Be sure to mention Dep't E-6.

Gargoyle Sales Corp.

The illustration accompanying this text shows a handsome, masculine young man, with a masculine haircut, dressed in casual, masculine, American clothes, including a sweater with his varsity letter on it. He is alert to danger. Behind him is an open window with the curtain blowing; he has apparently just entered the room that way. He is in the act of taking lingerie from a set of drawers, and undergarments are spilling out. (The girl is cool: a squash racquet and trophies lie about the room.)

Every detail counts.

Transvestites report, far more than any other group of men (including those with the other perversions), that they were put into women's clothes—usually by girls or women—as children. I do not believe, however, that a single episode of cross-dressing produces transvestism; other boys given this treatment are not thus damaged. I presume that only a boy who is already susceptible—some special uneasiness of gender development in the first two or three years of life—will need the perversion structure in order to preserve identity.

"To preserve identity." Against what? Against humiliation. And humiliation is, of course, a matter of identity, an attack on one's self-respect, the dictionary tells us. Only those strong enough to trust will let others in, allow intimacy. But if we have reason to feel unsafe (if, for instance, we were regularly humiliated in the first years of life), we shall be on guard, fearful of what others may find were we to let them in and how they will use what they find. So we seal ourselves off (Khan 1979), a process that dehumanizes us. Then, to be doubly safe, we dehumanize *them*. They convert to fetishes. For those who do not fear dissolution, intimacy is a joy. For those who do, there is an even more primitive threat: if I let someone in—if I thereby merge with that person—may he or she not, like an evil spirit, possess me, take me over entirely? Then, the great terror, I shall lose myself. It is against such fundamental menace that perversion is invented.

Note how the perversion preserves the trauma in its structure. In that regard, perversion is audacious.[12] More accurately, perversion *seems to be* audacious. One seems to take a risk in approaching the old danger. That is a central part of exciting experiences: uncertainty, a tense hum between the possibility of triumph and the possibility/memory of trauma, failure.

We saw this mechanism at work with the Bruce King in the pornography and our Bruce King who bought it: the danger is real for the fictional character and fiction for the real character. Our Bruce—the transvestite—simulates risk when he reads the story of Bruce King's trauma with the sorority girls. His excitement, as in all daydreams, is theater in that he knows in advance—has prepared the setting in advance—that he suffers the trauma only by identifying with a depicted character.

You think of examples to disprove the thesis. Take the exhibitionist. Does he not risk his reputation, his safety, his future when, in the real world, he puts himself at risk of arrest? Yes, of course. But, if my explanation is correct, he openly seeks that real risk because it measures his success in avoiding what

12. It is, from a different viewpoint, cowardly as well: like other daydreams, it pretends to confront issues but is actually used for deception and avoidance of intimacy with others and with oneself. Perversion, for all its masochism, is the refusal to suffer.

is unconsciously for him an even greater risk: humiliation. That business of defensive risk taking is familiar. We all know people who build active danger into their lives—bullfighters, football players, professional soldiers, swindlers—to bolster their identities, trying to prove themselves intact, strong (by means of the applause of the world and their corruptible conscience). The more violent manifestations of masculinity some men demand of themselves also exemplify this mechanism.

Once aware of this device, you find it anywhere. Bruce had a friend, A., a transvestite whom I have known for years. One day, at a resort, during a scientific meeting he also attended, I heard my name called as I was lying on the beach. Looking up, I saw rising from the water a vision in pink: pink bathing suit and pink hat with a fiftyish woman who was living dangerously to be so pinkified. It was A., yelling and displaying himself as on a stage before the audience of sunbathers; no one would doubt that he was calling attention to himself. He looked like a woman (a histrionic one, of course), but with one bizarre element. In the crotch of "her" bathing suit were several large pointed protuberances, looking like a penis shrub. Approaching me and the watching public, "she" reached into her bathing suit and removed coral pieces "she" had stashed there. It was some display.

Another example, also from transvestites, that exemplifies the same dynamic: when transvestite men sit cross-dressed in my office, they typically arrange their legs to reveal their upper thighs and a flurry of frilly, fluffy underwear.

These two behaviors—A. on the beach and B., C., D. in my office—have, I believe, the same function: the transvestite states the question, "When I am like a female, dressed in her clothes and appearing to be like her, have I nonetheless escaped the danger? Am I still a male, or did the women succeed in ruining me?" And the perversion—with its exposed thighs, ladies' underwear, and coyly covered crotch—answers, "No. You are still intact. You are a male. No matter how many feminine clothes you put on, you did not lose that ultimate insignia of your maleness, your penis." And the transvestite gets excited. What can be more reassuringly penile than a full and hearty erection?

Were we to study the role of humiliation in provoking psychopathology, we would find it at work wherever sadism and masochism appear—for example, in paranoid (sadistic) or depressive (masochistic) responses. My guess is that humiliation shapes erotic life only when the attack is aimed at those parts of the body/psyche concerned with erotic or gender behavior.

DYNAMICS

Let me review the dynamics[13]—the interplay of wishes, motives, interpretations, scripts, meanings—I extract from the data, such as in the descriptions above, of perversion. (Much of this account has been noted in other studies before mine).

Perversion is theater, the production of a scenario, for which characters—in the form of people, parts of people, and nonhuman (including inanimate) objects— are cast. The performance is played before an audience, the crucial member of which is the perverse person viewing (in reality, with mirrors, with photographs, or in fantasy) himself or herself performing. Transforming an erotic act into a performance serves to protect one's excitement from being ruined by anxiety, guilt, or boredom, to allow the creator to simulate reality without running the risks we all face unless we manipulate reality, especially real people. Perversion is a detour that, at best, leads asymptotically to intimacy: it never arrives. The dangers of intimacy in reality are too great. "Perversion is centered not upon the partner, but upon the 'sexual' act" (Devereux 1967, p. 154). That, I think, has always been the experience and therefore the expectation of the perverse person. The pain and frustration of earlier times live on unresolved, carried within, always a potential threatening force motivating one to resolutions that never quite work, to an undoing never quite done. How exciting it is, then, when erotism—which, in its biologic and psychologic fullness, leads to the greatest intimacy—is a defense against intimacy: risk surmounted.

13. But not expressed with the analytic vocabulary of libidinal stages, psychic energy, projective identification, castration anxiety, narcissism, archaic introjects, and so on.

Why do these attempts fail? Because they are scripted to harm the desired object, to bring restitution by revenge. It is not easy to get a safe and loving intimacy by means of anger and the desire to harm. How can you reach another person if you transform him or her, by means of your scripts, into something he or she is not, something less than full personhood? Even the pornographer's seemingly trivial airbrush removes the truth, the little blemishes that are unbearable, unaesthetic.

This is dehumanization. With it, because we cannot stand the revelations of intimacy, we deprive others of their fullness. We see them only as members of classes or as possessors of selected parts or qualities only. We anatomize them. And if even that is too intimate, we turn from humans to inanimate objects, such as garments, granting them a certain amount of humanness while not needing humans. By doing this in fantasy, for a moment, as long as we can write, direct, and produce the show, we avoid anxiety or, even worse, despair.

I have emphasized how one dehumanizes his object in order to feel safe enough to get excited. There is a price: doing so dehumanizes the dehumanizer—and that knowledge is not always unconscious.

The trauma in each perversion script—whether the story is told as a daydream, pornography, or performance in reality—is converted to a triumph. The attackers of earlier times are defeated, undone, unable to persist in their attack. Now, each new episode of the trauma is constructed so that the victim is not defeated, though the experience is carried out using the same essentials that had earlier led to the disaster. Now the victim is the victor and the trauma a triumph, the crazy optimism of a full erection. If the story is well constructed, one feels guiltless and without anxiety.[14] In this brilliant replay lies the idea that the old attackers have been thwarted and thereby humiliated—and humiliation is the fundamental experience that is exchanged in these episodes. By humiliating, one gets revenge for having been humiliated.

14. Consciously. The guilt and anxiety, that is, are out of awareness or, if still felt, are attributed to more acceptable causes. This latter is rationalization and can, for instance, change sinner to saint or fanatic and convert the infant guilt-ridden partricide into the adult proud regicide.

THE AESTHETICS OF EXCITEMENT

By now, I hope you see that a necessary aspect of erotic excitement in perversion is that one must keep oneself from knowing too much, from knowing what is going on, from knowing one's reasons, from knowing one's intentions, from knowing one's desires. The old trick of eating your cake and having it: how to keep your knowledge working for you and yet to turn your eyes away, to blur your awareness. How else can we sin? By definition, if we are not responsible—if we do not know what we do—then what we do is not sin. Sin requires consciousness, free will.[15] What makes perversion such an achievement is that this complex construction can be erected and used repeatedly. Yet one gets only the desired effects (movement toward pleasure), for the moment a detail is introduced that does not fit—because it tells too much or too little—it is dropped. And beyond daydreams, those who put their perversion into practice are rising to an even greater challenge, for the world is not always as easy to manipulate as a daydream or the act of buying pornography. So the real world, with its greater risks, yields greater excitement and, with a successful play of the perversion, greater gratification.

How intricate—more so than Freud's idea that perversion is the escape of an infantile drive, unmodified, into adult behavior—and how much a matter of aesthetics.

My hunch is that the main aesthetic task, as with so much of behavior, is to take knowledge and render it uncertain, ambiguous. This ambiguity is, I think, most pleasing when it is seamless, when it does not give hints that it was constructed, when it looks as if it sprang full-blown from unconscious depths. If it is not created spontaneously—miraculously—then it should look as if it was. Art. Artifice. If the painting looks like the work of a monkey, it is art only if it was *not* made by a

15. Are consciousness and free will in some way the same? Are they the same subjective experience? If we are conscious, do we somewhere feel that we created all we perceive? When we are driven—for example, by addiction or reflex—do we nonetheless feel responsible for feeling, sensing, that we are driven? The observer can see that our behavior is determined, not free, but we do not.

monkey; the shift in scripts, not the product, determines our response. Even absolute, platonic clarity, then, is ambiguous; the critic reduces it by wondering how was it accomplished, why, what were the intentions.

The exhibitionist knows he was humiliated, knows it was traumatic, knows it was a repetition, knows he is vulnerable to that humiliation, knows that in the humiliating attack on him are statements about himself he has always known, knows he wants revenge, knows he must pick strangers, knows the social rumpus is important. He knows so much. His aesthetic task is to keep knowing what he knows and yet to not know. (Freud called this "splitting.") So then we get mysteries and secrets and illusions and scripts. We get details that are thrown in not by chance but because they speak. And we get risks that are pseudorisks. The actor knows that.

We really do know that perversion is theater. If there were no mystery, secrets, and illusions, there would be—God forbid—insight. For perversion, insight is the death of excitement. It would require one to come to terms with the trauma and develop the ability to enjoy intimacy with someone else rather than deny it with a manic outburst, the perversion.

MALE VERSUS FEMALE

I cannot account for the differences between men and women in perverse behavior. (Today's social climate is not conducive to such a discussion, anyway, for the issues are too politically loaded to permit quiet reasoning.) I shall, therefore, simply throw out a few opinions.

1. Perversion is far more common in men than in women; women practice almost none of the official diagnoses. I do not think that this is merely a counting error—that women's perversions are hidden from the researchers. I also do not believe that women are less perverse only because they do not dare and that, when society treats women the same as men, women, now free, will be as perverse as men.

2. Testosterone (or whatever we should call the complex interplay of brain and endocrine organs modulated by andro-

gens) makes a difference in the erotic needs of men as compared to women. (The two groups—men and women—should be seen as two overlapping bell curves.) Especially from puberty on into adult life, most boys are driven by their erotic physiology more than most girls are. (This helps account, in addition to social factors, for the raging energy spent by young men in sports, violent crimes, car accidents, and warriorhood.) The drive becomes less intense with the years, but the demands on the psyche exerted by that intense erotic need in earlier years lead to different styles of erotic interpersonal relationships and help drive the fetishizing mechanism so obvious in males.[16] Listening to patients in analysis, I hear the urgency of most men's stiff cocks and its contrast with most women's greater capacity, even when excited, to wait, forgo, refuse if they feel it appropriate to the meaning of the moment. For men—the younger the more so—engorgement dominates engagement. But you do not have to be an analyst or even a researcher to know these truths. They have been questioned only in the past few years, and then mostly for political reasons. I am not saying that women cannot be erotically frantic; everyone knows they can. But does the need in most women come as much from the genitals as in young men? I doubt it. It is more likely to be erotomania, which is more a fire in the soul than in the perineum.

3. Fetishizing is the norm for males, not for females. Though women nowadays can admit to gazing on men's parts and can be as turned on to (what is called) men's pornography as men are, I get the impression that the view of a man's personality is a more reliable erotic stimulant for many women than is a woman's personality for most men. Men's pornography—heterosexual, homosexual, transvestic, whatever—does not depict relationships between people, does not describe desires for emotional intimacy, does not focus on affection and love. Women's does. Men are more worried about successful erotic performance than women are and tie

16. I want to note that conditioning plays its part too, augmenting the effects of the dynamics of meaning and motivation.

their potency to masculinity far more than women tie theirs to femininity. In almost all cultures of which I have heard, the definitions of masculinity tend in a macho direction, wherein manliness is the fear of being feminine and is expressed by the capacity to be cruel, uncommitted, physically dangerous, untender, and uninterested in the woman (the whole person) into whose reproductive organs—a complex land of mystery and miasma—the man is expected to plunge.

Women are afraid of men's physical strength and the paranoid irritability that enhances it, and men are afraid of women's psychologic strength and the patience that enhances it. Women are not afraid they might become less female if intimate with men, but men are afraid to merge with women because they believe that doing so threatens their maleness. Men of advanced technologic societies share with those from primitive places the fear—which can become terror—of women's interior and its habits, functions, desires, and secretions. Our first humiliator is a woman. I think that becomes unbearable to most males and bearable to most females. (The anatomic difference between the sexes creates more than penis envy and castration anxiety.)

Typically heterosexual males in our society, from age five on, forever press to get the clothes off females, seeming to require complete exposure, total revelation. Yet, if you check, you will find few men who can bear the sight of the unadorned nakedness; every girl learns that what drives men wild (as they say in the plummier romances) is anticipation, not total access to the flesh.[17] Castration anxiety contributes to this avoiding, but we understand better if we recall that identity stands behind anatomy. Men, that is, do not fear loss of genitals per se (castration anxiety) as much as they fear to lose their masculinity and—still more fundamental—their sense of maleness.

To save themselves, men avert their full gaze and shift into

17. Freud, however, expresses the majority view: "The progressive concealment of the body which goes along with civilization keeps sexual curiosity awake. This curiosity seeks to complete the sexual object by revealing its hidden parts" (Freud, 1905, S.E. 7:156). I agree with the first sentence. The second makes a complex matter too simple.

aesthetics. We see this at its most efficient in pornography, with its arranging in advance the settings, lighting, and poses, and in the ratings that cultures post, from era to era and place to place, for grading female fat distribution, skin color, facial configuration, carriage, and other aspects of secondary sex characteristics. This fetishizing of external appearances may displace concern about female genitals to other areas, but I think that males also "partialize" females so as to avoid the merging threatened by the acceptance inherent in unimpeded intimacy: if you get too close to a woman you'll be less manly. The classic cowboy movie—the Great American Myth—has the hero struggling manfully against the schoolmarm who tries, by tenderness, to lasso—castrate—him into civility.

I agree with those—almost everyone—who think that at high reproduction time (adolescence and young maturity) most males differ from most females in most societies. Though the bell curves overlap, young men are more driven toward orgasm than young women are.[18] As a result the two sexes simply do not understand each other, thereby increasing the already present hostility in males and masochism in females.

Perversion in men, I believe, is heavily influenced by these dynamics, but I do not forget that these gross generalizations are colored by my personality and are untested by objective studies. So, too, are the ideas of those who disagree.

Let us ponder women's pornography here.

But there is no pornography for women only, you say. There is just pornography, which, though supposedly made for men, attracts women as well. Newspaper feature articles report on heterosexual couples who go to porno cinemas or porno motels. And liberated women publicize their staring at men's pants and penises; they demand not only equal rights but equal drives.

Nonetheless, there *is* a pornography just for women, though it is not recognized as such. Even the millions of women who

---

18. Of those who arrive, more women are mulitorgasmic than men. I disagree, however, with those who believe that women in general, if treated right, are endlessly orgasmic.

use it do not know that the word for these delectable materials is pornography. "Best-selling author Janet Daily has written 79 romance novels since 1975. Almost 100 million books have been printed. Her technique, she told *Redbook* magazine, is to use innuendo without being too specific. 'You say "his roaming hand" without saying where it's roaming. The reader's imagination will supply that. To go too far in print is not romantic at all' " (*Los Angeles Times*, 19 May 1983, p. 2).

Yet they know the stories are—for them (but not for men)—erotic. They openly talk of "sexy" movies and novels, and some know they use elements taken from these stories as the basis for daydreams and at times for overt or (with inhibited women) cryptomasturbation. Such scripts are so far from the erotic dynamics of most men that men, including those who make the laws, cannot imagine excitement could ensue. I disagree with the insistence of feminists that the word *pornography* can be used only for typical male pornography. By that stance, militant women join their enemy—men—in demeaning women's erotic life. By not recognizing, even in the courts, that the material is important to the reading/watching woman, both sides deny her right to have her own unique erotic life. Here are excerpts from an article on the front page of the *Wall Street Journal* (Grover 1980, pp. 1, 14) (written by a man, of course; a lady's pornography is a gent's joke):

THE BODICE-BUSTERS:
A SURE-FIRE FORMULA
FOR LITERARY SUCCESS

Millions of Women Devour
Trite Sagas of Romance;
A Typist Gains Renown

By Stephen Grover

Staff Reporter of THE WALL STREET JOURNAL

NEW YORK—Shannon is the heroine of a 509-page historical romance entitled "Love's Promised Land." "Drawn by love from the plantation luxury of Mobile to the hellish heat of Panama," the cover blurb pants, "she found herself abandoned by the man to whom she'd given her heart—and at the mercy of another whose private desires would dictate her future."

As the author, whose pen name is Diana Haviland, puts it, "What happens to her shouldn't happen to a dog." Yet the escapades of Shannon and her ilk keep millions of readers—most of them women—turning the pages in fascination. These devotees of the historical romance constitute a huge market for publishers, one that has provided a highly profitable prop for the book business during otherwise gloomy times.

Historical romances—or "bodice-busters," as they are known in the trade—have always peppered the best-seller charts. But only in recent years have they been cranked out on a mass-production scale, using a formula that combines fail-safe literary devices and unabashed hucksterism to practically guarantee big sales. Indeed, the florid sagas—issued almost exclusively in paperback and always featuring a strong-willed adventuress heroine—have become publishing's answer to the Big Mac: They are juicy, cheap, predictable and devoured in stupefying quantities by legions of loyal fans. . . .

Meeting such demand is a prodigious task. Jeffrey Hohman, senior buyer for B. Dalton, a leading bookseller, says that of the 400 or so new paperback titles that appear each month, "at least a quarter and sometimes a third" are paperback original romances, gothics or saga fiction. "In terms of sales, they may not match the most successul paperbacks, but they constitute a very large market," he says. Nearly all the 10 major paperback publishing houses include an extensive line of historical romances on their current lists. . . .

"There are about a zillion books out there," says Andrea Cirillo, a literary agent who deals in paperback romances, "and each new title has about a month to make it." Thus, says Walter Meade, publisher of Avon, "the cover is awesomely important."

A successful cover can treble sales of even the least distinguished fiction, Miss Cirillo says. And, in the iconography peculiar to the historical romance, it provides a cryptic signal as to the contents inside. Usually the hero and heroine are shown embracing. But one category of cover, "the almost-kiss," says Rollene Saal, vice president and editor-in-chief of Bantam Books, "shows you that the sex is heavy. The other, known as 'a hugger,' is far less sexy and goes better with family sagas."

Otherwise, the romances are numbingly similar, rarely deviating from tried-and-true plot and character devices. The dashing hero and stunning heroine "are absolutely obsessed with each other," says Mr. Meade. And the plots chronicle their various meetings and partings in a dizzying succession of exotic locales. "The heroines move about so much," Miss Haviland says, "they practically live out of suitcases. Their love affairs are almost always consummated on ships or in hotels. . . ."

As far as I can tell from the titles, from the illustrated book covers reproduced in this article, and from being trapped in a few "women's movies," the hostility themes are present in these scripts but in different form from the male type: illuminated masochism and ultimate success in mastering the hero. *Sweet Savage Love, Whirlwind of Desire, Lost Love, Last Love, Southern Blood:* these are *Gone with the Wind,* not *Hustler* or even "Panty Raid." (If you want to be a pornographer, the Mafia will not muscle in when you publish your *Hustler* or *Penthouse* or *Playboy* for women.) Perhaps the ultimate putdown for women is that legislators, judges, and juries—and women, including militantly alert women—do not even know that women's pornography is pornographic.

"The biggest complaint we get about our adult films is from women, who say they're not female-oriented enough," says Andrew Wald, senior vice president for programming at ON-TV. "They don't want pornography; they want sensuality and eroticism, films where something is left to the imagination. There's a major shortage of product now which fits that mold. But the home audience—men and women—are going to demand much higher quality entertainment than has typically been available in an X-rated film." (*New York Times Magazine,* 13 September 1981, p. 36)

Men just do not understand.

CONCLUSIONS

1. Here are a remaining few thoughts/questions:

   a. Knowing that a central thread in the fabric of perversion is a fantasy of revenge tells us nothing about true danger in perversion. That estimate is beyond our understanding of dynamics.

   b. Does perversion have a positive function for society when anger is subdued to fantasy or to behavior that inflicts no harm on others in reality?

   c. How, when, or why are perversion and art interdependent?

2. The ideas in this chapter make up a system of explanations via scripts—that is, meanings, interpretations. But do not misinterpret my meanings: I do not discount the brain under the mind. Drives and the degree of their intensity power the play. (For psychoanalytic colleagues: I believe more in drives than in drive theory.)

3. I agree with those who let the actual harming of others, not fantasies of harming, be the criterion of morality and the law. Only fanatics equate thoughts with deeds. Though men's pornography depends on the theme of violation, a dirty thought is not a dirty act, and we have no unbiased data that very nasty thoughts lead usually to very nasty acts. (Rust is not steel though both are iron.) To label someone "perverse" says something about his or her psychodynamics, especially about a *fantasy* of harming. It says nothing one way or the other about the chances that dynamic will convert into activity that harms another person.

4. Beware the concept "normal." It is beyond the reach of objectivity. It tries to connote statistical validity but hides brute judgments on social and private goodness that, if admitted, would promote honesty and modesty we do not yet have in patriots, lawmakers, psychoanalysts, and philosophers. Except when being avowedly polemical, just give the data, do not summarize them by declaring they add up to normality. As a philosophic position (though I cannot recommend it as solid

truth), I—when sitting on the psychoanalytic perch and seeing the pieces and complexity of even the simplest seeming behavior—prefer to look on most everything as aberrant and then scale it all on degrees of aberrancy. In that way I express the awareness that all behavior comes partly out of our life history and contains elements of early, still unmastered traumas, frustrations, and other pains. The fact that the final product—the behavior—works well says little about the original events that were transformed into egosyntonic action.

5. Everyone knows that the desire to harm someone is bad; without wanting to be wicked, we would just be dumb animals attacking for food. But having the fantasy of harming is usually only a small part of one's total erotic experience. In the minor perversions—those called "normal behavior"—the hostility mechanism is a trace element, adding piquancy, fun, surprise. It works to keep pleasure from spoiling. An analogy may help. All living tissues share carbon as a common element, but living tissue is far more than carbon.[19] Despite the commonality, the differences are immense. (My heart sinks when people tell me my theory is that sexual excitement depends on people's being mentally or physically cruel.)[20]

We see that concept in another excitement: humor. Some humor is painful, some gentle, some malicious, some warm, some mocking, some insightful. But there is no humor without victims and victors, implied or manifest. One person's joke is another's insult. Both people have been touched by the hostile theme, but the one who laughs has gained an insight the other

19. The analogy is not perfect. I know that all living tissue has carbon but that not all erotic excitement has hostility.

20. An example of how someone can listen and get it all wrong: "While Stoller *has claimed* that all sexual excitement is based on hostility toward the sexual object, other researchers . . . [the author of this quote included] *have shown* sexual arousal to correlate with positive affective responses" (Heiman 1980, italics added). My feelings of being misused comes from the author's not noting how often I have written that (1) the hostility dynamic I have proposed is a hypothesis, not a law; (2) when present, it is often a whisper, not a roar, and only a part, not the whole; (3) I choose to put aside (but am not uninformed about) issues of "positive affective responses."

had to reject. Hostility, like the carbon atom, is a sine qua non, whether it is scarcely there or thickly larded in. Still, humor is far more than hostility. (Perhaps aesthetics is [or studies?] the means by which hostility is transformed from dangerous to safe.)

6. Non perversion is the real subject of my interest (perversion is only a device for finding dimensions, that is, for finding definition) and the issue I asked you at the start to hold as a silent support for this explanation of perversion. I do not define it by the anatomy used, the sex of the participants, its theater elements, or its aesthetics but by our acceptance of the selfhood, the humanness, of those we might need. No airbrushing. When we are accepting another (which requires accepting oneself), we can be intimate with (the body and personality of) another. You realize, then, that at the bottom of my descriptions is a moral, not a scientific issue. Perversion, I say, is the solution to a failure of intimacy, with my bias being that intimacy—letting a person be (per Hannah Arendt)—is good.

The nonperverse person does not powerfully fear intimacy, because he or she is not afraid that it will lead to a merging that swallows up identity. To be practical, we might best say "perversion" when one uses an erotic act for the purpose of avoiding intimacy—intimacy of personhood, not just anatomy—with another. But that thought brings us to affection, respect, warmth, acceptance, inner freedom, tenderness, and love, subjects even harder to discuss sanely than cruelty, revenge, humiliation, and hatred.

CHAPTER 2
Erotics/Aesthetics

Well, says the philosopher, physiologist, sociologist, or behavorist, let us please not fuss about sexual excitement; you get excited or you do not. It depends on the essences, such as beauty or attractiveness; it depends on the wiring and the hormones; it depends on social class, era, surplus value, economics; it depends on the conditioning, on chance contiguities. But I say not quite, in fact no: though they are all part of it, it's a matter of aesthetics. Or, putting the same thing differently, it's a matter of opinion, of biases, of styles, form, neuroses, interpretations, fantasies, meanings, taste. Of bad taste, actually, bad in the sense of poor and bad in the sense of immoral: for most people, no badness, no excitement (Is sex dirty? Only, Woody Allen notes, if it's done right.) It is, says the cliché, in the eye of the beholder, and almost everyone knows it.

To defend—against philosophers, biobehavioral scientists, and aesthetes—the premise that erotics is a matter of taste, this chapter expands on ideas published earlier (Stoller 1979) and glanced at in the last chapter. I shall try to link the special case—erotics—with the broader subject—aesthetics. In doing so, I shall use not only cognitive argument but also aesthetics—writing style, Americanized, rather unprofessional—to exemplify some of the issues to be examined. For, as in any piece written for publication, each punctuation mark, each word, the length of each sentence, each parenthetic remark, the grammar, and the rhetoric are governed by aesthetic impulses, whether the author is aware of that or not. (How, for instance, should I get to the next sentence?)

Look, in your mind, at this photograph. It is of a nude (or would "naked" be more provocative?) woman. No: a female;

girl; lady. Do you see? Already we are into aesthetics. Which word is exactly the right one—is pleasing, well formed, fits best, creates the desired effect, does so subliminally ("naturally": when something is "natural," it supposedly needs no explanation; a fine idea for destroying science) and therefore more deftly—to portray the micromood we want to produce at this point in the sentence? You and I are manufacturing an anticipation, and we want to do it exactly right. So, if we are limited to written words, every word counts, including the ones we think do not. It's all aesthetics. For the photograph is the same, whether we choose to describe the subject as girl, lady, woman, or female.

Let us play some more. We look at her; the print stays the same, but you are going to change. For I tell you: she is a starlet, a harlot, the farmer's daughter, your neighbor's daughter, you neighbor, unmarried, married, divorced, American, French, eighteen, twenty-eight, a farm girl, a city girl, five feet two with eyes of blue, six foot two with a size 12 shoe, the breasts are real (how about the shift that comes with our changing "the breasts" to "her breasts"; and what if we use the colloquialism "boobs"?), her breasts were augmented by a plastic surgeon (and why does he prefer "augmented"?). She is your sister, your daughter, wife, mother. She is married to the president—of the United States, of ITT, the university (which one?), the Kalamazoo Krackers Ko., the California Chamber Symphony Society. She is a student in your seminar on epistemologic hermeneutics, a cheerleader, an airline stewardess posing for *Playboy*, a mud wrestler. She is lesbian, straight, bisexual, oversexed, nymphomaniacal but frigid.

In fact, none of these is true. The reason her hand is hiding her genitals is not to simulate modesty but because she is an unoperated transsexual male.

No; that was a trick. (You don't laugh? Then laughter, too, is aesthetics. Why restrict aesthetics to art, especially when we cannot agree on what is art, what is a work of art, and who is allowed to be called an artist? The dynamics that underlie aesthetics may be the same whatever field you study: painting, sculpture, poetry, novels, theater productions, cooking, humor, gardening, scientific experimentation, high-wire acrobatics, debating, defecating, murder, or erotic excitement. Aesthetics is the study of adjectives and adverbs.)

And who are you who is watching? Male, female, boy, girl, man, woman, straight, gay, researcher, pornographer, born-again, astronomer, philosopher, Philadelphian?

Suppose, instead of this pose, she were nude (naked) but wearing high heels; a rear view, a side view, walking, sitting on the toilet (and doing what?), in her underwear—silk or cotton?

Who was the cameraman? What conjunction of planets and stars existed at the instant the shutter clicked? Would he have done better to use color film—Kodachrome or Ektachrome? Was the picture doctored to remove blemishes? What is the difference between a beauty mark, a mole, and a nevus; skin, hide, cutis, cuticle, integument, or epidermis?

Aesthetics all.

The complexity of simple pleasure: do you really think that erotic attraction is a matter of chemistry, thunderbolts, swollen phalli, enchanted evenings, or spinal reflexes? (You can see how that sentence is constructed to get effects. Different readers will respond differently.)

The dictionary (*Webster's* 1961) says that aesthetics is "1: a branch of philosophy dealing with beauty and the beautiful esp. with judgments of taste concerning them: a: the science of sensuous knowledge whose goal is beauty—compare LOGIC b: TRANSCENDENTAL AESTHETIC c: a particular philosophical theory or conception of art . . . 2: the philosophy or science of art; *specif:* the science whose subject matter is the description and explanation of the arts, artistic phenomena, and aesthetic experience and includes the psychology, sociology, ethnology, and history of the arts and essentially related aspects."

"Dealing with beauty and the beautiful": suppose something excites *because* it is not beautiful; that would be covered by aesthetics, wouldn't it? Who defines beauty? That, too, is an issue for aesthetics. At what point, with what measurements, on what scale are judgments such as "well made," "well applied," "perfect," "imperfect," "well contrived" promoted to "beautiful" and thus eligible for aesthetic consideration? When is a poem beautiful, or a car, a sea, a lima bean, a face, a cock, a rock? Cannot any object, any behavior, any mental state be the focus of aesthetic study? Aestheticians, as the dictionary hints, are beauticians; are beauticians aestheticians? Who owns the right to say?

The dictionary, in some of its meanings, links aesthetics to the beautiful but in others to art, which certainly includes more than beauty—whatever that is. It seems to me that pleasingness or an approach to one's sense of a perfect form are also connoted, so that there can be an aesthetics of, say, evil. Art, we have all experienced, reaches far beyond the usual criteria of beauty and health. Cleverness is a part of aesthetics, too: new, efficient, surprising ways of staying *within* the rules of the game played between audience and artist.

Collingwood, in his classic text (1958), is concerned that aesthetics, art, and beauty be distinguished. He and the dictionary disagree: "Aesthetic theory," he says, "is the theory not of beauty but of art" (p. 41). With the professionals in disagreement, let an amateur throw in three profundities: Art is what someone calls Art; an Artist is someone called an Artist (by himself or herself or another); Beauty is present when someone proclaims it is present. No more, no less. "There really is no such thing as art. There are only artists" (Gombrich 1956, p. 5).

I hereby appoint myself Aesthetician. And thereby—as self-assured as an art critic—pronounce as truth my conviction that the construction of erotic excitement is every bit as subtle, complex, inspired, profound, tidal, fascinating, awesome, problematic, unconscious-soaked, and genuis-haunted as the creation of dreams or art. I proclaim erotic excitement a matter of and for aesthetics (unless we are too fancy to admit baser subjects to higher consideration). We might even learn more about aesthetics from studying erotism than by working with refined notions such as Beauty or Art.

For this passage, then, I shall live dangerously—an excitement—and I shall look at aesthetics, a subject about which I have no formal knowledge or training, and shall use what must seem an unaesthetic activity: the psychophysiologic experience called excitement. Even worse, I make the case with *erotic* excitement as the example. Because, in part, aesthetics is a morality performance, I shall touch on the question of levels of awareness—conscious, preconscious, unconscious—in creating effects: who in me is responsible? Or should it be "what"?

Let's say we turned to pornography for insight. But would the fragments we used be pornography? Suppose they are not pornographic. (As noted in chapter 1, something is pornography if it *intends* to be pornographic—that is, to arouse. We should lable it pornography for its aspiration, not its success. In other words, a piece of pornography may not be pornographic: it depends, we all know, on who is reading, watching, listening. Recall your response to the Bruce King saga.) Suppose their intent is to arouse, and they do not. Suppose they are meant to be dirty, and they only amuse. (Comparable to the poor exhibitionist, who, on exposing his genitals to a woman, is greeted with amusement, not horror. What dismay, what disarray, what a loss of excitement: Delicate Construction Collapses.) Dirtiness is, of course, an aesthetic—also its twin, obscenity. We should not equate what is worth studying by aesthetics as something inherently finer, better, superior. Otherwise, we may be left only with ugly fights about Beauty.

Aesthetics—art critics to the contrary—is a matter of opinion. Beauty may be forever, but all the things that represent it will someday somewhere be someone's trash or, worse, be incomprehensible or, worst, be of no interest. "No," throbs the Romantic, "it is Art, and it is Eternal." (Capital letters count.) We make the same mistake if we think that what excites us erotically is a permanent and universal heritage of our species, not bound by culture and one's private history. There are few eternal verities in art or erotics. It's all in the interpretation, as everyone knows, and interpretations vary.

In other words, styles and taste are made, not born. An aesthetic conviction is an achievement, not inevitable or natural, as in "Natural Law." (Note for those who would misunderstand: of course I know that there is a somatic fundament to erotic excitement.)

Most of this is obvious and old hat, even to those who disagree. And allow me the aesthetic choice of representing these ideas by clichés. I hope it is also obvious, then, that the study of erotic excitement is just an example at hand for studying aesthetics, an example that, because it is concrete, universal, ordinary, and not burdened by millennia of philosophic discourse, can give a fresh view unencumbered by high-minded flummery.

An erection, penile or clitoral, is as heavy with fantasies as a cod with roe.[1] By fantasies I mean meanings, scripts, interpretations, tales, myths, memories, beliefs, melodramas, and built like a playwright's plot, with exquisite care, no matter how casual and spontaneous the product appears. In this story—which may take form in a daydream as one's habitual method of operation for erotic encounters, in styles of dress and other adornments, in erotic object choice, and in preference in pornography (in brief, in any and all manifestations of erotic desire)—I shall keep insisting that *every detail counts.*

Rapidity of response and the conscious feeling of spontaneity make one think that an aesthetic experience is not constructed, leading to an untested belief that the causes are nonmental, (amor non cogitur, they used to say), unplanned (for example, inherited), or that there are no causes: the thing just *is.* "People sometimes talk as if 'selection' were an essential part of every artist's work. This is a mistake. In art proper there is no such thing; the artist draws what he sees, expresses what he feels, makes a clean breast of his experience, concealing nothing and altering nothing" (Collingwood 1958, p. 56).

What difference is there, then, between the makeup of what is regularly accepted as aesthetic excitement, excitement in general, erotic excitement, and neurosis? Not so much. Content, mostly, more than structure. (Not just my contention, of course; similar notions have been argued in psychoanalytic circles from Freud on.) Note that I am not saying that aesthetics equals neurosis. Neurosis may participate, but it takes more than neurosis to make Mozart. (Unless you dislike Mozart, in which case what I call art you'll call neurosis or worse. Substitute Cage for Mozart.)

Not all aesthetic responses are excitement, of course. As with

1. Compare Kris 1952, p. 178: "The existence of annihilation fantasies behind comic gestures."

erotic life, one can also feel unadorned pleasure, sadness, boredom, anger, disgust—the whole crowd of affects, usually in a
state of mixedness. Two kinds of "mixed": (1) more than one
affect clearly felt at the same time; (2) one dominant with
others subliminal or unconscious. Caution: I am not thinking
here of creativity but only of the structure of excitements.

Let me tell you something funny, about men who get turned
on by lady amputees. (You don't think that's funny? Perhaps
you have no sense of humor.) These men—why no women?—
have started to organize and in doing so have named themselves. In this exercise in aesthetics, they have come up with
the term *amelotatist*, meaning one with an inclination toward
people lacking a limb or limbs. (You recognize that making it
into a Greek-syllabled state reduces one's guilt and shame: aesthetics is classy.) I quote from an anonymously written, unpublished monograph:

> The single leg, above-the-knee amputee is indeed the most
> popular . . . but there is another qualification: She must have a
> remaining stump. . . . [In the poll taken by the researchers] the
> SAK [single leg above knee] hip amputee got more first-place votes
> than the DAK [double leg above knee] with stumps. . . . the single
> leg amputee is more popular than the double leg, but the presence
> of stumps is more important than the number of limbs ampu-
> tated. . . . leg amputees took the first eight places in the ranking of
> means of all votes for a given type of amputee. The only variation
> on this continuity was the combination of one arm and one leg
> who [sic] took sixth place. . . . Those described as having congeni-
> tal defects ranked dead last. The amelotatist is no more immune to
> discrimination in this case than the rest of the population. . . .
> only 10% of the population [in the research] would choose an arm
> amputee first while 78% prefer the leg amputee as first choice.
> Eight percent chose arm-leg combinations and 4% preferred those
> with congenital defects. . . . For those who gave the single leg
> amputee as their first choice, other significant preferences showed
> up. He definitely wanted her to be using two armpit-type crutches.
> Wheel chairs and artifical limbs are out. A single crutch would do
> as a second choice and a peg leg or double forearm-type crutches
> would serve as third choice. Those who chose the single leg-at-hip
> amputee responded in the same manner, except they preferred the

forearm crutches over the single crutch. . . . The same group would prefer that the amputee's stump be exposed or partially exposed and that she be well-dressed. Casual attire would do, but full formals are not desired except by a few. It would be better if she had medium or long hair. Short hair is not popular. High heels are the next requirement. If you can believe all this with shorts or a swimsuit as a clothing style, you have the single leg amelotatist's preferences. When asked about how he liked her clothing altered when wearing slacks, he answered tailored, either open or sewn closed. . . . When asked to describe his ideal amputee, the respondents [*sic*] clearly preferred the blue-eyed, blonde, with long hair, about 29 years old, five-five and weighing 123 pounds. When describing clothing and shoes, the respondents split down the middle between the girl in a dress or skirt with high heels and the girl in shorts or swimsuit who is barefoot. Thirteen percent wanted her nude. They clearly preferred to picture her standing, even talking, posing, or walking. The only surprise was that 26% wanted to picture her alone, that is, not with respondent.

Note the author's aesthetic judgment in choosing the standard, late twentieth-century, Western society, even-toned, sensible, objective, scientific manner of reporting on the statistical relationships between women with amputated limbs and men jacking off. Today's magazines mix in an interview of the Secretary of State with photos of the boopsies.

Can't you picture an SAK arguing the merits of his preferences with a COLBA (combination, one leg, both arms)? The argument, depending on the participants' exquisiteness, might sound as scornful as in art, as elegant as in fashion, as fastidious as in bathroom ornaments, as restrained as in cuisine minceur, as manly as in bullfighting, as refined as in oratory, as scientific as in metapsychology.

DYNAMICS OF EXCITEMENT

Up to this point, I have felt on firm ground: anything can be given an aesthetic treatment. But now, whatever my rhetorical devices, I shall really only be sharing questions, hunches, and possibilities: I am not sure to what extent the dynamics of erotic excitement and other excitements are connected. (I am not playing the innocent, looking for advance absolution for dumbness and laziness; rather, I am trying to get your focused attention, trying to prevent you from discarding these ideas because I am unfamiliar with the vocabulary, concepts, literature, and authorities in aesthetics. If you are restrained from scorning the lack of scholarship, then you can better argue with the argument.)

And from lack of knowledge, I ask another indulgence. I can work well enough from the data with which I am familiar—people's erotic thoughts—but I have no comparable data on people's thoughts about the excitements found in the world of art. I must, then, leave it to you to extrapolate from my observations to yours—a dangerous device in confrontation.

Note that I am not discussing (do not know enough to discuss) the specific techniques by which the artist changes the raw material of his motives—desires, meanings, scripts, and so on—into the product that we accept as work of art. Those questions, of a different sort of "why" and "how," belong properly more to the branch of psychology known as aesthetics than to that we call psychodynamics.

Which is not to say that aesthetics and psychodynamics are totally different, just that each has its own rules. For instance, a recognized aspect of humor is efficiency and cleverness. One can define and describe the kinds of efficiency and cleverness that will please—exhilarate—an audience; and that discussion can be one of aesthetics. Or one can study why a culture or an individual comes to admire efficiency and cleverness, and that could be a psychodynamic study. At any rate, I shall not study these aesthetic aspects of art, humor, pornography, and so on.

What is excitement? (It comes from *citare*, "to put in motion.") Three examples from the dictionary: "Stir up (as a person or a hive of bees)"; "to energize (as an electromagnet): produce a magnetic field in." It is a dynamic tension: a buzz, vibration, an oscillation, a pulsation, a current, alternating with immense speed between two poles. It is not fulfillment, pleasure, an ending, but rather anticipation, a tease, a swarm of possibilities. Only because there are two poles—the two possibilities—can excitement emerge. But if we are to become excited, we must experience the poles simultaneously and also be placed pretty much equidistant between them. When the poles are switched on—immediately—then, like the energy that forms a magnetic field or the light in a bulb, we turn on. I could never list all the polar fields that might make an excitement, but they are such things as: aesthetic/anaesthetic, alive/ dead, active/passive, safe/endangered, unmasked/masked, brave/cowardly, loving/hating, loved/hated, kill/be killed, start/ not start, move/stop, clever/stupid, strong/weak, secrets kept/ secrets exposed, unbound/bound, I/not-I, in control/out of control, free (for example, from deception)/enslaved (by deception), sound/silence, accepted/rejected, broken/whole, triumphant/humiliated, shall I/shan't I, can I/can't I, will I/won't I (refusal), defended/defenseless, familiar/strange, clarity/confusion, movement/paralysis, constancy/inconstancy, time/timelessness, go/stop, permanence/change, knowledge/ignorance, simplicity/ambiguity, tension/relaxation, beginning/end, art/science, hard/soft, innocence/guilt, pleasure/unpleasure, actor/audience, on/off, in/out, up/down, light/dark, dexter/sinister, sane/crazy, erect/impotent, manic/depressed, male/female, man/woman, separation/fusion, seamed/seamless, true/false.[2] Perhaps the most useful is succeed/fail. With that one, certainly, you can see how aesthetics and erotics are related.

The next point carries me beyond safety. Aesthetics and erotics, in the minds of participants, are creations (attitudes, fantasies, and so on) whose purpose is to blur or avoid reality. Next step in the hypothesis: to blur or avoid reality by simulating some aspect of reality, including psychic reality, such as emotions.

The poles in the metaphor are markers limiting a territory within which the energy vibrates. Beyond the poles are experiences not of anticipation but of consummation, either present or guaranteed. Excitement is uncertainty; certainty brings plea-

2. "The unique combination of feelings which traditionally describes the aesthetic experience: a simultaneous force and calm (Nietzsche), vitality and ease (Berenson 1948), energy and repose (Stokes 1955)" (Rose 1980, p. 371).

sure, pain, or no response, but not excitement. Beyond too much lies fear/terror/panic, one's knowing something awful is occurring. Beyond too little is boredom. Straight through leads to pleasure. The task put to us in the experiences we call aesthetic is to constrict the situation so that, no matter how actively we move, we stay inside the poles. Otherwise, we are uneasy or uninterested.

Simulation, then, is the crucial word. Too much reality is just too much. But when we can control its dosage—when we can write the script, hire the actors, and direct the performance—the field of excitement is prepared. We do this in daydreams, works of art, pornography, and the unnumbered scenarios that unroll for us each day in what we call reality.

"Safety in the aesthetic illusion protects from the danger in reality, even if both dangers should be identical. . . . The maintenance of the aesthetic illusion promises the safety to which we were aspiring and guarantees freedom from guilt, since [in the artistic production] it is not our own fantasy we follow. . . . Art offers such socially approved occasions. . . . [However, the] intensity should not grow too much, but should be kept moderate. We are warned to remain at a safe distance. Too great an intensity of reaction may threaten the aesthetic illusion. . . . We touch here upon a problem which in the philosophy of art has played a considerable role, at least since Kant and Schiller, i.e., that the dispassionate spectator alone can appreciate beauty" (Kris 1952, pp. 45–46). Art is in the mind, says its protectors, not in the crotch (compare, Collingwood 1958, p. 37). Is this sanitizing of art truth or compulsive hand washing?

Must it be that an experience to which the term *beauty* can be attached should not be too intense? Otherwise the body is too much involved for the aesthete, whose aesthetic principle hides a flagrantly moral one. For these Oedipides, beauty can't be juicy.

The two poles are risk and safety, but the whole business is a fraud, an act, a performance, a masquerade, a disguise—no matter how much the author of each life proclaims about truth.[3] There are moral issues here. Let us say that when our deceptions are unconscious we are not liars, not in a state of full responsibility. The moral issues arise when one can, even if it is difficult, grab one's motives if they are conscious even for just a flash. What shall we do with daydreaming, where we know that one is quite consciously deceiving oneself, inventing a story known to be untrue, embellishing it—that is, putting on the aesthetic polish—from motivations one knows are different from what is portrayed in the story line? Yet, for all that falsity, tissues swell. Fantasy converts to physiology. And how much do we do that all day long, not just with daydreams? Is not all entertainment constructed that way, including the entertainments some use to romanticize the real world, distorting everything from casual encounters to war?

What is portrayed is danger. Why say *portrayed?* Is not excitement the response to anticipating true danger with the outcome still unclear? It depends. For the excitements we are discussing here (aesthetic excitements) the situation is staged—arranged, produced (in the publishing or theater sense)—by the individual. One gets the idea, sketches in the plot, casts the players, writes the detailed script, and mounts the production. The final form may vary—a complex habitual piece of behavior; a symptom; an idea or image subjectively experienced as unexpected, unplanned, spontaneous; an irruption or epiphany; a belief; a (conscious) daydream; a published—that is, disguised, transformed, intricate—daydream, such as a novel or play; a complex crypto daydream, such as nonfiction or poetry; or synesthetically transmuted daydreams, unconscious scripts, and script shards, such as paintings, music, sculpture. If the subject matter is erotic and intends to excite, the product, if published, is pornorgaphy.

What determines the production's form is first the creator-producer and second the audience. By audience I mean either

3. Though the practice of art may be a search for truth, I want to repeat the familiar wisdom that the artist searching for truth is often (usually, always?) also a liar. That in itself should make for some excitements.

the audience the creator imagines or the audience that actually shows up, as, for instance, with a play or a painting. (Though even in that case, the audience is imagined: what the artist believes is his audience and what the individuals making up the audience are feeling are two different—sometimes *very* different—states.) Let me try this on: a sine qua non of what will be categorized as aesthetic is *audience*, real or imagined (compare, Collingwood 1958, pp. 118–19). More than that, a work of art becomes a work of art only when it is created by both the artist and the audience.

Can there then be excitement without an implied or perceived audience? I think so. That type of excitement will be of a sort that does not arouse aesthetic impulses and that is not created from an aesthetic intent. It is the true (that is, genuine, nonscripted, nonornamented, nonperformance-modified) form that the second type—aesthetic experiences, aesthetic excitements— simulates. The essential factor causing true excitement is oncoming but not yet present, true/nondramatized trauma. One's fate is still in the balance. When the odds are greatly against us, we are terrified. With better but still poor odds, we are anxious/ excited. An estimate around 50/50 promotes an uncertainty/ excitement, and improving odds introduce a few sparkles of pleasure (but not consummatory pleasure) into the experience. Lowered odds move us toward dread, favorable odds toward relief or joy. From these beginning definitions, we can see that *excitement* is, like all other words used to label affective experiences, a generic term. It only approximates the specific experience; one cannot always or completely distinguish fear and anxiety, or pleasure and good times, from excitement.

Some, probably, can convert any dreadful experience into one they manage to experience as a game (for example, by denial)— that is, they wrench the scripts into new shapes. Most people, however, cannot convert from true to aesthetic excitements such situations as that of soldiers moving up to combat or civilians hearing enemy bombers approach.[4]

---

4. A footnote for completeness. Reality is, of course, only what we know is reality. And so an approach to combat has different reality for the soldier

Because unadorned fear is hard to bear and carries in itself the hint that we can go out of control, we do what we can to make it less unpleasant. Fear (a feeling that indicates we think the odds are poor) then changes to true excitement (which, along with threat, has its promise that we have a chance) to aesthetic excitement (in which we are now the masters of the action, since *we* now decide what is reality). We make what is for us true reality less real, more bearable. Excitement, then, is a continuum of anxiety/fear into which has been poured the possibility of pleasure, especially of mastery. Here, to reduce oversimplifying, is another case. An experienced actor, before the curtain rises, may no longer suffer stage fright but now feels excitement. Anxiety has been modified by his memory of previous survivals, even successes, perhaps triumphs, toward mastery.

True excitement, in summary, occurs when we are weighing the odds between danger (trauma) and safety, without introducing illusion to shift the odds. Aesthetic (including erotic) excitement is, however, theater. An anticipated audience is crucial, serving to mask that the drama is staged.[5] Beyond that, the audience—imagined at the time of creating, real later—serves as conscience (corruptible, of course; that's the art). For another set of poles between which vibration occurs are such judgments as: well done/badly done, acceptance/rejection, true (when something is false/false (when something is true),

who has never been there from one who has. For the first, the reality has not been completed; there may be enough romance in the expectations that he may even sing brave songs. His excitement takes place in his imagination, on a stage, perhaps influenced by movies he has seen. The excitement is still aesthetic. On being introduced to reality, he next approaches combat with a grimmer excitement, the kind I am calling true. You can be sure that though we, in the safety of intellectual exercises such as this, have trouble separating true from aesthetic excitements, there are billions of unfortunate people who daily make the distinction.

5. "Aesthetic *form* . . . calls for an active contract with the audience. To begin with, we might say that it requires on one part the capacity to trust and from the other side that it be trustworthy. [It also requires a mutual taste for conspiracy.] A readiness to participate responsively calls for assurances of safety. . . . Serious breaches of this contract can be disastrous" (Rose 1980, p. 356), such as telling a joke and having no one laugh.

knave/hero, open/secretive, deceptive/insightful, well performed/poorly performed, smart/dumb.

Do aestheticians talk of the corruption of conscience as a necessary quality for an aesthetic experience? I guess not. In fact, the manifest content of aesthetic discussions among academicians, I suspect, is built on good-conscience concepts: ideals, perfection, purity, beauty, essences—experiences from which the dross of falseness, illusion, anger, humiliation, trickery, and secrecy have been removed—unless about an artist we do not admire.

True excitement, then, is defined by the reality of the risk and is made up of two simultaneous and opposing judgments regarding an oncoming danger: I shall be all right/I shall not. An aesthetic excitement is defined by its pseudorisk: if I control the production, then I make sure that what I represent to myself as danger is only pseudodanger. Therefore, the oscillation is a piece of theater, and my task is an aesthetic one only: how to create enough effects that I transiently lose my awareness that there is no genuine risk. This, then, is art, artifice, artifact, artificial, artful (as in "the artist" and "The Artful Dodger").

Fenichel (1945, p. 463) writes of the process of erotizing anxiety. I now see that process as a defense by which we convert oncoming true trauma into scripted trauma: simulated trauma, mastered trauma. One can get addicted to that sport. Chronic worrying would be an example. By forever anticipating trouble, one hopes to prevent its unexpected visit. Maybe the best of all simulations are those that occur under real circumstances. Then, as in, say, shoplifting, hang gliding, or hanging oneself to get an orgasm, real danger is nonetheless incorporated into a scenario, like going to a whorehouse rather than a library to find characters for one's story. Cheap thrills, safe thrills. Triumph, not trauma. Performance.

The theory, then, that we go to art, such as the theater, for catharsis—to experience the truth and thereby purge ourselves—is unlikely, a conceit: "We read novels, look at pictures, go to the theatre in order to interact and take a position in relation to them. At the least they act like magic rituals reassuring us that nothing is new, nothing has changed, all is safe and well, we never left home. At most, our sensibilities are refreshed by an exciting and sometimes anxious [pseudo-anxious] trip, from which we return safely but forced [pseudoforced] to look at our familiar self and world in some [simulated] new ways" (Rose 1980, p. 368). I suspect that most simulators are not looking for true education but are teaching us how to use intellectualizations, rationalizations, fancy insights, aesthetics arguments, badinage.

That, however, is the nasty side, not the whole of it. That the dynamics of behavior have roots in the traumas, frustrations, and defenses of childhood does not mean that much of daily life cannot be conflict-free. I ignore such reality now but nonetheless recall that there is a huge literature pointing up nonneurotic sources of creativity. For instance:

> Because of the historical development of psychoanalysis, as well as Freud's personal tastes, the analytic view of aesthetics has traditionaly been that of defense. Aesthetics was a way of paying a bonus to the censor in order to gratify a forbidden wish in a somewhat attenuated form. Scarcely, if at all, distinguished from a neurotic symptom, dream, or joke, art became trivialized [as I am doing herein] as a diversion. . . . The essentially aesthetic quality of form, including, of course, musical form, was ignored. (Rose 1980, pp. 353–54)

> The coexistence of primary and secondary processes on all levels, in moment-by-moment functioning, and the two-way traffic between them, implies that fusion and dedifferentiation take place continuously and not just once upon a time at a certain developmental stage. What was initially a fragility of early ego boundaries may become an adaptive flexibility, and one that functions autonomously. Though this may recall the earliest fusions and separations it does not signify that the aesthetic experience involves a regression, a nostalgic journey. It is precisely the close experience of the past without regression, the sensuously textured past contemporaneous with the present, expanding the moment with greater dimensionality and a heightened sense of transience, that distinguishes the aesthetic experience from the merely sentimental. (p. 369)

For most of us, unadorned reality would boil our eyeballs. If we are to learn anything that is true, we may find that only a roundabout approach is possible. Perhaps, even from infancy on, our desire to know the truth is also a constant pressure. We can't stand it, but we also can't stand living without it. Maybe we are not completely crazy: who, of those who buy tickets to war movies, would also buy a ticket to the war?

What troubles me is less that we stage our excitements than that we deny we do so. We deny we are responsible for our plots, beliefs, scripts. We thereby claim we are innocent or at least ignorant; we do not know, we say, what we are doing. ("Before the photo session started I was fully clothed, but before I knew it, I was posing nude," the ex-Miss America is quoted, in a news report, as saying.) And when accusations fly, we willingly feel guilty all the time rather than admit our true guilt. The trick is to confess to the wrong thing.

Everyone knows, at least everyone who daydreams knows, that daydreams function to alter reality—to undo traumas and frustrations, to provide instant though transient mastery, to disguise safely (which nowadays can even include what seems to be no disguise). It is no news that daydreams can be one source of art.

Kris (1952) writes of this transforming of danger, via daydreams, to mastery, even triumph. He tells of a boy who, frightened by a dog, "relives the pleasurable experience of the conquest of danger in his daydreams. The delight of the triumph explains why play and daydreams can be repeated time and again" (p. 32). That is simple enough: the daydream serves to bring pleasure, not excitement. Who would refuse pleasure? But Kris stops his exploration too soon. He does not note that when older, that boy does not settle for simplicity, for unadorned healing of trauma by fantasy. Instead, he develops a penchant for excitement; he is into aesthetics. Now in his daydreams (including purchased daydreams, such as books, movies, and television), he has introduced the appearance of uncertainty and thereby gets to excitement, even thrills. Simple reparative work is now childish, obviously, trashy; it lacks aesthetic punch. If, then, undoing the trauma is a triumph, aesthetics is the introducing of still another triumph: taking on the challenge, as in art, of a task of many and subtle dimensions, with high risk of failure in the eyes of an audience—oneself or others—and yet succeeding. Minor success is marked when one survives by managing rules (that is, talent), and great success is measured by one's survival after breaking rules (genius).

The point here, once again, is that aesthetics is a game. Like chess or football, it simulates by manipulating the symbols of danger. Kris misses that in his discussion of danger and triumph. His is a more innocent view of aesthetics, art, excitement.

Aesthetic mechanisms, then, are (among other things) techniques used similtaneiously to disguise and to communicate this trauma-to-triumph defense. When the creator (artist, pornographer, masturbator) packages his product well, his audience (which includes himself) is also stirred and for more or less the same reasons as was the creator. The trick is to prevent too much insight from arising in either party, for—the mechanisms understood—there would not be excitement, only wisdom (or arousal and unadorned pleasure, or guilt, anxiety, anger, despair, boredom).

Kris misses this mechanism, too. As does Freud, who, impressed that people repeat their traumas, said he had discovered a new biologic imperative—repetition compulsion (later, when he made entropy an instinct, to be called Death Instinct). Repeating our delights is only part of it. I believe that the dynamics of excitement, because insight is missing, must be replayed to infinity. As a cure for trauma, aesthetic excitement is as effective as scratching is for poison oak. It bears repeating.

Kris points us to other interesting issues, but I shall defer going in those directions, preferring for the moment to let him lead me to talk more directly about erotic excitement and to use that discussion in this effort to understand aesthetic experiences better. "One might . . . ask to what extent the aesthetic attitude is limited to the reaction to art. To attempt more than speculation would mean to enter into areas of research which are particularly difficult to approach. Our expectation, however, is that psychoanalysis supplies useful equipment for these investigations and that the process of psychoanalytic work in practice and theory might continue to improve the value of the tools which we have to offer" (Kris, 1952, p. 63). I am trying to do that with erotics, as he did with humor (see below). Here is a summarizing statement.

Erotic excitement, as in its aesthetic forms, for example, pornography, private daydreams, psychodramas acted with prostitutes or spouses or other willing players, is created and/or heightened for most people when one has built up a script in which uncertainty of outcome is portrayed, when danger is possible and work must be done to prevent a bad outcome. That work—aesthetic mechanisms—consists of putting into scripts these elements in greater or lesser amount: safety factors, mystery, secrets, risk, illusion, reversal of trauma or frustration to triumph, revenge, and dehumanization/fetishization (Stoller 1979).

By safety factors I mean elements in the story used to disguise the underlying dynamics I am describing so that the process that leads to the experience of excitement is not interrupted by unplanned anxiety or guilt. By mystery I mean converting the known to the unknown and converting the unknown to the inexplicable—supernatural, wondrous, beyond investigation, beyond question. By risk I mean depiction of risk, which is really pseudorisk: the main character in the story is at risk, but the daydreamer, though idenfitying with the main character, is not. By revenge I mean retaliation in which we overpower, if not humiliate, those we see as current representatives of the ones who, in past times, harmed us by humiliating us when we could not defend ourselves. By illusion I mean prestidigitation: tricky fingers, deception of one's self, and the keen pursuit of an audience—co-conspirators—willing to share the same deceptions. By secrets I mean information consciously kept to prevent others from knowing the truths we quite consciously know about ourself. By dehumanization I mean reducing another person to one or another favored body part (anatomization) or to a cliché ("all men are pigs") or to nonhuman status (fetishization). Obviously, these techniques are all powered by hostility. Only when these dynamics of excitement work as planned, as in a well-told joke, does pleasure come. Let us look at humor. It makes a nice bridge between reactions to art and erotics.

KRIS ON HUMOR

The most respected study of aesthetics by an analyst is Kris's *Psychoanalytic Explorations in Art* (1952). It has helped me for years, but recently, on returning to it after organizing my ideas on erotic excitement, I felt that he sometimes does not bite deeply enough.

Let me take his views of humor, a subject he uses extensively to explicate aesthetics, to measure our differences. We disagree in that Kris does not see hostility and defenses against recognizing it as being central in humor. (He wrote this study before Grotjahn's [1958], which insists on the importance of hostility in all humor.) To me it is clear that, without someone who is put down, there is no humor, though the audience must be protected in the depiction from feeling too sadistic or too attacked as it identifies with the parties in the script. To test this hypothesis about humor, we need only take the situation out of its frame—a told joke, a movie or play, a magazine's cartoon—and picture the same event happening in the real world. Then, without the safety factors, the hostility shows more clearly. Kris is far less innocent than, say, this older analytic view: "Humor is never sadistic" (Dooley 1934, p. 50). But, like Freud, he does not go all the way and claim there is a sadism—a humiliating of someone(thing)—in all humor. They find hostility only in the sharper forms of humor, those labeled, for instance, wit or caricature.

The right word for the form the hostility takes in humor and erotic excitement is humiliation, which word/affect connotes not only attack but that the victim, in some part, agrees with the attack. Without humiliation (for example, were the victim to react with pride rather than shame), the attackers have failed to harm their victim's essence (self) even if they tear off his arm. Note how an audience can switch its allegiance to the victim who cannot be victimized.

Kris, I believe, leans away from seeing the hostility that energizes humor. He does this throughout his exploration of art. For instance: "Among the many works of art that have come to us from earlier times there is not one which may be said to serve exclusively or even predominantly aggressive purposes" (p. 143). That cannot be unless one is dealing with the manifest content of the work of art rather than the artist's motives— conscious or unconscious—while at work. Yet Kris would surely not describe art, as do Beauty fans, as a form that does not provoke.

Here is another case where I find Kris prefers to emphasize the more benign aspects:

> One might suggest that the element of suddenness in this economic process [of creating the comic] is responsible for the nature of comic pleasure. We know what happens if sudden relief occurs: The energy held in check by the inhibition suddenly becomes superfluous and is ready to be discharged in laughter. . . . But Freud did not confine the essence of the comic to its economic function. He recognized another of its properties in what he calls the relation to the infantile, to the pleasures and pains of childhood, to childhood itself. . . . Under the influence of the comic, we return to the happiness of childhood. We can throw off the fetters of logical thinking and revel in a long-forgotten freedom. The perfect example of this type of behavior is pleasure in talking nonsense; here we handle words as we did when children. (p. 205)

I offer a less wholesome, more complex hypothesis: we do not simply repeat the traumas and joys of childhood in humor, erotic life, and art; we *simulate* repetition.

The only adults who talk nonsense are brain damaged. And I doubt that many children, from the moment they first acquire words, talk nonsense, when when they babble. Infants, before they have words, can alter the sounds of their crying in ways that show they have most cunningly sized up the situation. Is it not guileless to believe that "under the influence of the comic, we return to the happiness of childhood?" At best, we might say that we *try* to do so or partly do so, or do so but also-much-more-than-that-in-the-same-instant.

Beyond that, I doubt if much of the laughter of children is innocent. I prefer Hobbes, whom Kris quotes: "The passion of laughter is nothing but sudden glory arising in ourselves from

sudden conception of some eminency in ourselves by comparison with the inferiority of others *or with our own formerly*"
(p. 208, Hobbes's italics). Why, since Kris knows this, does he
stress the innocent joys of humor? (I modify Hobbes only in
recalling that "formerly" is, in us all, "at present" as well.)

Kris goes on: "Hobbes, in my opinion, is more akin to Freud
than any later psychologist, although Freud takes economy in
expenditure not superiority to be the decisive element in comic
comparison" (p. 208). I disagree with Freud in that I believe
both are equally necessary; remove either "eminency by comparison with the inferiority of others"—that is, hostility—or
economy, and no humor remains. "Economy" by itself does
not entertain us but only makes us feel its producer's cleverness. (I am ignoring the subtle differences between wit, comic,
and humor; they have much in common. See Freud [1960,
p. 236] for his view of their differences.)

Kris slights another point. He believes that when we identify
with a victim, we do not laugh. I would say, rather, that we
laugh *only* when we identify with everyone in the joke, including the victim. Keep in mind that when you are laughing, you
are laughing at yourself. If you are not laughing at yourself,
you are not laughing. (Though I have not checked carefully, I
think I have voiced no joke, double entrendre, hyperbole, or
sarcasm in my life where the joke was not also on me.) But
whether, on so identifying, we laugh or gnash our teeth depends on aesthetics: how and when we identify, what form the
identification takes. If it is too complete and too intense, no
space is left for laughing at ourselves. Is wryness the important
aspect—overt or subliminal—in feeling amused? If so, that
means I have a dim awareness that I am *all* the characters in
the script. Perhaps what happens is that, with laughter, identification is moving into consciousness, and the movement
itself—toward freedom—adds to what Freud and Kris call the
"release of mental energy." (Laughter is a sign of insight: the
one inside us who gets us to laugh is the one who already has
the insight.)

So when Kris says, "Enjoyment of the comic entails a feeling
of complete security from danger" (p. 209), I feel he misses an

essence, that the comic depends on a sense of danger. Risk (pseudorisk) is foreplay for aesthetic pleasure, and only when the safety factors have been deployed so that we glimpse (preferably suddenly, as Freud noted) that we are not in danger can we break loose our pleasure in the form of laughter or other joy at an artist's succeeding. (Success: the experience of taking a risk and not failing.)

Kris, again chained to innocence: "When in fact does a child find an experience funny? . . . A preliminary condition is *complete* [my italics] control over the function in question. An absurd movement on the part of another person will seem funny to a child *only* when it has itself mastered the movement. . . . Laughter may denote superiority [Hobbes], but it denotes something else as well. Not so much '*I can do it better*' as '*I can do it*' " (p. 209, Kris's italics). Not quite: the excitement followed by laughter occurs not when the child has mastered the action, as Kris says, but only when he has mastered it not so totally that there is no awareness left that he could still fail. For the child, as for us, laughter includes, "I succeeded. I escaped."[6]

Yet, along with his blander explanations, Kris knows how tension energizes humor: "Our sense of the comic is preceded by an experience which can be compared to a kind of examination, to a resistance test if you like. We do not necessarily relive the entire form or situation in our infantile development; a fear signal, however faint, may take its place. A feeling of anxiety over our own powers of mastery, or more accurately, the memory of an averted, superfluous anxiety, seems to accompany the comic" (p. 209). With this insight he shows he was wrong to claim the child needs "complete control" as a preliminary to being amused.

Kris demonstrates this dynamic in the French *drôle* and German *komisch*, words for "comic" that also "denote anger or surprise," and how "*drôle* has undergone a transformation of meaning from the uncanny to the comic," as in the case with our *funny*, which can mean "comic" or "odd." Risk and safety.

6. Compare Grotjahn on "infantile pleasures such as exhibitionism, nonsense, and play on words" (1958, p. 13).

He says, "I suggested calling this peculiarity of the comic the double-edged character of comic phenomena" (p. 214): the two-pole oscillation that links excitement to aesthetics.

Kris cites "the mechanism latent in all comic": "Relief is achieved by a previous increase in tension" (p. 214). Correct. But we need to know more: what is the nature of that tension? I have suggested one part: that the tension is more precisely to be called excitement; that excitement is an oscillation; that the oscillation is between success and failure; that, in aesthetic excitement, the person experiencing the excitement is also its author and has, in advance, scripted a pseudorisk guaranteed to work out well and therefore lead to pleasure. This does not bring us to understand the differences between excitements (for example, erotic versus comic) but only gives us common denominators.

My contribution, however, can keep us from another of Kris's mistakes, when he describes the psychology of the grotesque as different from that of the comic (p. 204). He is again making the error of aestheticians who presume that there are eternal verities, such as grotesqueness, rather than seeing that one person's grotesquerie is another's humor (as in the case of, for example Lenny Bruce). I find an experience grotesque when not enough safety factors are present: I am too close to the trauma. You may find the same situation more protected and, being enough removed, laugh, even if nervously.

An essay by Kohut shows that some of the dynamics of aesthetic excitement I have sketched may apply to another experience—music. "With this background of security the musical ego[7] can now playfully repeat the original traumatic threat and enjoy it. A minor increase of tension is created by the musical movement into dissonance and followed by enjoyable tension relief as the music returns to consonance. Thus the playful mastery of the threat of being overwhelmed by sounds becomes an enjoyable ego activity which contributes to the total enjoyment of the music" (Kohut 1957, p. 392). Does this description not also fit humor?

7. Why do theorizers think their theory is stronger when they fortify sensible ideas with jargon?

CAUTIONS AND CONCLUSIONS

Most aestheticans would say (though more aesthetically): keep your dirty analytic fingers off our subject, as if knowing that a painting is made from pigment reduces the triumph of the art. But their concern is warranted; those who are not careful come to believe that the psychodynamic origins of art and aesthetics explain art and aesthetics. That is not the aim of this chapter, which, when it touches on art, is about a response—excitement— to creative acts, not about creativity.

In the hope of forestalling confusion, let me make some declarations:

I am not studying art or aesthetics but excitement, the dynamics of excitement, whether it is caused by erotics, humor, art, or whatever.

My suggestions seem obvious, not much new. I have said only that the particulars others find are more generally true than they thought. Freud and Kris (and plenty more) saw that hostility could be present in humor; all I have done (following Grotjahn) is to say that it is always present. Others (for example, feminist groups) have said there is hostility in all pornography, by which they mean only men's heterosexual pornography; all I have done is to suggest that hostility is present in the rest of the erotic scripts and daydreams of both men and women. Others (for example, Genet [1964, p. 7] and the dictionary) know that excitement is an oscillation; I add only that the oscillation is between danger and safety. Others know that what is sometimes called tension is, more precisely, excitement, a tension to be found in a variety of experiences, such as appreciation of art or of humor; I add only that these different tensions have common denominators. Others know that erotics is a matter of taste; I add only that erotics is as much a matter of aesthetics as is art.

Some may still insist that I find nothing more to art, humor, erotics, aesthetics, than excitement; or that, despite disclaimers, I confuse excitement with pleasure; or that I blur the separation between art and response to art; or that I think that showing the primitive, neurotic energies of excitement reveals the truth about art; or that I do not appreciate the sophisticated, complex, skilled, synthetic functions that put the pieces—archaic and advanced, gross and subtle—together in the final product; or that I cannot see that the process of creation is more than the crunching together of its component parts and dynamics (Rose 1980, p. 369); or that I believe the dynamics described here are all that excitement consists of; or that I think hostility equals humor or hostility equals excitement.

I am not saying that the published form of erotic excitement—pornography—is art, only that pornography has its aesthetics. I agree with Collingwood, who distinguishes art from other creative work by their purposes. Art, he finds, is not craft, representation, magic, or amusement. Whatever may be the fate of a work of art, its purpose lies only in the artist's mind: its purpose is *to be*, that is, to be an expression of the artist's mind. But craft, magic, amusements, and aesthetic excitements are meant to influence; they have purposes beyond that they are simply to be. So too, of course, with daydreams, including pornography. Art, then, is not "the skill to amuse people, or in general to arouse emotions in them." Instead, "art is the activity of expressing emotions" (Collingwood 1958, pp. 117, 118). Art lies beyond the dynamics I describe. It is likely, therefore, that, as in "erotic art," the less an artist has pornographic intent, the fewer the people who will find the work pornographic.

My theory of the dynamics of aesthetic excitements has its dark side—trauma, humiliation, revenge, deception—but these are dynamics only. We are far from informed if we do not also experience the aesthetics, especially the conflict-free quantities and qualities. The following are different: a murder portrayed in the theater, a murder in a myth, and a murder in a joke. Each stirs different feelings in us, though each has a murder as the common denominator.

I hope these explications help. I do not mind being wrong, but I do not want to be misunderstood.

CHAPTER 3
Centerfold

This chapter carries forward the discussion of the aesthetics of erotism. The clinical data come from Olympia, a centerfold. I use her, first, to exemplify the subliminal communication of unconscious fantasies that passes between people engaged in erotic adventure and, second, to reinforce the hypothesis that, in our culture, men fetishize—dehumanize—women in order to be erotically stimulated. That women do this with men and that this mechanism is needed for sexual excitement in general, not just for heterosexuality, are issues not reconsidered now. The argument, you now know, goes like this.

From infancy, people experience frustration, trauma, and other pain inflected by those to whom they turn for intimacy, dependence, love, sensual gratification, and clear-cut erotic desire. The resulting conflicts and attempted resolutions are visible to anyone who looks at infants, children, adolescents, or adults. The resolution that most affects erotic life, is, I think, revenge and its partner, the sense of righteousness that rationalizes cruelty. Dehumanization is revenge, a triumphant act offered by men in most societies as proof of masculinity, an undoing of a sense of victimhood and weakness vis-à-vis the category of objects (for example, women) one desires. It aims to prove to ourselves and to inflict on our objects the magical belief that we can reduce people to less than they are. We do this in two ways. Either we ignore our awareness that people are human like us and focus only on certain anatomic parts or on partial aspects of their personality, or we turn our backs on humans entirely and desire the nonhuman, such as a garment.

To preserve their damaged erotic capacity, people create and, as the years pass, polish up daydreams, private and published, conscious and unconscious. And they move these daydreams into the real world, finding partners for the action. For these scripts to work, to cause physiologic change, one must deceive oneself, hide one's intentions from oneself. If not, excitement is replaced by either anxiety or boredom. Especially useful in the task of deception is the representation of risk in the script. Excitement is a buzzing oscillation between, among other things, the sense of danger and a sense of mastery leading to gratification. If the mastery comes without effort, for too many people it does not include excitement. To prevent such dullness, mystery—the illusion that raises something merely unknown to the grandly supernatural—is coveted by those who need it to sustain flagging interest.

Perhaps because the illusion of uncertainty—the appearance of risk—is heightened if the game is played out as if it were beyond one's own scripting and direction, pornography provides a safe lift; even better—more pretense of danger—is to collect in the real world players whom one chooses because they show, in their behavior, that they will perform within the limits of what is needed or who otherwise indicate that they can be manipulated into taking the assigned roles. Those who are outside these limits are consciously felt as either uninteresting or too frightening. It would seem useful, therefore, to look at the psychologic "space" between people engaging in an erotic performance in order to observe their ways of communicating—of ordering each other about, of bargaining, of teasing and gratifying, of measuring risks and safeties: what is that plaything in the centerfold saying to her audience of men, and what are they saying to her?

As wise men say, it takes two to tango. So the trick, when you are afraid, is to touch without touching, to steal intimacy but not to be caught at it either by others or by yourself. To understand this subliminal, interpersonal communication, we must hear not only from the fetishizer but also from the fetish. Olympia's remarks to me, though a bit novel, can point us toward general hypotheses about excitement and can alert us to the similar but less obvious dynamics that society avoids looking at when it calls behavior normal (as in labeling it simply biologic: men look at women because it is natural to do so; is that not explanation enough?).

She was not a patient but rather a volunteer for an interview before a medical school class. The subject of the lecture was hysterical personality, and I had asked residents if they knew someone in treatment who could represent the histrionic, erotized quality of that diagnosis. None did; but there was Olympia, an acquaintance of one resident's girlfriend. She eagerly agreed to be interviewed.

As you will see, she is constructed to be a fetish. Since childhood, she has experienced her body as an object to be displayed to an audience. In adolescence, she consciously set about to recreate its appearance so that it would be a product on which she could capitalize. She does not sense her interior self as a formed identity or as being contiguous with the body she inhabits. With conversion reactions she negates body functions and parts almost on command. If it were not for the secrets to which she alludes, or for her sense of humor and the intelligence that supports it, I would not have known, when talking with her, that anyone was home. In the brief time we had together (an initial interview, one before the students, one on videotape for future classes, and a final talk), she revealed only flashes of her childhood, but they suggest we need not be surprised that she turned out as she did.

For the sake of this discussion, let us ignore questions about dynamics and diagnosis. My focus is not on how she was invented, what motives energize her, or how we might assess her pathology (for example, hysterical personality, borderline personality), but simply to see out of what she is formed. She may then serve in our task to clarify the general rules that make the fit between voyeur and exhibitionist exact enough to unleash excitement.

INTERVIEWS

S: Tell me about yourself.

O: OK. One thing I have to my advantage is that I am totally without shame. Nothing shocks me, surprises me, or embarrasses me. I can be very blunt and very honest. Someone can ask me anything and be very direct with me; it never bothers me or offends me. [These statements are now being rattled off almost as a set speech, the speech of a star being interviewed for the hundredth time: to give the effect of normality, competence, breathless enthusiasm, earnestness, intelligence, and professionalism.] I'm trying to establish myself as a sexual star and have been working to create my skills as a sexual type of entertainer. I've paid a lot of attention to observing what a person's response is in entertainment. You don't decide what an audience wants: rather, you fill a void that's there. I try to keep myself receptive to what they want to see and keep myself as archetypal [a nice word for a fetish] as possible, to say a little about myself in each thing I do so that each person in the audience will see what they want to see.

I've always been fascinated with go-go. Because what I'm really fascinated with is dance. Nude dancing is the most credible dance form, because you're actually doing something that makes sense: there's no beginning, middle, and end with a story being told. Everybody knows what you're doing. Lots of times dancing loses credibility because it looks like a bunch of fruits prancing around. But I am interested in my dancing because of the sexualism in it. From what I've seen, sex really does rule the world on all levels. That seems to be the strongest thing in any human—that sexual drive. My choreographer told me one time, "We have a lot of work to do; cut out your sex life completely so we can rechannel your energy." It was true. We progressed about four years in six months. My interest in go-go dancing started from about five years old. I can remember standing on a pillow and doing burlesque routines. There wasn't a drawer in my room that wasn't broken from my taking it out and standing on it until my feet went through. Then I would build huge colossal things from upside-down chairs and tables and drawers on top of the bed. Then I would strip. Or sometimes sing. There wasn't an audience. I'd do it for myself. The reason I like working on stage is to create illusions and fantasies. I do that for myself. And it's nice if an audience can share them too, because I am getting appreciation for the illusions. But mainly I do it for myself. I don't think it's exhibitionism, because I don't feel naked when I have my clothes off. Instead, I have always thought it was that I was entertaining people. What else would I be doing if I was standing on the lawn and wanted to do something? The major reason I don't feel naked is because I'm confident with my figure. I can go up on stage and take all my clothes off and feel just as comfortable as I do right now. But if I had to go up on stage and tell my deepest personal secrets, that would make me feel naked. But not my body: what's so different about *my* body? There are billions of versions of it. All women have the same equipment I have.

All the time I was growing up, my mother said, "Aren't you ever going to learn how to sit like a lady? We're so tired of looking at your underwear," never realizing that that would be my fortune. All the random incidents in my life, all the people I've know, everything that's happened ties into now. Just recently, someone told me that he's never seen anyone so happy in his life.

My memory goes way back. My first memory was [at] six months. In the memory, I don't remember my mother; I don't remember myself; there's no people; there's no action. All I remember is the bathroom. With all those early memories: no event and no people.

I remember, when I was around four, whenever I had to tinkle, my father'd take me to the men's room, because he didn't think I'd be safe in the ladies' room by myself. I remember standing by the urinals, watching all the men tinkle; that was one of my favorite forms of entertainment. He and my mother believed that children wouldn't be safe going into a public rest room by themselves: if you sent a four-year-old kid into the ladies' room by herself, you don't know who might be in there. There might be some kind of sex crime, for instance. My mother had pointed out to me in the newspaper where little boys had gone into the rest room at gas stations and had their peepies cut off by some razor-wielding fiend who's hiding out in there. I don't think they were as concerned about a sex crime as much as the permanent mutilation involved with it. They're both very, very naive: they were sure that in public rest rooms, if you send a child in by themselves, there is always the possibility that a mutilating homicidal maniac is waiting.

S: Even in the ladies' room?

O: I'm sure there are women mutilators as well as men mutilators.

S: More memories?

O: There was quite a while that I thought I was a dog and would go potty in the yard. I was terribly disappointed when I learned that I wasn't. I was sure that I was a dog because I felt very, very close to my pet dog. So I would sleep under the porch. I never found my identity in physical likeness. I had quite a bit of difficulty as a child. I was suicidal for a time, because I never felt attached to my body. I just felt completely detached from my body; I felt like a completely separate entity from it. I still see my body as a tool, something to be used.

S: Give me an example of how today you sense not being attached to your body.

O: I don't feel pain.

S: What do you mean, literally?

O: I really don't feel pain. If something feels sensual or very, very good, I have heightened experiences, like taking a bath or caresses. But pain: I'll cut myself or get bruises and never even notice. With my dancing, I don't feel any pain. I think what it is is that I have pain but don't allow myself to feel it. I have a kind of memory in the back of my mind that has been there for some time, but I never let it move forward consciously. I keep it a subconscious thing, a limiting thing.

S: Have you ever been paralyzed?

O: Yes. I used to have a thing where I would begin to lose consciousness, a fainting spell. I never went completely under. I would just lose the sense of feeling or control of my body. I would be unable to see; my vision would black out completely. I would be unable to hear anything. If I spoke, I wouldn't be able to hear myself speaking or to feel it being done. It would just be totally closed under. I would feel a heavy weight just pulling me down. I think it might have been a metabolic kind of thing. Once I had pressure to complete an art project and couldn't think of anything. So I paralyzed my right arm and side, couldn't move it in any way. But I didn't worry about it, because I know it was just tension. As soon as an idea came for the art project, I had full use of my arm again. I paralyzed my vocal chords because of my Spanish class; as soon as I dropped the class I was back to normal. Once, out of tension, I blinded myself. For four days. The doctor decided it was a brain tumor. When I broke off my engagement, which, ironically, was to an optometrist, my vision came back.

I have only been engaged once. Because I don't think it's for me. I don't like making sacrifices for an involvement I would have to make: I wouldn't want to have to ever cancel a dancing lesson or anything. Because my business is to model, sing, act, and dance. They all fall in the category of entertainment and the trick is to make them all work together. I've developed an incredibly close relationship with people who are involved in it—my manager, my choreographer, my dancing teacher, singing teacher, the woman who draws up the advertising work that I use in the trades, the songwriter, the costume maker, my photographer, the guy who writes up biographies on me and publicity releases and lines that I should drop in certain situations. Oh—and a financial backer. We're all involved in the same thing—creating a certain sexual image. And they're as much a part of that image. I remove myself from myself. I see myself as a commodity. They are as much me as I am. We're all equal pieces of the pie. All I am is the physical likeness in the act. Without them, I would be nothing.

S: Who are you?

O: The real me doesn't have a name, doesn't have a face. It doesn't have that spark of life or whatever.

S: The person who goes by the name of Olympia is not you exactly, is that right?

O: No, because they haven't named *me*. They've named my body, my [public] personality. It's hard to understand, because there aren't words to describe it.

S: Should you have a name?

O: No. Although Olympia is talking to you, Olympia would be nine or ten feet under the ground and rotting if it weren't for me—the part of me that's the spark of life, a small part of the collective unconscious, and the sum total of actions. Twenty-five girls send their pictures in to *Raunch* magazine, and each has the same unique idea. But if I'm going to succeed, it does me no good to do a hundred and five *Vogue* layouts: people will never know who I am; that way, I'm just an anonymous face, but by dealing with *Raunch*, they always identify me, and I'm established as a personality. With the pictures of me, there's a name, there's a story; they build up a personality. And people read it. If they have a circulation of four million, they figure twenty million read it. So that's twenty million people, at least in the month of July, who will know me as the Lovely Lilac of L.A. And my name.

S: So you look on yourself—on Olympia—as a corporation, in which different people do different things? Your contribution is to put that body out there——

O: Yes, because the physical is the instrument by which the performance is put on. Entertainers aren't born, they are created. All entertainers are put together. And I do have someone who's put me together: my manager. He tells me how to dress, what style of makeup, just everything. If I weren't put together, I never really could have cared less about my physical appearance. As a result, I looked very, very dumpy because I didn't have any identity. As a child, I never had any kind of image or appearance. Just to live.

Then I realized if I was going to succeed, I'd have to be put together. I am trying to establish myself as a particular personality. That's what's nice about *Raunch*. Though I plan to play a part, the reader doesn't know that. They think that's me and that's my name. So now, I have much more credibility with people. I say things and people listen now, even though I'm the exact same person I was five years ago. The main centerfold is saying that. So it must be important. I had a terrible problem as a teenager; there was a terrible, terrible waste occurring. There was no way I could reach millions of people so that they would say, "Yes. She did brush her hair today!" [Laughs] I've always needed to be a legend.

So I got right down to business. I starting pushing. It worked. I was able to get parts in films. I started dancing. When I first started, I was really terrible. But I realized that if I let talent stand in my way, I would never accomplish it. Everyone admitted I was the worst dancer they had ever seen. And no one could imagine how anyone had that much nerve to stand up there and dance when they were so awful. But I had a huge following, and I was making a fortune in tips, I tried so hard. Go-go.

When the man who is now my choreographer came in the first time and saw me, he realized that he couldn't find a bigger challenge: there was never going to be a worse dancer. It was like *Pygmalion*. I became the best dancer there.

I sit in the kitchen with my choreographer, and the guy that writes up the things for me, and the woman in the advertising; we sat there and decided, now what is my personality going to be? We decide it will be this and that, but we leave the space open, trying to make it as archetypal as possible. What type of speech, what kind of walk, what's her childhood, what affects a certain demographic but not another demographic? The same way you market any product; the same way as this cigarette. The same way you market a package of cigarettes, we are marketing sexual personality. A person that appeals to the sexuality in everyone.

S: Are you interested in sex for yourself or only as a product?

O: Oh, I have the same desires as everyone. But at this stage of the game, I feel that sex only takes away that same hour that I would be on the phone to my costume maker, for instance. I barely have enought time to sleep and eat as it is. I don't have the time. When

I do have the time—and who knows when that will be, maybe in a year—I have the same desires everyone does.

The sexuality in me extends in all areas of my life, particularly creativity. I write a bit, and I'm a big fan of science fiction. And I realized one day that the biggest part of female sex organs, the most important and best part, isn't what's there, but what isn't. It's the space, it's the void. I was thinking about how all women don't have the same fears of actual physical inadequacies that men do: it's what's not there that counts, not what *is* there. Wouldn't it be interesting [science-fiction story she may write] if there were a linkup, that people are linked up to everything in nature. Like a black hole in space so that on the day that a black hole in space became activated and began to suck up the whole universe, all the vaginas in the world also became activated to sucking to a lesser extent: pulling up the carpets, the little knicknacks, and all of them turn themselves inside out and disappear.

So I will talk to the medical students. What a story for a TV talk show: to ask me about my sexcapade, and I say, "By the way, I was interviewed by 150 students about sex." As far as being an entertainer, it gives a chance to do something for the real me. I honestly believe wholeheartedly the statement that the whole is larger than the sum of its parts. So I feel the more of my parts have been exposed to the public, the larger I will become.

We talk again.

O: I'll start with my mother. She and I are very, very close. She has been a real source of inspiration to me to see how it does pay off when you apply yourself to things. She's a very, very humorous person, very warm. One of my best friends, my mother. She's very attractive; still gets checked for her identification to get a drink in a cocktail lounge. She is thrilled about my career. She had a great deal of artistic talent when she was my age. Amongst her talents was acting. She always regrets missing that opportunity. So she is living through my experiences; she's thrilled with them. She's incredibly supportive. In fact, she's got everyone she knows buying *Raunch* magazine. She says it's the best centerfold ever. She has seen an advance copy and is just thrilled. My father's an absolute fool. We don't get along at all. So I avoid him. Like one time he told me that I had cadaver appeal, that I could look forward to growing older so that I would become interesting, that what I had going for me now was attractiveness and a body—nothing more than cadaver appeal. He could have said it a little more tactfully.

S: Was he ever close to you when you were little?

O: I've never been close to anyone in my life. I keep my distance. As much as I was close to anyone, I would say we were close.

S: Tell me more about you.

O: I get bored very, very easily. So I have to seek out the bizarre in life and new experiences. If there's a carnival, I'll drive hundreds of miles to go see the freak show.

My sexual life started when I was very little just looking at organs. My mother was always free about nudity. She was always nude around me. I remember spending a lot of time looking at what she had. She would play jokes. She'd put on a hat and gloves and belt and nothing else and say, "Good bye, I'm going to the store now." It was a very, very familiar thing to see her nude. When I was six months old and sleeping with her, I woke up with a scream because I had bit her on the ass. I had found that interesting. She told me about it.

Her body appealed to me in that I knew it was a sexual organ. It was interesting, and my vision was drawn to it. I don't know if it appealed to me as far as actually doing anything about it. I was fascinated. I just about gave myself eyestrain looking. As far back as I can remember.

S: What were you looking at or looking for?

O: Just trying to look through the hair to see what was there. She didn't make any big deal about it. She just went about her business. And then, with the other girls [friends], we'd look at each other. And that was a big bore. So we'd look at the boy next door. But I'm sick of it now, from working as a medical assistant in a free clinic and in nude dancing. At first it was fascinating, but it's something you get used to. It was fascinating to discover that each one was different. It's more distinctive than their faces. It's easier to recognize people from the other end than from their face. It got to a point where it was a turn on. Labia were the most interesting parts of the whole body, because that's where the difference is. And that is the most interesting.

I didn't have as much interest in male genitals as female. My interest in the female, I think, was in trying to understand myself. At the clinic, when I finally had seen enough and learned enough to understand completely everything I had and how it works, I became bored. With me, I take it more for granted, not as interested in detail. There is just no mystery to what men have. It's right there.

S: What is the biggest visual turn on you've ever had?

O: It's the one wearing the mask. Because there's a uniqueness about it. And it's anonymous. A mask of some kind: I was wearing one, and they were wearing one. I was always wanting to do something different with him. So we decided to wear masks; we both agreed there was an appeal in it. No matter how free you are with another person, you're aware they are watching you—your expressions, what you're doing. But when you face is covered, you don't have to worry what shows on your face. And there is no point looking at the other person's face because it is covered. So it is just pure physical pleasure for pleasure's sake—anonymousness. And you couldn't do the same in black darkness, because you would not be able to see the body. You have to mask facial expressions. Just a mask to cover up. I tried with eyes covered. But that is no good, because then you can't see out and see the other's body. The mask should just hide facial expressions: the other person's facial expressions, and [so] that they can't see yours. Sometimes, you might feel a particular way, but you have to force a big smile for your partner's sake, for their security. With a mask, you're freer.

Fragments from our TV interview. Just before taping began, as we were talking together, she looked in the direction of the camera behind the one-way window and noted that she has sometimes enjoyed videotaping her sexual encounters. Then:

O: I don't know if you ever tried this: I have a boyfriend with a videotape setup. It was terrific. It's really nice to be able to watch what you were just experiencing. There is something about photographing it that made it more enjoyable than plain watching it. I could see what I was doing and tried to work on it and get it better. Things like, "Gee. Next time, I'm taking my underwear off." Or, "I'll put my hair up from now on; look how raggedy the ends are." That's picking up the little things, but basically, it's fun to watch actual sex activities.

S: Are you ever dissatisfied with your performance?

O: Oh, yeah. If it's a bad camera angle and if the camera isn't moving, you have to move in front of it. You get something which at one angle would be quite lovely. But you get in a bad angle: I might look a little bit cruddy.

S: When there is no camera and you are having sexual relations, are you still on camera?

O: Yes. I'm on camera twenty-four hours a day. I never felt attached to my body. I felt I would have much more freedom as a part of the collective unconsciousness, as a spirit, if I were freed of the physical limitations in a container like this [body]. Without the container, I could totally disperse and be in a billion places all over the universe at the same time. But it's not just a container; it's a tool for accomplishing things. It helps us to physically identify ourselves to other people. And we decorate the outside when we dress, style ourselves, carry ourselves. When we dress ourselves and when we carry ourselves, we can give any kind of appearance we like. That's why female impersonators are usually much more feminine and put together than actual women, because women just take it for granted since they are a female body. Whereas a female impersonator will study all the feminine movements and style of dress.

S: Did you study that?

O: Yes. I've studied all that.

S: Are you a female impersonator?

O: Yes. Because I'm a natural clod. I feel that I'm a female impersonator. I like to joke because I don't have that natural femininity. My coach told me: why didn't I try a wig on? So I'd put my wig on and come to class. It would be crooked on my head with a point up at the end and the bangs hanging down in front, my eyelashes up to here, my nail polish smeared all over. None of those things that seemed to come so naturally to some women ever came naturally to me. I always thought I had the grace of a truck driver but I discovered that it's not a matter of gracefulness, it's a matter of knowing how to do things by studying. For example, I could show you two ways of sitting on the floor, one graceful like an accomplished dancer and one like a clod.

S: Which would be you?

O: Hopefully, the studied one.

S: But that implies it's not you.

O: But it's an accomplishment. What purpose am I here for, if not my accomplishments?

S: *Who are you?*

O: Who? Olympia Dancing-Doll: The Sweet with the SuperSupreme.

S: What the hell is that?

O: That's the title of my act. And all the years they told me, wouldn't

I ever learn to sit right, they were so sick of looking at my under-wear. And it came to be my fortune, at least with *Raunch*. With underwear and without underwear. But it's always in the same poses I was in as a kid.

S: So you have an unfair advantage.

O: Lewdity comes naturally to me. Lewdness for lewdness' sake.

S: You don't look that way now. Am I missing something or is the "lewdity" an act?

O: Oh. The lewdity is an act; that's why I do it. I become bored very, very easily.

S: Have you ever in your life been real?

O: No. Because everything I do I can see it as part of a movie scene. When I go to the grocery store, it is act 1, scene 3: "At the Grocery Store." It's not, I just went to the grocery store. It is either in a film or on stage or something I will eventually write.

S: So even now, when you're on stage with an actual television camera here, there's another stage on which this is taking place.

O: Yes. What else!

S: Is there ever a moment when a feeling slips through that has not been observed or studied or controlled or planned?

O: I don't think so. When I was growing up, my father would say, "Look at it this way. Imagine how good it's going to look in your autobiography." So I got used to thinking of everything in terms of being written.

S: [I point at her] This is a body. Is it your body?

O: Yes.

S: Are you your body?

O: No. I'm not my body but *it* is my body.

S: How does it feel inside your body? *You* are inside your body. Am I wording it right?

O: No. I'm not inside it. The actual me is just different degrees of energy. As far as a body, a personality, a voice, and a mental process is concerned, they are for me to make use of. They are something for the energy force to propel for the sake of actions. So I am "The Sweet with the SuperSupreme." "Strip the Starlet": that's the name of my act.

DISCUSSION

Because this series of centerfold beauties has an *n* of one, we need not fuss about reliability or validity. One could even suspect that Olympia is in a class of her own; she certainly is unlike anyone else I have met. But there is relief at hand for those who scorn reports from a single case. The publisher has found a far larger sample and done the computations for us. First, the hunch: he looked at Olympia and saw her exuding output. Then he funded a pilot study to test if she could transmit her signals onto film. After the prints, the project: he came up with the resources to pay for a press run in the millions to accommodate the millions of men out there who would detect her messages. Finally, a program for extended confirmation: he performs the experiment month after month with different women as the fetish. In other words, his research design is effective; he will make money. He and his customers understand the psychodynamics too elusive for the uncorrupted mind of Science.

I need not be too smug; we cannot believe that most women whose profession is to exhibit—models, starlets, exotic dancers—are as disconnected internally as Olympia. She fits my argument too well. But who doubts, after endless study of hysterical personality, that the diffusion of identity is, beneath the acting and exaggeration and to a milder degree, its essense? A quotation from Anaïs Nin (a bit jazzed up by Nin's hysteria-transmuted-to-art) can stand for the mass:

> As June walked toward me from the darkness of the garden into the light of the door, I saw for the first time the most beautiful woman on earth. A startlingly white face, burning dark eyes, a face so alive I felt it would consume itself before my eyes. Years ago I tried to imagine a true beauty; I created in my mind an image of just such a woman. I had never seen her until last night. Yet I knew long ago the phosphorescent color of her skin, her huntress profile, the evenness of her teeth. She is bizarre, fantastic, nervous, like someone in a high fever. Her beauty drowned me. As I sat before her, I felt I would do anything she asked of me. Henry suddenly faded. She was color and billiance and strangeness. By the end of the evening I had extricated myself from her power. She killed my admiration by her talk. Her talk. The enormous ego, false, weak, posturing. She lacks the courage of her personality, which is sensual, heavy with experience. Her

role alone preoccupies her. She invents drama in which she always stars. I am sure she creates genuine dramas, genuine chaos and whirlpools of feelings, but I feel that her share in it is a pose. That night, in spite of my response to her, she sought to be whatever she felt I wanted her to be. She is an actress every moment. I cannot grasp the core of June. (Nin 1966,p. 20).

Such people know they are lost. So they are vulnerable to those who promise them a connection. They are not just willing to serve as fetishes; they have no other options. Their need is as fierce as addiction. The fetish wants quickening; will that not happen in the stabbing aliveness of sexual excitement? Imagine: *millions* of men!

Olympia certainly does not care to know, though she does know, that they use her as their whore, cheaper than the cheapest, an uncomplaining target. They deal with a female who, being only a piece of paper, is defenseless and unthreatening. (You cannot say, can you, that even the most enslaved woman-in-the-flesh is not just a bit dangerous.) We can guess that some women who rent out their femaleness feel less benign about it than Olympia does, that many even despise men. The less one is by nature a fetish, the more upsetting to be treated as one. (We should not wander now into the thicket of mixed motives bedeviling those who nonetheless choose such work.)

So, though Olympia is a rare one, if we place her as a point on the continuum of histrionic women, we are back on familiar ground. She represents an instance of the current interest in the repressive side of society's rules for femininity. ("Society" here is a generalization for pornography, parental attitudes, ladies' magazines, advertisements for beauty products, fiction, movies, and so on.) Olympia, she tells us, is a commodity, and she knows she is being sold for erotic use. She ignores the hostility inherent in the bargaining that takes place between her and her audience and feels the price is worth the reward.

To repeat, pornography sells well and in doing so covers my failure in experimental design. By the time the publisher has put Olympia out there, a lot of data on men's erotic ideals for women have been scanned, calculated, and printed out. She now fits soft-porn myth, an archetype, she says; she no longer is just a lost, scrambled, real woman. What was pathology is now success. And, in submitting to the fetish-making machinery, she has an unfair advantage (as also does a mannequin who is mentally retarded or deranged) over more normal girls dreaming of stardom, for she does not have to contend with the inner life of the woman who has not felt herself from childhood to be a nonperson.

The point here is obvious: though sexual excitement is experienced as an automatic, uncomplicated, natural (with implications of both biology and theology) phenomenon, it is actually dense with meanings at all levels of awareness. We should not let ourselves put the subject aside, to presume that the apparent spontaneity of excitement indicates an experience needing no explanation beyond the reach of biology or conditioning. Psychiatry has good cause to be pleased with the advances brought by, say, physiology, pharmacology, or learning theory. But psychiatrists[1] are forgetting that meaning also moves behavior, especially everyday behavior such as excitement. If you think sexual excitement is not complex and not the product of your earlier life, of fantasies, of meanings, try again the exercise we practiced in Chapter 2 with the imagined photo of the nude. Observe Olympia doing her number, and depending on who you are and who you tell yourself she is (your daughter, wife, sister, mother), the same performance will appear different to you. One's excitement can be moved about like a piece of furniture.

In this regard, and related to Olympia's insight that she is a female impersonator, the following offers confirmation (Buruma, 1984): "Influenced by nineteenth-century European ideas about naturalism, attempts have been made in the past to have women play female roles in the Kabuki theatre. It simply did not work; they looked too natural; they lacked the beauty of artifice; the only way they could achieve the desired effect was to imitate men impersonating women" (pp. 116–117). Recall Mae West and Marilyn Monroe (who have a strong gay following).

---

1. In this book, *psychiatrist* is not synonymous with *psychoanalyst*.

Once alerted to the underlying motives of Olympia's audience, we can better appreciate the mixed feelings of a teenage girl who must adjust not only to the physical changes of puberty but to the discrepancy between knowing that her body is just a female body and the apparent madness in the males around her who overvalue her secondary sex characteristics without caring who inhabits them. And so the hostile undercurrents flow. Puzzlement and humiliation must be mastered or she will be stuck in a grossly passive position. How does one deal with undeserved fame?

Changing times spotlight an aspect of these dynamics. In the way that formerly outrageous words no longer incite us and strong metaphors turn to clichés, so nudity's power has been reduced (and not, I think, just because of habituation, as in an experiment with rats). A tougher pornography is required these days to sustain the risk, the attack on one's sensibility, that is needed for excitement. It is not so easy now for voyeurs to live dangerously. But, fortunately for the preservation of the species, women still clutch their skirts when the wind blows.

CONCLUSION

There are psychologic experiences that, because familiar, are taken for granted, as if what we feel tells all. Such is excitement. If we are curious, however, we explore to uncover meaning, for meanings are motives. In trying to find how sexual excitement works, then, we want to know what each participant brings to it, what each imagines the other brings, what signals each transmits, and how each interprets the signals. And when we study the way things are rather than the way we think they ought to be, the obvious—though lied about, unwanted, denied, and negated—appears: sexual intimacy is threatening to so many people. They anticipate attack and humiliation that would reduce them to reliving traumas and frustrations never outgrown.

To master the imagined dangers of intimacy, then, they turn to reducing the full humanness of erotic partners, to fetishization. This is made easier by those willing to be fetishes. The dumb blonde—bubble-headed, bubble-busted, bubble-butted, soft, supine, and stupid (or pseudostupid)—has always been a staple for the erotic equation: masochisma matches machismo. In helping us test these hypotheses, Olympia serves us well, for she is even grosser in expressing that she is a fetish than the average woman. But Olympia is not so odd that we are not reminded how these dynamics work in the everyday world. (Nothing looks ordinary under a microscope.)

Pornography is, for men, their revenge on women.

That nastiness—cruelty, desire to degrade others—is an essential aspect of pornography is no argument for suppressing girlie pictures. We shall not thrive on laws that, in the absence of a destructive deed, penalize us for our thoughts. On the other hand, we should not forget that this aspect of the putative sexual revolution is financed by masturbation, a practice that can leave a lot to be desired, and that masturbation, though proclaimed so by the current philosophers of sex, is not always an uncomplicated, unmotivated, undynamic paean to human freedom.

CHAPTER 4
Functions of Obscenity

We should spend more paragraphs on obscenity, pornography's sibling. The two share a lot genetically: their differences are more aesthetic than psychodynamic.

CATECHISM

What is obscenity? Whatever someone says is obscene. What good is obscenity? It lets everyone—the righteous and the guilt-laden—hate (themselves and others). If obscene, then of course tempting. If tempting, then not merely desirable—sensual—but forbidden or at least disapproved.

Clear enough: obscenity is murky, as ill-defined as the feelings it arouses. Recall, for instance, how the meanings of *obscenity* overlap those of *perversion, pornography, dirty,* and *sin,* conditions of sensual pleasure to which hatred (or violence, brutality, cruelty, shaming, insult, hostility, anger, aggression, dislike, teasing, jesting—a continuum of lessening rage) has been added. And hatred? The desire to harm. Harm? To humiliate, debase, violate for revenge. Revenge? To punish others with punishment that I say they deserve and that I deny I deserve.

CONNOTATIONS

Feel the word *obscene.* When aimed at us, we sense the attack in it. Something, we think, is being forced on us, something outside us. To experience something as obscene, we must *feel* shocked. A shock is a blow, as if we have been physically struck, our body's response thereby bringing full conviction (righteousness) to the sense of being attacked. We will not recognize that it is inside us as well, that *we* want its voluptuous promise ("the renegade flesh" [La Barre 1980, p. 258]) and that *we* force it on ourself. But should we not feel attacked, the situation is simply incomprehensible, humorous, foolish, or— the truest absence—unnoticed, but not obscene. Obscenity is a form of unaccepted desire.

I agree with the relativist: to be obscene, something must be obscene *to someone*. Nothing is inherently obscene, though disgust, a closely related experience, is present in humans at birth (Basch 1976). Obsceneness and disgustingness, however, are not synonymous. Disgust is in the nose, mouth, and gorge; it has to do especially with smells, tastes, and palpable qualities of objects. The obscene is more in the mind than the mouth, starts out more as an idea than as nausea, and moves one toward retention more than ejection. Were the obscene simply disgusting, we would hold no conferences or trials on obscenity.

Another closely related word is *unclean*. But we know that the obscene is more than unclean. Just as, if something were simply disgusting, we would avoid it, if something is unclean we can do likewise or wash up. To raise the disgusting or unclean to being obscene, we need a further quality: obscenity is (creates) a form of excitement, an anticipation of danger.

OBSCENITY AND EXCITEMENT

Let us add more poles to our list of excitement's oscillations: goodness and evil, Heaven and Hell, aliveness and deadness, buoyancy and boredom, pleasure and pain, clean and dirty, food and feces, obscenity and shame. For to be obscene is exciting: will we get away with it? If we would use the obscene—not everyone needs to—we must know what we are about and weigh the acceptable against the forbidden. To do so requires us to understand what society in general and the present moment in particular can bear: we imagine our audience in order to decide if we can get away with it. As with mother and naughty baby, who will win the battle of the excrements? Taking risks with obscenity starts very early, and if parents make enough of an issue, the battle becomes a lifelong theme in the search for autonomy. Obscenity tries to turn the tables, a risky business in which the meek hope to humble the mighty. It is a political act, a declaration, an engine of separation (rupture of symbiosis), an accusation, an excuse, a renovation. It is to be revolting—revolt but not revolution. Victim is to become victor by dumping the dark, moist, smelly, hidden, mysterious, swollen interior's contents onto society's sin-sniffers. That struggle has no point unless we can entice others into opposing us—audiences that judge our naughtiness. Here we find a link with humor (Adams 1977, La Barre 1980), art, and the erotic, where what is gentle, audacious, cruel, or obscene is a matter of aesthetic judgments and skills. One person's obscenity is another's pornography is another's joke is another's research study.

DYNAMICS: MOTIVATIONS: SCRIPTS

Obscenity, then, is a planned assault on an audience. It is exhibition, theater. So we are not suprised that, like perverse exhibitionists, those using obscenity are titrating danger against safety in a social arena and may also be prone to seek punishment (Lenny Bruce again). For, even in being caught, one has won. One has goaded the authorities, forcing them to admit that one *really* exists. (The imaginative reader again can make connections back to the traumas and frustrations of earliest childhood and the development of permanent patterns—character structure—that unendingly repeat these themes.) But obscenities are fragile. We know that they vary from era to era and from place to place. We remember how the British lost *bloody* and we are losing *shit*. Robbed of intensity, obscenity stops being obscene, is no longer excitement for the jaded.

Obscenity is a game. It works only when both sides know the rules, some of which are expressed by the most subtle cues. It is part of the oldest game of all—the children against the parents. Each player understands the motives; the moves are familiar and the outcomes predictable. The game ends, of course, if you no longer need to play. If one party recognizes what is happening and opts out, the structure collapses, as happens with the exhibitionist when the woman chuckles rather than calling the police. And if both sides see it is a game (that is, do not want to attack and be attacked), the result is humor, not obscenity.

Another quality of obscenity is secrecy. Presume that when people—judges, philosophers, political and religious leaders, or just folks—declare something is obscene, they are also telling us their dirtiest secrets.

You probably know most or all of the above; I suppose each of these points has been made before by one or many authorities. So you know that societies (that is, people—individuals soaked in history) need obscenity (1) to improve moral tone; (2) to keep evil hidden but alive inside ourself; (3) to maintain within us the tension between the allowed and the forbidden, that is, to relieve boredom; (4) to provide scapegoats; (5) to keep rebellion alive; (6) to exteriorize, a bit disguised, what we think—consciously, preconsciously, and unconsciously—about our interior; (7) to shame others as a way to avoid feeling shame ourself. Those who need hate to justify themselves need obscenity. Depending on your disposition, you can either attack those you experience as obscene—and thereby obscure your own obscenities—or be obscene and provoke the punishment you seek. No wonder the courts have trouble regulating obscenity.

SUMMARY

What is obscenity?

A matter of aesthetics
A temptation
An excitement
Hatred
A desire to harm
An assault, insult, invasion, violation
A shaming maneuver
Risk taking
Punishment

An undoing of childhood frustrations and traumas

A search for autonomy

Revenge

Triumph, with victim becoming victor

Rebellion

Depiction, evocation, performance

Illusion: word become flesh

A sensual, sadomasochistic dance in which each partner knows the movements that excite the other

A biopsy containing the history and present structure of the society and of the individuals who give and receive the obscenity

CHAPTER 5

Problems with the
Term "Homosexuality"

Let me now begin shifting toward the second main theme in
this book, the first being the dynamics of excitement: can we be
confident that the observations we report are the foundation of
the dynamics we describe? Moving through these chapters, I
shall become more impatient with the way we analysts define
our terms, select our data, shape our writings, and create our
theories. The erotic practices that serve as examples—homosexuality, transvestism in women, erotic vomiting, pedophilia—were chosen not by design but by the happenstances of
patient referrals and of invitations to take part in professional
meetings. (I have little experience in treating people in any of
these categories.)

This chapter should be unnecessary, for the ideas are obvious and simple to state and do not rely for their logic on a
complex theory and/or technical language. Perhaps, then, my
main point is to have the reader share my surprise that the
obvious is still obscured.

What is obviousis is that the word *homosexuality* has been
used in so many ways that, unless one clearly says how it is
employed at a given moment, the surplus meanings stifle our
understanding. For instance, until recently analytic theorists
unquestioningly called both nonerotic feelings of friendship
and an erotic desire for someone of the same sex *homosexuality*
and said both experiences were at bottom the same. (This
issue is reviewed and corrected by Ovesey [1969]). We were
thereby instructed not to be fooled by illusions: the instinctual
imperative (said to be "bisexuality," "anality," or "orality,"

and now—the latest fashion—"narcissism") is the same; only the defenses differ.

But that sensible logic can be misused. To be safer, let us recall rules that, in the clinical situation, can help us discover the truth embedded in behavior's disguises. Here—with the admonition that careful observations can be the safest anchor for theory— are five guidelines: (1) different appearances may indicate different origins of behavior; (2) similar appearances may have similar origins; (3) a major lesson that psychodynamic studies bring to psychology: different appearances may hide a similar origin; for instance, disgust and fear may both stem from erotic desire; (4) similar appearances may have different origins; for instance, erotic excitement may result in one person from disgust and in another from fear; and (5) the most difficult to abide by, the one that inhibits, and the one that geniuses can ignore but that the rest of us should not: similar is not yet identical; the differences may be as crucial as the similarities.

To make these suggestions work, our judgments will depend on clinical skill, that is, careful observation. We must watch to see when, by means of rhetoric that uses *essentially, really, in fact, truly, without doubt,* and the like, behaviors that are different are alleged to be the same. This observation in regard to "homosexuality" is a major concern of this chapter. To protect ourselves from the error of equating similarities, we should use, as is done in much of medicine, the differential diagnosis.

For example: two pubescent boys are enthusiastic fellators. Each, during his performance of this act, is consciously erotically excited. The sense of an erect penis in his mouth is sensually pleasurable for each boy, and he resonates with conscious-preconscious-unconscious memories/fantasies of oral pleasures from birth on (tempting some to use clinically sloppy labels, such as "orality"). Each boy believes in a well-known dynamic of homosexual behavior—that his sense of existing, of intactness, of self is enhanced by the semen he is about to drink. But one of these boys is on his way to becoming an effeminate, homosexual hairdresser in Los Angeles, whereas the other will become a masculine, heterosexual warrier/hunter in New Guinea.

DATA AND PSEUDODATA

The last example is obvious. No one would confuse the two acts—in which the same anatomic parts are used in an erotically intense experience—as being the same in meaning or origins for each boy. Yet the analytic literature is crammed with judgments about "the homosexual" and "homosexuality," using a logic that needs to equate homosexual impulses and acts as being, at bottom, made from the same stuff. To obscure things further, a highly abstract, theory-laden, speculation-soaked, scientistic, pseudoexplanatory jargon is offered—and accepted in psychoanalytic circles—as the clinical evidence: "narcissistic and prenarcissistic disposition," "withdrawal of libidinal cathexis," "extremely strong fixation," "intense unneutralized aggression," "overflow of primary narcissism with hypercathexis of the physical and mental self," "inability to bind the original instinctual energies and to transform them into a potential tonic energy," "archaic and primitive psychic mechanisms," "insufficient self-object differentiation," "a primitive ego utilizing incorporation to a high degree," "highly ambivalent cathexis," "pregenital archaic superego formations," "narcissistic homeostasis," "massive intrusion of infantile object cathexes which overwhelm the reality ego," "archaic objects cathected with narcissistic libido . . . which are still in intimate connection with the archaic self," "fixation on archaic grandiose self-configurations and/or on archaic over-estimated narcissistically cathected objects," "cohesive archaic narcissistic configurations," "a regressive movement which tends to go beyond the stage of archaic narcissism," "sexualization of the pathological narcissistic constellation," "the narcissistic equilibrium that depends on the analysand's narcissistic relationship to an archaic, narcissistically experienced prestructural self-object," "cathexis of ego functions," and so on.

Are there ego functions that have no cathexis? What does a narcissistic homeostasis look like? What visible manifestations distinguish a cohesive from a noncohesive or partially cohesive or quasi-cohesive archaic narcissistic configuration? How does a cohesive archaic configuration differ from a cohesive narcissistic configuration? How does a cohesive archaic narcissistic configuration differ from a cohesive archaic configuration? What do all these words mean?

Where are the direct observations that supposedly are the data from which this vocabulary has been developed? Would one's colleagues, on seeing the behavior, agree to apply the same abstractions drawn from this list? Dynamic theory indicates that *everyone* passes through, and more or less retains part of, primitive and poorly controlled phases of behavior and thinking. To account for differences, then, and especially if we want to say that someone—say, a heterosexual—is normal as contrasted with someone else—say, a homosexual—we need to show that one of these people is more (or less) under the sway of a dynamic than is the other person. It is not enough just to find an archaic dynamic; the strength, timing, and intrapsychic ambience of the dynamic must be quantified. Consider the following words (psychodynamic discourse is studded with them): unseen but present in the unconscious, extreme, intense, marked, profound, overwhelming, archaic, primitive, moderate, severe, insistent, largely dominating, exclusively, semidelusional, crucial, high degree, intolerable, intimately related, easily, in all instances, to a great extent, the most classic examples, has a potential for, is prone to, is susceptible to, a considerable degree of, decisively, relatively, classic, quasi-normal, and normal. These are all good terms, but it is difficult to know, when coming across them in a sentence in the literature, to what observations, what measurements in the real world, these words refer.

The desire to solve riddles—to search and discover (and to read descriptions of other's explorations)—is one of the keenest intellectual pleasures humans have. In this detective work, psychoanalysts are always at risk since we constantly, in our practice, try to make the invisible visible. That work, taking place against desperately clever resistances (themselves, mostly unconscious), finds analysts often struggling with, and in danger of succumbing to, the temptation of grand explanations. At those times, we substitute the vocabulary of theory, in that way forcing reality to yield a truth or two (as, for instance, when we say that homosexuals have more archaic cathexis of X or Y than do heterosexuals).

And then the sophisticated theorist, to calm such complaining, recalls that there are no facts and no reality, only concepts and interpretations. The theorist knows that an interpretation is simply a belief about an element of reality; the clinician's "facts" are limp organs until they are infused by theory. But I still think that I cross the river on a bridge, not an interpretation of or a theory about a bridge. Theory led to the ability to build the bridge, but my interpretation—as is everything, unprovable—is that a bridge is not just a theory.

When talking about those people with conscious homosexual erotic preferences, it is better to talk of the homosexualities rather than of homosexuality. Beyond that, there are as many different homosexualities as there are heterosexualities. Perhaps even less acceptable is the idea on which I keep hammering: that I do not find heterosexuals in the mass to be more normal than homosexuals. When it comes to the expression of sexual excitement, *most* people, whatever their preference, often appear to be quite hostile, inept, fragmented, gratified only at considerable price, and deceptive with themselves and their partners. Are there reliable reports to the contrary?

My homosexual *patients* are, by anyone's measure, disturbed; that is why they came for help. These patients have islands of heterosexuality scattered in their ocean of neurosis, and all want to uncover their heterosexuality. But it is silly to find in these patients the proof that urges toward heterosexuality are present in *all* homosexuals in the same mix and degree or with the same prognosis. Likewise, because no authority can present raw data as evidence, we should not say that the mere presence of homosexual erotic desire guarantees prepsychotic, "narcissistic," or other severe character states. Many of us read the data from some patients and friends to reveal no more narcissism—as if there is a way to measure the concept—than is in heterosexuals.

Extreme femininity/effeminancy in males and extreme masculinity in females most likely[1] occur with homosexual erotic choice; the less extreme the gender aberration, the less surely will there be homoerotism. Analysts, like less educated folk, sometimes confuse these gender (masculine/feminine) attributes with erotic issues when judging homosexuality, in the inaccurate belief that visible cross-gender impulses inevitably signal homosexual erotic choice, even if the latter is not consciously experienced. This mixup is yet another clinical mess that could be resolved with better observations.

In the analytic writings that discuss the behaviors covered by a differential diagnosis of cross-gender behavior (for example, transvestism, primary transsexualism), the nouns *homosexual* and *homosexuality* eventually crop up. They are used wittingly by analysts to indicate that whatever the later consequences in gender behavior or erotic choices, the origins and mechanisms of the behaviors composing the differential are fundamentally the same (because these origins and mechanisms are "archaic," "primitve," or "narcissistic"). I would rather say that *some* of the dynamics are found in some of these different kinds of patients and that some are not or not to the same degree.

Anna Freud (1965) makes this point in regard to the development of homosexuality in males. She reviews factors that may be etiologic:

> The individual's inborn endowment . . . the individual's narcissism which creates the need to choose a sexual partner in the image of himself . . . the links of homosexuality with the oral and anal pregenital phases . . . the overestimation of the penis in the phallic phase . . . the influence of the excessive love for and dependence on either mother or father or extreme hostility to either of them . . . traumatic observations of the female genital and of menstruation . . . envy of the mother's body . . . jealousy of rival brothers who are subsequently turned into love objects. (pp. 190–91)

---

1. I use "most likely" here not only for the sake of this sentence but also as an excuse to interject this footnote, a reminder that so many of my clinical generalizations are not backed by large enough numbers of people studied to be more than guesses by an experienced observer: no guarantees.

But, she warns:

> Notwithstanding such numerous and well-documented links be-
> tween infantile past and adult present, the reasoning cannot be
> reversed and the reconstructed data cannot be used for the early
> spotting of homosexual development in children. . . . These ele-
> ments, which undoubtedly are pathogenic influences in the past
> of the homosexual, can nevertheless not be used for the progno-
> sis of homosexuality if they form part of the clinical picture of a
> child. Far from being abnormal or even unusual manifestations,
> they are, on the contrary, regular and indispensable parts of
> every boy's developmental equipment. . . . In other words, that
> certain childhood elements in given cases have led to a specific
> homosexual result does not exclude a different or even the opposite
> outcome in other instances. Obviously, what determines the direc-
> tion of development are not the major infantile events and con-
> stellations in themselves but a multitude of accompanying
> circumstances, the consequences of which are difficult to judge both
> retrospectively in adult analysis and prognostically in the assess-
> ment of children. They include external and internal, qualitative
> and quantitative factors. (pp. 191–93)

To see why, in the presence of "certain childhood elements,"
the outcome may be either homosexual or heterosexual, we
must do the detective work—the careful observation—alluded
to earlier. Let us keep trying to go where Miss Freud points, to
find in exact detail the events "external and internal, qualita-
tive and quantitative." And that is what we have not done well
so far. We need more than a vocabulary of undefinable concepts such as "deneutralized libidinal cathexes" or an author's
insistence that something we cannot observe was nonetheless
present in extreme, absolute, archaic, potential, or narcissistic
form when he or she was there. So, when we say "homosexuality," let us always say what we mean: cross-gender behavior?
erotic object choice? nonerotic object choice? And let us make
clear if we are referring to consciously (or preconsciously) experienced behavior or only unconscious behavior.

Further, let us be careful whom we label as being "a homosexual," for that is not the same, necessarily, as saying that a
person is homosexual. The shift from the adjective to noun is a

shift to a statement about a person's totality, his identity, and that may not be accurate. The data from New Guinea illustrate this obvious thought.

My argument for this chapter has thus far had one main theme, that careful observation reduces confusion about the meanings of the term *homosexuality*. The only other theme—to be considered now—is the contemplation of meanings that underlie *homosexuality*, that is, "normal" versus "abnormal." The bottom line in most psychodynamic discussions of homosexuality is that homosexuals are abnormal, whatever creative contributions they bring to a society. This *abnormal* can make no sense without a comparison group that is normal; the heterosexual serves this purpose for analysts and moralists. Though no one would claim that all heterosexuals are normal in erotic or gender behavior, the given in the argument is that heterosexuals can still serve this function of *the normal* and *the natural*.

It seems to make sense to consider heterosexuality natural and therefore normal. If one argues from animals and evolution, we must admit that almost without exception, when it comes to erotic (if that is the right word) behavior, animals are heterosexual. Humans being animals, it follows that heterosexuality is our natural state. In addition, a species for which heterosexuality is not natural could be at risk.

But let us look more closely at the word *natural* and not take it for granted. It has both the biologic connotation of intact function, of a highly efficient machine, and the morality-tinged meaning of "approved" and "good." *Natural* implies inherent, biologically sound, inevitable if not disrupted, grounded by the laws and mechanisms that move chemical, electrical, physical, and other natural processes. Animals are heterosexual by instinct, by biology. Man is an animal; therefore, man is heterosexual.

From a procreational viewpoint, penis-in-vagina is the only natural orgasm inducer. Yet a different "natural," the physiology of orgasm, runs its inevitable course just as briskly in night dreams, masturbation, copulating with donkeys, hair despoiling, coprolagnia, or smelling dirty shoes. And a normal penis in a normal vagina, the two being as purely natural as God with his severest commands could desire, can be connected to remarkably weird or cruel fantasies. The word *natural* has supported a lot of sinning.

A psychoanalyst, to maintain that heterosexual behavior is natural, must ignore the discoveries of infant/child development, from Freud's first descriptions of that necessary, universal vicissitude of development called Oedipal conflict to the present. Though I find it hard to believe that the heterosexual "impulse" found in other animals does not carry into human biology, when we learn to measure, not just speculate on, such matters, I presume this quality of behavior will be found to be like so many others: less bound, in our species, by rigidly stereotyped biologic mechanisms and more open to the complexities made possible by the cerebral hemispheres and their functions—thinking, fantasy, choice, deception, defense, and so on.

Are there data to contradict the opinion that heterosexual preference is, in both male and female humans, an accomplishment rather than a given? Words such as the following resonate with the evidence of generations of data collecting showing that heterosexuality—not just homosexuality, necrophilia, flagellation, doraphila, and hemothymia—is a compound artifice: separation, individuation, defense, fixation, regression, anxiety, mastery, repression, vicissitude, depression, anger, envy, dream work, unconscious, secondary process, disavowal, identification, amnesia, ego, superego, self. Are there really psychoanalysts who believe that human psychic development proceeds "naturally" with preprogrammed facility?

Though we are familiar with conflict-free aspects of development, some originating in biologic anlagen and some in conflict-free interpersonal relationships, are qualities as intricately complex as heterosexual object choice or gender behavior appropriate to one's sex to be ascribed in humans to "natural" causes? What evidence is there that heterosexuality is less complicated than homosexuality, less the product of infantile-childhood struggles to master trauma, conflict, frustration, and the like?[2]

2. Freud raises some objection (1905, p.104).

As a result of innumerable analyses, the burden of proof (providing demonstrable evidence) has shifted to those who use the heterosexual as the standard of health, normality, mature genital characterhood, or whatever other ambiguous criterion serves one's philosophy these days. First, one has to list the tests—agreed on, definable, measurable (no "deneutralized libidinal archaic narcissistic cathexes," please). Then come the controls, then the counting, and then the conclusions. Thus far, the counting, if it is done from published reports, puts the heterosexual and the homosexual in a tie: 100 percent abnormals. This suggests, at the least, that we really need better sampling techniques.

By no means am I alleging that the same events in infancy and childhood can lead equally to either homosexual or heterosexual preferences. Nor am I suggesting that there are not early—"archaic"—influences that are necessary for the development of some homosexualities and that these may be different from those that lead to a heterosexual commitment. I am only asking that no one try to win the argument by the device of representing heterosexuality as "natural."

To make their writings clear, clinicians should announce their biases. So let me here express my morality-invaded opinion. When I am all alone and not trying for clarity, I consider a person healthy if he or she gets along well with others—without a lot of anxiety, lying, crippling psychologic symptoms, inhibitions, or hatred, open or disguised—takes responsibility for his or her actions, uses his or her talents effectively, and is dependable. This is a cliché-ridden, uninspiring, unpsychodynamic-sounding list of virtues; but then I am considering here only intrapsychic and interpersonal health. A description such as this one includes, perhaps, several heterosexual and homosexual people.

If only we could legislate that none of us, when pronouncing publicly on human psychology, be allowed to use—either openly or by implication (not even a raised eyebrow)—the concept "normal." On the other hand, I do admire the word *abnormal*, which I use, perhaps with indefensible moralistic intent, when on the subject of erotic desire, in order to imply impulses, fantasies—conscious, preconscious, unconscious—to harm one's object.

Maybe we approximate the truth better if, in regard to erotic behavior, we assume that most people are abnormal. At least, then, we shall be less polemical.

CHAPTER 6

Theories of Origins of Male Homosexuality: A Cross-Cultural Look

Professor Gilbert H. Herdt co-authored this chapter.

Among those who do not believe in a primary somatic cause, it is commonly held, analytic theories and data to the contrary, that homosexuality—in fact, erotic behavior in general, whether aberrant or normative—is the result of conditioning by pleasurable erotic events, especially first experiences around puberty, with the behavior reinforced through repetition of those pleasures as time passes. Though such encounters can play a part in erotic development, we disagree with the importance given this factor by learning theorists.[1] Left out of that explanation is an appreciation for the power of early nonerotic events in shaping the character structure that, once formed, in itself and weightier than chance encounters, leads people to erotic preferences. In ignoring how personality shapes desire, these theorists also ignore the importance of fantasy, failing to understand that fantasy not only is an aspect of the way desire

1. There are a number of schools of learning theory. In recent years, the failure of the extreme models to explain human behavior has led more and more, especially among clinicians, to explanations that admit to the power of meaning—of fantasy—in moving people's behavior. However, to focus our argument, here we shall use "learning theorist" as a straw man against which we set out our ideas. But by using exact quotes from authorities generally accepted by learning theorists, we want to indicate that we have pretty fairly represented the published authorities on erotic behavior. There is no point in reviewing the spectrum of positions in learning theory—from none to considerable—of belief in fantasy and inner meaning as motivators of behavior. The chapter is written, for the sake of the argument, only to highlight differences.

presents itself but also can lead to—be a cause of—desire. (We shall use *fantasy* here with its conscious, preconscious, and unconscious connotations, not as learning theorists do, as synonymous with daydreams or other conscious imagery.)

Though the manifest content of this chapter discusses only male homosexuality, we want the interested reader to extrapolate our ideas to the greater issue of the origins of erotic behavior in general and beyond that to behavior at large—the chosen ground for conflict between psychodynamic and learning theories. In this sense, our data, explanations, and line of argument on homosexuality are meant to serve only as an example.

We shall not review here psychoanalytic or other non–learning theories of the origins of homoerotic desires or argue for one or another analytic explanation. Instead, using data gathered from the Sambia, a New Guinea tribe, we shall present ideas that challenge and weaken nonpsychodynamic positions or at least require a redoing of the explanations of learning theorists that would make their accounts look more like those already used by analysts. In addition, we shall discuss findings of developmental circumstances, pre-Oedipal and Oedipal, in this tribe that fit those predicted by analytic research and that would be seen by the learning theorists as coincidental or unimportant.

Let us first sketch in our argument, after which we shall review the observations. A major difference between learning theorists and analysts is that learning theorists either do not explain behavior as resulting from meaning or concedes significance only to consciously comprehended meaning. There is little room for private, idiosyncratic, gradually-developed-from-infancy-on, illogical, fantasy-laden, drive-impelled—much less unconscious—mental experience. Instead, explanations are carried by concepts that are purposely emptied of most mental content: aversive conditioning and positive reinforcement, cognitive dissonance, stimulus pairing, extinction, approach-avoidance learning, avoidance behavior, appetitive conditioning, contiguous association, evoked responses, single-trial learning, sensitization, desensitization, reciprocal inhibition, habituation, differential conditioning techniques, generalization of reinforced responses, counterconditioning. We do not deny the studies that validate these mechanisms; many ego and superego elements and functions—for example, the development of preferences in morality, music, cars, carpets, hairstyles, or vitamins—are examples of states of mind in which the just-listed processes, ignored by analysts, participate. Our disagreement comes when learning theorists continue to use these factors, of such narrow range, in specific cases as full explanations of behaviors and especially when their vocabulary serves to deny that subjectivity—our experiencing ourselves as people, that is, creatures moved by our meanings—is important.[2]

An analyst would agree with the behaviorist that, for instance, if a mother disparages her son's interest in certain games and her influence is not modified by the boy's father, the child is not likely to excel in those games. (We also need, of course, to explain those who become athletes under similar circumstances.) Still, an analyst would disagree that the lasting form—character structure—these interchanges take within the boy can be explained by a learning paradigm alone. We would add much more from what we know about other aspects of this boy's relationships with his mother and father—for instance, how, intrapsychically, he constructs an inner reality made of his versions of how he believes his parents are constructed and who he believes himself to be. And we, in contrast to the behaviorists, see that by far the greater part of this mental work is unconscious and resides in the form of fantasies, not only in such nonmental forms as reflexes and contingencies.

The behaviorist, for instance, says that the choice of an erotic

2. Rule: behaviorists who do not believe in intention—desires, motivations, fantasies, meanings—as a mover of behavior are not allowed to get angry at those of us who disagree with them, since that anger would be evidence of intention—desire, motivation, fantasy, meaning. Nor are they allowed to argue against us unless they can show that the anger and the planning are not backed by motivations such as desire. The neurophysiologist who feels subjectivity is an illusion and mechanistic—explainable by cells, synapses, and chemistry—is not allowed to feel that feeling, since such feeling and its accompanying thoughts *are* subjectivity. You are not allowed to stake your existence on what you say does not exist.

fetish is fortuitous (that is, mechanistically determined: *desire* is not a favored word in learning theory): if the fetishist-to-be is in a state of arousal and, by chance, puts on his mother's skirt, then that random contiguous association leads to transvestism. The analyst, however, questions why the boy was sufficiently interested to first make the experiment; why in one case there is instantaneous and powerful excitement and in another no further interest; why perversions are much more frequently found in males than females; why some people report that the first experience with what is now a central feature of their excitement was then traumatic, only later to be transformed to pleasure.

In brief, the behaviorist paradigm omits the perspective that behavior is usually made up of—is the final manifestation of—several complementary factors: biologic drives and their modification from infancy on by interpersonal and then intrapsychic factors the purposes of which are expedient (that is, they serve to defend oneself and still preserve both pleasure and reality). Ours is a form of exploration more complex than, though in some ways not in disagreement with, that which says a behavior once hit on by chance will be repeated if it brings pleasure and avoided if it brings unpleasure.

Let us focus now on homosexuality. We shall use that term here to stand for erotic preference—need—for a same-sexed person, and we shall presume, without discussing the issues further here, that there are numerous homosexualities, varying in their etiologies, subjective states, and manifest behaviors. By *preference* we imply a commitment and therefore a complex of organized motives, beliefs, fantasies, and behaviors that can be summarized in words such as *character structure, personality, self,* or *identity.* It is our hypothesis—one that all analysts probably share—that such a homoerotic commitment is not simply a product of chance encounters at susceptible moments.

This chapter should be read not only for its ethnography or its contentions about origins of homosexuality but to support the idea that psychodynamic and learning theory explanations of behavior can be argued using specific examples, not just rhetoric and theory.

We shall now look at the Sambia to find data that serve to

test the behaviorist hypothesis that repeated pleasurable homoerotic experiences cause homosexuality.

BACKGROUND DATA

Hidden in the mountains of the Eastern Highlands, Papua
New Guinea, is the Sambia, a tribe of some 2,300 people. We
here use the ethnographic present of the first years (1974–76)
Herdt (1981a) studied these people. After 1979 (when Stoller
visited briefly), the culture was rapidly changing.

Because of constant war, treacherous terrain, awful weather,
severe protein deficiency (few animals and birds, no fish but a
few eels) and strong potential for starvation, no medical care
other than that of shamans, and an acceptance of killing other
humans, it takes a lot of luck, fierce masculinity in the men, and
a steady heterosexual impulse for the Sambia to survive. Yet the
route to this survival is via overt, obligatory, institutionalized
homoerotism for all boys, from childhood till taking a wife. All
males are coercively required to indulge in exclusively homosexual—homosocial and homoerotic—activities from age seven to
ten until they are married. During this period of obligatory homosexuality, females are severely taboo to initiates, not only as
erotic objects but in any way. (Girls are likewise forbidden to
interact with unrelated or initiated males.) They are not to be
touched or looked at, and even food and other objects they
handle are dangerous; the closer the blood relationship, the
more dangerous the patterns of conflictual male/female relationships common throughout Highlands New Guinea.

Until first-stage initiation at around age seven to ten, boys,
when not with other boys (preinitiates), are mostly with their
mothers and other females. At the same time that fathers are
distant, mothers are close to their children. Both men and
women are not defined as full persons without children. Men
disparage women. Beyond that, sons are valued more than
daughters, for despite the tension between the sexes, sons
grow up to be hunters and fighters, the admired members of
this men-admiring society.

So, almost always, close bonds form between mothers and

sons, a condition the men allow—custom expects it—but that increasingly bothers them. This tension, building up for years, emerges at the first-stage initiation. The men, in certain ceremonies, rage at the women for having scolded and polluted the boys, thereby endangering them (Herdt 1981a, Read 1965). The boys are taken from their mothers and sisters and spirited into the forest, where the secret rites of creating manhood begin. Now, via an often brutal and terrifying initiation, each boy is resocialized by the men so that he will grow to be manly, a warrior, a husband, and a father.

At the height of the first-stage initiation, he is told the secret of Sambia maleness: one remains only the shell of a male unless he drinks as much semen as possible. The boy then must suck postpubertal boys' penises often, ingesting as much semen as he can during these years.

The second phase begins with a later initiation that is presaged by puberty: the boy now becomes the person sucked. From this point on, a bachelor must not fellate other males. This is taboo, for one would then be stealing semen needed by the younger boys. But, in addition, neither youths nor men report any impulse to suck penises. The erotic pleasure is in being sucked (even though, at the same time, the male nervously recognizes that he is being depleted, made less manly, inching toward the femaleness from which he emerged). So now, and for years until the approach of marriage, he will be constantly fellated by the younger boys. During this time, females remain taboo—their glances, the objects they use, their touch, their bodies, and most of all their female secretions—until the bachelor, with the onset of the processes that lead to becoming married, in the late teens or early twenties is thrown into intimacy with his wife.

He turns to heterosexuality, and though memories of the erotically exciting fellatio persist, heterosexuality is the only accepted behavior. Further homosexuality is negatively sanctioned, and a man who insistently indulged would risk being despised as a "rubbish man." The taboo on being fellated by boys after one enters the ritual series of events and stages— there is no single ceremony—that make up the marriage process is far less absolute than, say, revealing various ritual secrets to females. So some young men continue, with rapidly decreasing frequency, to use boys erotically. In addition, one enters genital heterosexuality by spending the first weeks of betrothal-marriage to one's menarchic bride with fellatio, not vaginal intercourse. Only a few mature married men ever again sample the boys.

From this description can be abstracted a definition of sexual aberrance among the Sambia. (They have no categories of perversion—fetishism, transvestism, sadism, masochism, and so on—because no such erotic behavior is known. In addition, there is no anal intercourse, hetero or homo; Sambia find odd the rumors they hear that, in other New Guinea tribes, men do so.) We divide the concept of "sexual" into two parts: gender behavior (masculinity/femininity) and erotic desire.

Gender aberrance would be manifested in men by a lack of commitment to warriorhood, hunting, marriage, fatherhood and by the presence of interest in or visible behavior the society defines as typical of women (feminine), an interest either in dressing in ways untypical of men or—even worse, and unheard of—in dressing as women do.

For *erotic* behavior, the criteria for aberrance in mature men are simple: persistent homoerotic behavior and low interest in heterosexuality.

CASE MATERIAL

Two men suggest the normative and the aberrant. The first, Moondi, typifies the way Sambia men experience desire for women. Some express it (in word and deed) more and some less, but Moondi will serve well enough to convey the fact that the heterosexuality is a genuine enthusiasm, as much (and as complicated) as in societies without institutionalized homosexuality. The second is Kalutwo, a man the Sambia recognize as sexually aberrant (though they have no vocabulary for such aberrance). Herdt has used these two as informants over a six- to seven-year period—dozens of conversations ("interviews") plus just being with them in the hamlet in ordinary daily circumstances. Both have deep, almost therapeutic relationships with Herdt, who has long since been tested and found trustworthy.

Moondi is nineteen, anticipating the state of marriage. He comes from a happy family, with parents who are congenial and respect each other. A girl was picked for him years ago, and as she approaches menarche (around seventeen to nineteen with the Sambia), he has learned who she is and has begun daydreaming about her. He is forbidden to look at her, as are all young men with the girl arranged for them to marry.[3]

M: Suppose I really looked closely at her face; then I could make up a good daydream. But I haven't seen her very well. So I only can think of parts of her face. I sometimes sit down and think: the nose of my woman is like this; it goes down and curves up a little bit. And I think, "Oh, that's really nice." And I think, "At night we would sleep together and do it, what all the *nupos* [married initiates] do. [Talks fast] They screw in the mouth. [Voice exhilarated: the sense of a happy confession]

   Sometimes I think, "Suppose we [he and his girl] made a house. We'd sleep in it, and when I wanted to, I could shoot her in the mouth. And she'd feel excitement from being with me."

H: In your daydreams do you see her face or that of some other woman?

M: Hers. In the daydream, she's got a cloth which she covers up her face and her skin with. She covers her breasts completely. I haven't yet actually seen them. She hides them. [Sambia are modest, both males and females.] Sometimes I look at her and she acts in a certain way . . . I don't forget. So when I make up a daydream about her, I picure her face and her smile.

H: When you do that, does your cock get hard?

M: Yeah! [Said as "of course!"] Whenever I think about her [like this] I get hard. All the time.

H: When did you start having these feelings?

M: When they marked me [for marriage to her]. [In the house portrayed in this daydream] we can sleep and we can play around. I

3. The following transcript of part of an interview with H. (S. sitting in, quiet most of the time) is edited in four ways: M.'s sentences have been made to read more easily, by removing hesitations and repetitions, for example; most of H.'s questions and comments are deleted; paragraphs that add nothing or are unrelated to the present theme are deleted; and S. is not an audible presence.

can hold her breasts. When I do that, she can feel something in herself, some kind of excitement to make her feel good. [Pensive] Yeah, we can do that, and I can ask her, "Can we do it [sexual intercourse]?" [Lowers voice; slight quiver] And she says [whispers], "Oh, that's all right, we can do it." And I feel real excited. I really like sleeping with her. I ask her softly. She's not far away. We're close together. [As he imagines this gentle lovemaking, his voice is tender. In contrast is Weiyu (see Herdt 1981), a powerful, mature warrior, who also worked with H. on his fantasies. No tenderness there; just wham, bam, push it in. Forcing a woman to have sex, something short of rape. That's the excitement for Weiyu. Moondi, you can see, is different. Yet both are heterosexual.] She says, "That's all right. We can do it." And when she says that [in the daydream], I feel my penis hard. [Pause] I was thinking, "Why don't I get married quickly so I can do this?" I think, "I want to sleep with her." And it gets hard.

H: In the daydream, when your cock is hard, is it in the mouth or down below [vagina]?

M: [Reflecting] Sometimes in the mouth and sometimes [lowers voice] down below.

H: It's only now [recently] that you're getting another kind of daydream? [In earlier years his daydreams were only about boys.]

M: Yeah.

H: Now, the other one, about screwing initiates——

M: That belonged to before, when I was a new bachelor; then I used to imagine the boys.

H: Where is that fantasy now?

M: I have it, but less and less. I don't have sex much with the initiates anymore. Before, yes; when we were down at Yellow Valley [during his third-stage initiation, when it was expected of him]. I used to do it lots of time with that boy who was sweet on me [a small first-stage novice being initiated at the time of Moondi's third-stage initiation]. But now? Not at all. I don't do it [have sex] with the boys now.

H: Could you?

M: I think that . . . no, not at all. I suppose if I felt I wanted to, I'd do it.

Let us review and orient this fragment. We are talking with Moondi, a bachelor, who is moving toward marriage. We choose him for our report since he is a typical young Sambia man. He is male, the sex preferred by parents, since only males can defend the hamlet against the unending threat of destruction in war. At age eight, he is suddenly removed from his mother's doting attention and, via brutal and terrifying initiation rites, is resocialized by the men so that he will grow up to be manly, a warrior, a husband, and a father.

The process begins with the first-stage initiation, when he enters the phase of semen drinking. He has only a few years to do so, however, for with his third-stage initiation at puberty, he may no longer drink semen but is to offer his penis to the next cohort of boys. At the same time females are severely taboo.

Whatever reverberations lie hidden within these overt experiences, we know that from the start of their erotic lives and for the years of their peak orgasmic capacity, these young men are propelled into intense, obligatory, praiseworthy, powerfully gratifying homoerotism. At the same time that males are positively reinforced as the only sex objects, females are negatively reinforced. They are not just forbidden. The taboos are nailed down by the dread created as the boys now learn how vaginal fluids cause illness (if not ritually treated) and eventual death— the consequence of being infected by even a droplet of menses. Yet Moondi, who at nineteen learns the identity of the girl he will marry, begins—without deprogramming—to create powerfully erotic heterosexual daydreams. And if he is like other Sambia men, he will desire women the rest of his life, without ever forgetting his homoerotic joys. In fact, by becoming initiators and teaching about homosexual fellatio to sons and other new initiates in later years, these men are reminded of and have reinforced for them the positive value of semen and homoerotic activities.

Probably if Sambia society allowed adult married men to be homoerotic, some, as in our society, would be bisexual. But those like Moondi would not; they love their lust for women. And it is that lust—with its depth and breadth—that the behavioristic account says should not be there. As Moondi exemplifies and as hundreds of hours of interviews, gossip, and bull sessions with other men revealed, desire for women is—for all its vicissitudes—as gripping for Sambia men as it is anywhere else.[4]

Could this just be bluster by men denying that they are really homosexual? We doubt it as we think of their desire for multiple wives, of the occurrence of adultery despite severe taboos, and of men's drive for intercourse, so strong that even the terrors of female fluids cannot halt the heterosexual tension. And finally, were that heterosexual need weak, it would be further subdued by the men's awareness that every ejaculation of semen advances the deterioration of one's manhood. (Intercourse with women is thought to be more depleting than that with boys.)

Only those fevered by theory would argue that, appearances to the contrary, Sambia culture is *really* homosexual. The fact is it takes a lot of homosexuality to be truly homosexual there. We found only one case—Kalutwo—who fits that label as we would apply it at home.[5]

Kalutwo is an unremarkable-looking Sambia man now in his mid-thirties, whom H. has interviewed periodically since 1975. He was reared and lives as a biologically normal male (which he is). Though K. has technically been married four times, each marriage failed prematurely, and he has been increasingly stigmatized for those failures. What is even more strange among the Sambia, K. not only fears women but prefers erotic contacts with boys. He, therefore, unlike other Sambia, comes closest to being a homosexual in the Western sense of that identity.

K. was traditionally reared and still lives in that traditionalism. But even in this regard he is deviant. Though he fought in several battles, as must every male, he stayed in the back lines, no fighter. (Nor, he admits, did he aspire to be one.) He is indifferent to hunting, which adds to setting him apart from other men. Instead, he prefers gardening, a respectable pursuit, but more for older men and, of course, women. And,

4. At any rate, by the kind of gross inspection that leads to most impressions about other cultures, we do not see the erotic lives of adult Sambia men as more swayed by overt homoerotism than are those of men in Western society.

5. The following description of Kalutwo is from Herdt 1981b.

more glaringly deviant, he is now, after four failures, unmarried and childless. With his enthusiasm for other male activities and social relationships decreasing, his peers disparage him even more these days.

Still, K. presents a tough, stiff-lipped, traditionalist-type, masculine facade. He always wears a grass sporran, warrior bandoliers, and bark cape: the ancient insignias of a true warrior. But he is cold, distant, and uncomfortable in public; secretive; avoids children; is quiet, emotionally flat, and moody; with dull speech, though people watch out for his sarcasm. these traits are deviant but not quite out of the range of traditional Sambia masculinity.

Below this sullenness, however, lies greater aberrance. He has no manly achievements: no battle scars or heroic deeds, no impressive hunting record, no oratoric skills or powerful ambitions, no female conquests (not even a few) or wives with many babies. His marital status is abnormal; in a society anchored in valuing marriage as the bedrock of adulthood, he is an unmarried, aging bachelor now, who has almost never had any form of erotic experience with women (wives or other) and has none now.

In short, K. portrays in his dress a tough warrior, but he cannot bring off this performance since his own needs undermine it. So he is disparaged as a "rubbish man"—and not always behind his back—for in Sambia society merely seeming tough is not enough to prevent a man from being stigmatized as a masculine failure; he must *demonstrate* manly achievements.

By almost any indicator, K.'s childhood was unusual compared to that of other Sambia men. His parenting was, by Sambia standards, bizarre. Little is known about his mother, who died twenty years ago, except that she was a conscientious gardener who disliked crowds. She eventually avoided contact with men. She had had three children by her first husband and was an older widow by the time K. arrived. Two children died, leaving K.'s eldest sister as her mother's chief companion. Some time thereafter his mother began a liaison with a married man of a neighboring hamlet. That man—K.'s biologic father—subsequently rejected her for reasons still unclear, though he was married and had several adolescent children. This kind of rejection seldom occurs, since the product—a son—would normally be desired and claimed by his father, not left to become a fatherless bastard. (There is not even a category term in Sambia for *bastard;* that absence reflects the strong cultural bias for heterosexuality only in marriage, and the wish for heirs, including adoptees.) So the Sambia, who are prudish, prize virginity, expect faithfulness in marriage, and outwardly condemn promiscuity, came down hard on K.'s husbandless mother when her pregnancy became noticeable. She protested, pointing to the father, and appealed for marriage to him. In such circumstances, one would expect the man to have taken K.'s mother as a second wife, but he did not. He disclaimed involvement or responsibility, an ominous rejection, for it labeled K.'s mother as immoral and meant that she would have no economic support in rearing the boy. She was condemned by all, and her brothers, who might have helped her, publicly insulted and beat her. She was thus left to live in isolation with K. and another widow at a pig-herding house well removed from the hamlet.

This history—of a liason that led to a morally offensive birth, humiliation, banishment, and bastardization—dominated K.'s childhood. He grew up without a father or acceptable substitute. Unlike what should have occurred, none of his mother's brothers stepped in as an appropriate masculine figure. In fact, to worsen matters—and here we see how familial guilt and conflict were built into the child's environment—K. was told his father was dead, and the man's true identity was hidden from the boy. It became a family secret. Having been treated shabbily, his mother was thereafter bitter toward all men, withdrawing from community life, including contact with men.

K. participated, as prescribed, in all initiations, but his response to them was strange: he feared and resisted them. He says, for example, that he faced the first-stage initiation wishing he had been born a *girl*, remarkable and unheard of with other Sambia men. Though his first response to doing fellatio was fear—that is how most boys respond—within a day he was enjoying it, his pleasure made up of shame, a sense of danger, and sexual excitement. Despite fear, moreover, he had an erection with his *first* fellatio, an extraordinary response that no other Sambia has reported. He was an avid fellator for years. When, in puberty, he was initiated a bachelor, he eagerly switched to being fellated. He enjoyed copulating with and daydreaming about boys. He never stopped using them.

Married late, K. was not active in the arrangements, though by custom and personal motivation he should have been enthusiastically involved. He would not consummate the marriage. Bored after a long wait, his wife left him. Three additional marriages went the same route.

K. was never at ease discussing his erotic behavior and life history. He described with discomfort the type of boy who turned him on and how it happened. It was harder for him to express his feelings about women. But he could not even mention his desire for prepubescent boys: he wanted to suck them off! H. learned of this only when several initiates told how K. had tried to reverse fellatio roles with them. It is strongly taboo but not unheard of for a backsliding adult man to let a boy drink his semen, but for an adult to suck on a boy is simply shocking. This reversal is, for Sambia, fundamentally immoral. No one performs fellatio on prepubescent boys; for an adult to go for boys when they have begun producing semen is to steal semen the society needs to reserve for the boys, who grow strong and manly only by its ingestion. So K. fiercely avoided this subject, and when H. brought it up, he fled. Above all else, the one act that makes no sense to the Sambia is that he—an adult—sucks boys' penises. There is no category for that. It is outside their culture and comprehension. To us it is a primal urge of his, a homosexual commitment based on the disasters of his childhood. He would be a homosexual anywhere, independent of the culture's erotic customs.

LEARNING THEORIES OF SEXUALITY

We quote representative authorities on learning theory:

> According to classical learning theorists, who generally follow Hull's (1943) drive-reduction model (e.g., Kinsey et al., 1948, 1953; Marquis, 1977; Miller and Dollard, 1950), eroticization occurs via the following sequence of events: (a) An individual experiences an

originally neutral stimulus, (b) that stimulus is paired with an increase in sexual arousal, (c) the arousal-stimulus pairing is reinforced by a reduction of sexual arousal (e.g., by orgasm) and (d) the originally neutral stimulus becomes a conditioned erotic stimulus capable of eliciting sexual arousal in the future. In short, according to classical learning theory, the arousal and reduction of sex drive are intrinsic to the eroticization sequence.

In addition to sex drive, classical learning theorists have also emphasized the facilitating role of masturbation and sexual fantasizing in eroticization (Marquis, 1977; McGuire, Carlisle, and Young, 1965; Miller and Dollard, 1950). Masturbation and fantasizing [daydreaming] are frequent sources of unconditioned erotic stimuli. Because masturbation and fantasizing frequently lead to orgasm, they can also develop secondary reinforcing properties.
. . . There is also evidence that adolescent erotic stimuli form the basis for an individual's adult erotic orientation. Two reasons have been offered for the formative nature of adolescent eroticization. First, one's earliest sexual fantasies, especially those accompanied by orgasm, may be more dramatic than later experiences (Sarnoff, 1976). Future sexual fantasies may be built on an individual's first and most dramatic fantasies. If an individual develops an early fantasy about men, for example, he or she is more likely to notice men in sexual situations, be aroused by men, conjure up more fantasies about men when sexually aroused, and thus eroticize even more male-associated stimuli. Second, the influence of early erotic fantasies may be enhanced by the development of sexual self-identity during adolescence. (Storms 1981, pp. 341–42)

Or:

It has been strongly argued by McGuire *et al.* (1965) that the nature of the first sexual experience, followed by orgasm, is crucial for the establishment of the direction of sexual orientation, and they cite several cases in support of this theory. It is particularly relevant to our emphasis on the importance of incubation of behavioural experiences . . . that McGuire *et al.* also emphasized that the deviant behaviour is maintained by the fantasy of the behaviour becoming a cue for sexual response (such as masturbation). . . . It may be that learning involving only a single trial, or a few trials, does occur in at least some individuals, and it may further be that such brief learning is the more likely to be crucial in determining the direction of sexual orientation if it occurs at a particular, and hence critical, stage of development. The stage at which secondary sexual characteristics are developed would be an obvious candidate for such a critical period. (Feldman and MacCulloch 1971, p. 170)

Note the absence of a belief that meaning and fantasy (other than daydreaming) may motivate erotic choice. In this learning theory, if someone is exposed to a stimulus, the stimulus becomes erotized because of its chance contiguity with erotic arousal that is the result of the increased sex drive of puberty. It becomes a fixed behavior when reinforced over time by masturbation (in the case of Sambia youths, by the fellatio-induced orgasms). There is no space in the explanation for awareness that the pubescent child is also primed by previous life experiences—events in the real world that have been remembered and transformed, via fantasizing, into personality.

A brief detour regarding fantasy. When analysts use that word, we do not mean just "daydream," as learning theorists do. We include far more: all the motivated transformation of perception. In this sense, then, we are simply agreeing with those who, for millennia, have said that one cannot perceive reality but only a private, individualized, idiosyncratic version of it.[6] Even something as simple as looking at a tree is an act modified in all its dimensions by our fantasies of what trees are, what that tree is, what the color green means to us, why we prefer maples to oaks, in what ways we identify with the tree as sturdy or old or bent or young or well rooted. (And to further exemplify the process, why did we pick those qualities when you, were you writing that sentence, would have picked others?)

Storms (1981) contrasts his variant of learning theory—the erotic orientation model—to dynamic theory.

> In terms of social psychological development, the erotic orientation model differs in several ways from sexual inversion [psychodynamic] theories. Most inversion theories attribute homosexuality to early childhood experiences resulting in sexual identification with the other sex. The erotic orientation model, in contrast, posits that the eroticization process underlying homosexuality occurs pri-

6. But we are not agreeing with the platonic version that says there is an Ultimate Reality for which mere mortals' realities are just shadows.

marily during preadolescence, much later than the early childhood experiences cited in most inversion theories. Further, the
erotic orientation model places considerably more emphasis on
the contribution of one's peers (sexual experiences with them,
emotional attachments to them, exposure to sexual information
from them) than on relationships with parents. . . . the erotic
orientation model hypothesizes that homoeroticism develops out
of normal, commonplace experiences that occur to nearly everyone during the period of homosocial bonding. It is proposed that
some individuals simply have stronger sex drives during this period and thus eroticize these homosocial experiences to a greater
extent than others. (p. 351)

Learning theorists, then, emphasize that homosexuality is an
expected outcome when, with increasing sex drive around puberty, one's first great erotic excitement and resulting orgasm
occur with homoerotic activity. When these "positive reward
conditioning" factors are linked to "the occurrence of *unpleasant* heterosexual experiences which have led to heterosexual
avoidance," there is a powerful synergy toward homosexuality
(Feldman and MacCulloch 1971, p. 170).

Analysts, too, believe that positive and negative reinforcement ("pleasure-unpleasure principle") shape erotic choices.
But we disagree with learning theory's big-bang hypothesis
and its tendency to ignore that infancy and childhood also
contribute. Most of all we disagree with explanations that leave
out fantasies, meanings, and scripts—conscious or unconscious—as motivators of behavior. We therefore disagree with a
theory that omits an awareness that the traumas, conflicts, and
yearnings children have regarding, for instance, one or the
other parent contribute to some people's later choice of same-
sexed erotic objects (Fenichel, 1945, p. 327).[7] (Learning theory

7. It is painful to see how antipsychoanalytic critics sweep aside the idea
that infancy and childhood contribute to adult behavior. By using a question-
naire and one or two interviews with adult subjects, including the parents of
child subjects, or by no more than superficial observation of children sitting in
the reseacher's office, the critics reach their conclusions. No in-depth studies,
no techniques for trying to get below the surface, no interest in defenses or the
struggle to see behind them, no systematic infant observation, no extended

has not faced the paradox that came to unsettle Freud creatively more than any other issue: "the economic problem of masochism"—why humans search for, need, and enjoy, even erotically, suffering.) But the fundamental flaw of the learning theorists cited above is, perhaps, their not seeing that erotic experiences can be the final common pathway—the successful compacting—of myriad earlier nonerotic experiences, memories, and fantasies going back to earliest life (Stoller 1979).

Learning theory therefore leads to what seem to us tortured explanations. A text on social learning theory cites a paradigmatic case:

A 17-year-old male [reported by McGuire et al., 1965] was highly sexually stimulated at seeing a girl dressed only in her underwear. Thereafter, he frequently masturbated to the mental imagery of the scantily clad girl. Eventually the memory of the girl's characteristics faded, but advertisements and shop-window displays of women's undergarments continued to serve as strong masturbatory fantasies. After a period of several years the erotic potential of these fetishistic objects had increased to the point where he no longer showed interest in girls, but rather derived his sexual stimulation almost entirely from women's underwear which he bought or stole. (Bandura 1969, p. 519)

---

looking at families in interaction. "The basic question at issue is whether a sexual orientation contrary to the one at birth can be superimposed by [sex] assignment and rearing. The evidence most prominently put forth in support of such a contention has been found unacceptable" (Zuger, 1980). And who in all the world is the authority he cites for finding the evidence unacceptable? Himself. Another example (pointed out by Gagnon in his book review [1981] of Bell, Weinberg, and Hammersmith's *Sexual Preference*): The authors "have drawn the controversial conclusion that there is almost no correlation between early family experiences and adult sexual preference and therefore that sexual preference must result from an early, presumably biological propensity for either homosexuality or heterosexuality. They based these conclusions on the answers given by their adult respondents to questions about their lives from their preschool years to about age 19 . . . [p. 10]. The idea that adults can answer such general (and distant) questions about their childhood as whether their mothers were 'hostile' or 'strong' with sufficient accuracy and detail flies in the face of all recent research on memory. . . . the present and may influence the memory of the past more than the past influenced the present" (p. 37). Freud said this in 1919 (p. 193).

Aversion to heterosexuality, chance turn on to an aberrant object—a person of the same sex, clothing, copulating flies, whatever—and reinforcement of the pleasure by repetition in masturbation. The example chosen to represent the process— the seventeen-year-old male who was "highly sexually stimulated at seeing a girl dressed only in her underwear"—reflects some of the weaknesses in the argument. First, such a story is not found in other transvestites, who, if masturbating to the image of a girl in underwear, try to see themselves as the girl. But more important is the load of information hidden in that "eventually." How and why did "the memory of the girl's characteristics" fade, and how and why did "advertisements and shop-window displays of women's undergarments" increase, after several years, "the erotic potential of these fetishistic objects"? Why did his erotic focus shift from female anatomy to its immediate coverings, a move that suggests to us a shift in meanings: what does the flesh say to him and what does the underwear say? The answer the researchers give— reinforcement of aberrance by frequent masturbation—hides the great question: what really happened inside the boy? Which leaves us with the problem of *why* this boy became fetishistic to women's clothing when all those other hardy teenagers who look at "scantily clad" females do not.

DISCUSSION

It is neither our purpose nor within our competence to argue the compatibilities of learning and psychodynamic theories. But we believe that someone some day will show how both perspectives are present simultaneously in some behaviors (for example, fantasies reinforce conditioning and vice versa). It is not for us to worry that many learning theorists cannot accept the idea of repressed unconscious forces, especially that unconscious fantasies can move behavior. But it ought to be easy enough—and quite useful—for analysts to systematize and absorb theories and data of learning theorists. We use some of these ideas all the time anyway.

For instance, identification consists of more than just unconscious oral incorporative and introjective processes. We also know that children and adolescents choose aspects of identification because of positive and negative reinforcement by significant people in close relationships and by the culture at large. We would not understand the development of superego functions without such knowledge of the influence of parental and societal attitudes. Or take the desensitization that occurs in working-through, in which patients become less frightened of an aspect of themselves or of the analyst in part because, each time the feared quality is experienced, no harm follows. The first try may be done consciously and courageously. When to the patient's surprise there is no trauma, the next time takes a bit less courage. The phobic aspects diminish. Or, to point to another huge area where we need both theories of explanation: the transforming of children into social beings who spontaneously and automatically reflect the styles and customs of a culture. This shaping of behavior, we all know—having had it done to us and having done it to others—is certainly, whatever else it is, a process of reward and punishment. We analysts are, of course, uneasy that when learning theorists talk of, say, desensitization, or positive and negative reinforcement, the theory behind the words excludes the play of fantasy, as if the processes were the same in planaria, pigeons, and people.

An example from Sambia experience returns us for a moment to our data. Even in homosexual circles in our society, we do not hear of men who fetishize other males' mouths, comparable to the fetishizing of women's bodies by heterosexual men. In fact, despite the importance of mouths as erotic organs among homosexuals and heterosexuals in our society, one does not hear at all of the fetishizing of mouths. Yet Sambia males, in erotic reminiscing, go on and on about the shapes and aesthetics of mouths. On the other hand, though there is an aesthetics of penis appearance among homosexuals in our culture, there is none with the Sambia. For them the penis is a semen conveyor. It is at these points of precise observation, where technical vocabulary and theory give way to clinical reality, that we could find the proper proportions for mixing psychodynamic and learning theories to explain a piece of behavior.

There is another tendency found from more to less among learning theorists: selfhood is denied. Instead, we have modeling, physical contiguity, cognitive rehearsal, signaling systems, learned and unlearned habits. The vocabulary, sentence structure, rhetoric, and concepts plead for acceptance as objective, scientific. (Analysts do this too.) Objectivity, we see in the writings of the grand old behaviorists, requires that one not recognize mental life—fantasies and feelings, meanings and interpretations. Writing and thinking this way has become a style—the clanking language of mechanisms—whose purpose is to stimulate the reader to responses extracted of feeling. And so we get phrases such as "the increment of habit strength accruing to a response through cognitive rehearsal, indexed as an increase in the intensity or speed of the response on the next exposure of the person ["the person": what is that!] to the external stimulus" (Feldman and MacCulloch 1971, p. 174). Or: "The observed CR is the resultant of two opposing tendencies; extinction will be observed if the decrementing tendencies are greater than incrementing ones, while *incubation* will be observed if the incrementing tendencies are greater than decrementing ones" (Eysenek, quoted in Feldman and MacCulloch, 1971, p. 171). (It is rather like analysts on the trail of cathexes.) How would they deal with "envy," "despair," "rage," "humiliation," "joy"?

A woman puts in her closet a sachet given her by a lover. On returning from a long trip with him, during which their relationship became embittered, she opens the closet and is nauseated by the smell. Is that nausea due to her being conditioned to become nauseous at the perfumed smell of the sachet—a reflex—or does the stimulus—a scented odor—have a new *meaning* that sickens her?

In a typical report by Havelock Ellis (1942, pp. 35–36), we find a vivid language, with each sentence connoting complexities of human experience—the way life is really lived—for which learning theory simply cannot account. "I admired pretty feminine foot-gear," "intimate friends of my parents," "a beautiful and powerful girl," "always daintily dressed, and having most lovely feet and ankles," "a most distractingly coquettish manner," "she playfully stepped upon my body," "scrunch," "no description can give any idea of what I felt," "glee," "flashing eyes, flushed cheeks, and quivering lips." (What would be the behavioristic analysis of "I admired"? Or even of "I"?) Ellis's kind of writing reflects a belief, as Freud's did and as all clinical reports should, that, in our subjective experiences, subtle, subliminal, sometimes unreportable details are crucial for creating the desired effects. If that is true in our appreciation of, say, music or a properly baked cake, then why not for erotic life? There is no adequate behavioristic theory for the origins or experiences of the subtleties of desire—and without these aesthetic choices, where is desire?[8]

With these kinds of cases, we think the obvious: the excitement and orgasm are so rapid and intense, so visibly set off by the stimulus, that we shall not explain "the first time" as being the chance contiguity of excitement with whatever just happens to be occurring at the moment. Rather, the descriptions suggest that though a precise event set off that first erotic charge, the person excited was already prepared for the stimulus. There is, for instance, the young man (and there are innu-

8. This is not to say that Ellis was not a learning theorist. Long before the behaviorists we cited, Ellis too had inherited the idea that chance contiguity explained aberration: high-sex-drive-adolescent-boy-with-erection and dainty-footed-brown-silk-stockinged-high-heeled-slippered-perfectly-frank-and-charming-girl-with-crunching-foot produced a lifelong erotic aesthetic. Or: "In a case of Moll's the development of a youthful admiration for the nates in a coprolagnic direction may be clearly traced. In this case a young man, a merchant, in a good position, sought to come in contact with women defecating; and with this object would seek to conceal himself in closets; the excretal odor was pleasurable to him, but was not essential to gratification, and the sight of the nates was also exciting and at the same time not essential to gratification; the act of defecation appears, however, to have been regarded as essential. He never sought to witness prostitutes in this situation; he was only attracted to young, pretty and innocent women. The coprolagnia here, however, had its source in a childish impression of admiration for the nates. When 5 or 6 years old he crawled under the clothes of a servant girl, his face coming in contact with her nates, an impression that remained associated in his mind with pleasure. Three or four years later he used to experience much pleasure when a young girl cousin sat on his face; thus was strengthened an association which developed naturaly into coprolagnia" (Ellis 1942, p. 64).

merable others) "who when he once chanced to witness a woman urinating experienced voluptuous sensations. From that moment he sought close contact with women urinating, the maximum of gratification being reached when he could place himself in such a position that a woman, in all innocence, would urinate into his mouth" (Ellis 1942, p. 61). Or "the curious case of a sexually hyperaesthetic nun who was always powerfully excited by the sight or even the recollection of flies in sexual connection, so that she was compelled to masturbate; this dated from childhood" (p. 73). Even if we argue that, as a child, she was sexually aroused and at the same time, flies were buzzing around, we would still have to explain why her memory seized on the flies as the stimulus for all the rest of her erotic life. Should we not wonder why, out of the thousands of neutral stimuli in the ambience at the moment the erotic lightning strikes, the child/adolescent chooses a particular one for the subsequent fetishism? The analyst, however, suspects that, for this girl, flies had a special meaning, that they stood—despite their manifest neutrality—for more highly charged objects and circumstances. In other words, we believe that "meaning" is more motivating here than "stimulus." And no matter what the *etiology* of a piece of erotic behavior, once the subjective experience "I want" appears, an S—R explanation is at best incomplete.

How then shall we sketch in our explanation for the heterosexuality of Sambia men and the homosexuality of Kalutwo? And why no others like K.? Learning theory does not account for the heterosexuality. Yet the essentials it claims for setting the direction of erotic choice (McGuire et al. 1965, Marks et al. 1965, Rachman 1966, Bandura 1969, Feldman and MacCulloch 1971, Rekers 1978, Storms 1981) are all present in the Sambia homosexuality: (1) first orgasmic experiences (2) lustfully repeated and thereby reinforced as often as possible for years from puberty on (3) enthusiastically approved by the society's authorities, myths, mores, and rituals (4) with terrifying negative reinforcement for any other erotic choice (females). Yet the bachelors, once the signal is given, switch over to equally lustful heterosexuality. Something else must be going on; we need a better explanation.

It is there, though still incomplete, in the boys' childhood experiences, which, both for the heterosexuals and for K., fit analytic descriptions of the origins of heterosexual and homosexual preferences. We would expect the typical Sambia youth to be defended against the pull toward homosexuality produced by the powerfully gratifying, socially approved homoerotic behavior of Sambia adolescence if, in childhood, heterosexuality was the official standard of the culture and if the boy also constantly observed families—not least his own family—in which the men, despite their fear of women's bodies, clearly expressed their erotic pleasure in women. We would also expect that the men, especially the boy's father, would not block the communications that let a boy know he can identify with—would even enjoy identifying with—heterosexual men, in particular his father. In addition, we would expect that the women—married and unmarried, mothers or not, but especially his own mother—would show (with whatever reservations, anger, and despair) their need for and enjoyment of men. Finally, there would be peer relationships that encourage identifications with masculinity and behaviors defined as masculine. And these predictions are borne out in the data (Herdt 1981a).

Still, all those cultural factors—all those urgings that the boys identify with men, all that positive reinforcement—are not enough (just as they are never enough in other places, other eras). More fundamental is the creation by Sambia men and women of an Oedipal situation, however stressed. The ingredients of boys' classical positive Oedipal situations anywhere are (1) breaking free from symbiosis, with its primary identification with mother, (2) into a separate person with a sense of being a male, (3) so that one desires to have mother more than to be a mother, (4) a passion mother somewhat encourages but basically forbids, (5) since her son cannot serve certain of her needs as a father can. (6) A father will not let his son displace him; he has the power to stop his son. (7) So the boy's hunger for his mother must wait for a later time and other females. (8) This delay is made easier when his father is available as a man worthy of identification. Though the mothers are closer to their sons and for longer than the fathers like, the boys' excessive identification with their mothers is avoided. The boys do separate from their mothers, who point them toward masculinity via identification with their tough, admired fathers.

And the fathers, though distant in those first years, have three techniques by which later they radically, acutely, and traumatically try to turn the boys from the women to the men: the initiations, the semen drinking, and the terrifying taboos on physical closeness with females.

For all the spectacular differences, Sambia boys and those of our culture who will be heterosexual proceed along a similar Oedipal path. In each case, they leave the mother-son symbiosis and develop a distinct sense of self. That done, they can turn back to their mothers as separate objects of their desire. Then, with fathers too powerful to be resisted, the boys are forced to defer return to the embrace of women until the society allows it exogamously.

Sambia men, probably because they know it from their own boyhood, say that their sons' masculinity is threatened by too much intimacy with the mothers. And without skilled and tough men to hunt birds and animals (protein), the hamlet would soon be weakened; without fierce warriors, the hamlet could be destroyed by the fiercer, ever-waiting enemy warriors. Unquestionably, then, the Oedipal situation must be well managed—must be tuned to the local conditions—or the people are not fit to survive.

Kalutwo, on the other hand, had none of these advantages. He was not wanted, and he was never accepted. His father not only denied him but was never present either as an object to be admired and identified with or to be loved. K. was exclusively with his mother, the two so ostracized that he had little to do with—much less acceptance by—his peers. We believe that a boy in such circumstances yearns for a good father more than anything else, and it is common knowledge among analysts that one of the contributions to some of the homosexualities is a hopeless, awful yearning for an unreachable father. Then, too, if at an early age, a boy is not picking up his culture's techniques for expressing masculinity and heterosexuality—the constant learning that goes on among peers—another important contributor to gender identity is missing. So Kalutwo, with his depression, sense of worthlessness, and already aberrant gender behaviors (for example, fear of the rituals that are to make the boy manly) had less chance to desire to be heterosexual. He was homosexual long before puberty. The initiations came to late.

As compared to the rich details that emerge in a psychoanalysis, these more external, narrative, reality-based, fantasy-impoverished data are not very satisfactory. Nonetheless, the fact that they point in the same directions already described from analysis-derived situations serves as at least a mild cross-cultural confirmation of some of the dynamics.

With both the Sambia and us, there are many impediments to this developmental scheme (more gross with them, more subtle with us) and manifold points where it can be damaged or fail. (There seems an almost perverse impulse in these cultures to make the process difficult.) Yet the Sambia—even more than we, as our technology loosens the demands of family dynamics—must have powerful forces at work to ensure heterosexuality and masculinity. For them, under constant threat of Stone Age man-to-man warfare and murder, it is a matter of life and death that these two qualities be present, but that no longer holds in most parts of our society. So the reinforcers among the Sambia are heightened, dramatized; no exceptions. Every boy must participate in all the rituals, which, for all the expressions of fear and hatred of females and the massive homoerotism, aim toward Oedipal resolution and heterosexuality. We feel, however, that the process would fail were it not for the early, substantial, wholesome heterosexuality the boys have with their mothers in the first years. Even though the men sense that the boys are too close to their mothers and that this is a threat to the development of masculinity, that dynamic is counterbalanced intuitively in the culture by the masculine and heterosexual reinforcers sketched above.

An example: Starting with the first-stage initiation, boys learn that women's bodies are not just taboo but poisonous. We believe that there would be no heterosexual Sambia men and therefore no Sambia if those teachings were instituted in the first year or two of life. But it is only after the Oedipal situation has been allowed to reach its height—the first initiations, you recall, are undergone only at age seven to ten—that the boys are both warned of and forbidden to approach the terrible dangers of female bodies.[9] Before that, females were as pleasure promoting as they also can be in our culture. Therein, we feel, lies the root of the heterosexuality that is strong enough to resist both the taught terrors of women's bodies and the wondrous sensations ("reinforcement") of the institutionalization of fellatio.

From our perspective that a rich and complex early childhood plays its part in erotic decisions of later childhood, puberty, and adult life, we analysts disagree with learning theorists. What seems to the naive observer a spontaneous, unprepared, unconditioned first response of excitement in, say, puberty is in fact an experience (not just a response to a stimulus) that falls on already prepared ground. And that prepared ground—"character structure," "self," "identity"—is so strong that it will participate somehow in all erotic learning and choosing. That, we think, is why all Sambia males except Kalutwo can be heterosexual, despite the overpowering positive reinforcement of homoerotic pleasures. Were that not so, the Sambia would have long since disappeared or changed their customs.

How would the behaviorists we have cited explain the genuine heterosexual enthusiasm of the Sambia men, who have no orgasmic or other body reinforcing of heterosexuality until, in late adolescence, they experience their wives? And how can one, using orgasm-reinforcing theory, explain the appearance of heterosexual pleasure after those years of homosexual fellatio? What was the reinforcer of women and their bodies if not the fulfilling closeness of infancy and childhood? And what of the terrifying negative reinforcements regarding femaleness, the life-threating power of women's parts and juices (Herdt 1981a, b)? Those latter fears are created—taught—and forever frighten males, and yet those destroying pollutants cannot stop desire.

---

9. Though pre-Oedipal boys everywhere may dread femaleness, few theorists would say there is no difference in quality and quantity of response between unconscious fantasy and terror in reality.

After intercourse, a man goes to the forest and drinks the white sap of certain plants to try to replenish the lost semen. And he regularly lacerates deep into his nares with razor-sharp grasses to flush out some of the pollutants taken in by contact with his wife. Yet he returns again and again to a woman's body, unable to forgo heterosexual desire.

Could one say that the heterosexuality of Sambia men is only a facade, the result of cultural demand, that they give up homoerotic pleasures only when forced to do so and only to fulfill the role of husband and father? We presume that this factor contributes with some Sambia, as it does in all societies that taboo homosexuality; Herdt confirms this view in unpublished case studies. We need not put Sambia men on the couch to hear them tell of homoerotic desires. But we found these desires no keener than those we detect in our culture; in fact, far and away the majority of Sambia men have no active homoerotic desire for boys. And among the older bachelors—those who are fellated—almost all are avid to get on with heterosexual matters.

Cognitive learning theorists and social anthropologists might argue that Sambia males are not really having a homoerotic experience. They are just conforming to custom and ritual; or they are making the best of a situation in which they are threatened by the mature warriors; or the fellatio experiences, though producing erections and orgasms, are primarily a game. In other words, this is not a spontaneous act but rather a performance with a precise set of rules, clearly defined as not truly erotic and openly recognized as an essential step to heterosexuality. We have no question that, to varying degrees, depending on the boy, but far less than such statements intend, these elements are present. (They are an aspect of the issue we mentioned earlier, that erotic excitement is partly the compacting of nonerotic elements.) There is enough truth in these ideas that, to make a joke, for hyperbole, or for a Ph.D. thesis, one could say that ritual, authorities' power, bargaining, and other game dynamics are the essence of erotic development for most adolescents in most cultures.

But our Sambia friends would not recognize a description of their experience (nor would you of yours) that emphasized only those points. They (and you, unless terribly deprived by nature and imagination) add lust, a phenomenon broader and more compelling than a reflexive momentary excitement from erection and orgasm that are without meaning or object. *They do not just accept fellatio; they want it.* These homoerotic activities are not routine or simply an obligation one is pushed to by the culture. Quite the opposite. Almost all boys indulge with fine erotic enthusiasm. They daydream about and plan their episodes of fellatio, judging the physical attractiveness of the younger boys with as much keenness as do heterosexual young men with females in our culture. The desiring and the doing go on all the time, exactly the reinforcing that, in learning theory, predicts lifelong homosexuality.

To us, knowing how intense is the homoerotic desire in Sambia bachelors, it is racist ("ethnocentric" is the prettier word) to force theory on the facts and, in effect, tell the Sambia that their excitement is just a game or just ritual. The boy-fellator, increasingly as he approaches puberty, is eager to suck, and the youth is eager to stick it in. True, the boys know that marriage, heterosexuality, and procreation are goals of the ritual; the learning theorist would be right to point to those prospects as powerful reinforcement for the heterosexuality that results. But, even if theory gets complicated, one must not deny these people their awareness of their pleasure.

Though few boys—Kalutwo is an exception—are enthusiasts when first sucking the bachelors, they become more eager. The degree of interest varies from boy to boy, but when it comes to being sucked, the youths commit themselves fully to the homoerotic pleasure, even as they realize that each emission of semen must in time lead to decreased manliness and eventually deterioration of one's body. We know only one exception, a man socially and erotically aberrant because he is happy to be married to his two wives and openly expresses his pleasure in intercourse and intimacy with their bodies. Other Sambia men may love sex with women, but they nonetheless fear women's bodies. It is unknown to other Sambia, but this man never participated in sucking bachelors after the first ritual experience and never indulged in being fellated.

The Sambia appear by no means to be unique in respect to ritualized homosexuality. In a recent survey of the literature, Herdt (1984) found that such practices were far more wide-spread—occurring in some 10 to 20 percent of all Melanesian societies—than previously believed. Many of the social and behavioral characteristics noted above for Sambia appear also as thematic patterns in these other groups. In most groups, homosexual intercourse begins at an early age, though, as among the Marind-anim of southwestern New Guinea (Van Baal 1966), the erotic mode is anal intercourse, a more frequent practice in New Guinea than fellatio. In none of these societies is it reported that homosexuality persists aberrantly after the appropriate age. Even among the Marind-anim, who permit older married men to ritually inseminate boys, Van Baal (1984) takes the view that the man performs this task more out of duty than pleasure. For, like Sambia, Marind-anim men are enmeshed in many ideologic and behavioral hostilities to women, but they nonetheless show every indication of lusting after them. We believe that eventual research will confirm that early nonerotic relationships with girls and women outweigh adolescent homoerotic stimuli in the development of these sexual patterns.

CONCLUSION

For the particular subject discussed here—male homosexuality—we reviewed data that contradict the belief that lasting homosexual preference necessarily follows if, in homoerotic circumstances, one's first orgasm is powerfully reinforced for years. We found, rather, that the roots of Sambia heterosexuality were fixed in pre-Oedipal and Oedipal occurrences, and we presented a case in which homosexuality followed when a boy—Kalutwo—was not thus protected. However, in disputing behaviorists' explanations of erotic choice, we are not trying for a debating victory. Neither the nature of our data nor our lack of training in learning theory allows that. There is still too much unknown regarding sexual life, and professional xenophobia delays exploration.

Let us end by underlining a larger issue of which our ethno-graphic data are only an example. Learning theorists do not accept analysts' commitment to or findings on the power of infantile and childhood interpersonal and intrapsychic experi-ences and do not—at least in their writings—believe that non-erotic, sometimes even traumatic or frustrating, events influ-ence erotic choice. They also reject the analytic view that these experiences, in the form of unconscious fantasies, exert their influence years after they occur. We think this rejection is a mistake and expect that other reports such as ours will improve our understanding of the origins not only of erotic but of other behaviors and—a powerful addition to the search for such ori-gins—help learning theorists and analysts to work together.

CHAPTER 7

Transvestism in Women

The structure supporting erotic excitement suggested in the last few chapters holds, as I have said, more for men (in general) than for women (in general). The most visible difference—underlined in men's versus women's pornography—is men's preference for fetishizing and women's for a relationship. That difference is also reflected, I think, in the fact that women's erotic neuroses rarely take the form of the perversions of our formal classifications.

Keep these ideas in mind as you read the next two chapters, which are about perverse women. In neither of the perversions to be described can I make out the mechanisms that are easy enough to see in more common perversions. So I presume that, still beyond our reach, clues to further understanding of perversion and of the erotism of the two sexes are hidden in these conditions.

The first is transvestism—fetishistic cross-dressing—in women. As described here it is so rare it is almost nonexistent. Still, let us look closer at this previously undefined phenomenon; perhaps a rarity like this can lead some day to new ideas, to help us understand larger issues of sexuality—of erotism and identity.

To delineate the behavior, I have only three cases on which to draw—one from the literature, one known only through letters, and one who was in treatment with me for years.

THE LITERATURE

The literature on transvestism in women is odd in two ways. First, the authorities do not agree, in talking of men or women, on what they mean by the term. Some use *transvestism* (*transvestitism*) to refer to any act any time in which a person puts on apparel belonging to the opposite sex, some to fetishistic (erotic) cross-dressing, some to both of these behaviors equally. And some simply give no definition, probably presuming that the matter is clear and without challenge.[1] Even the meaning of *fetishism* in women is unclear,[2] as Bak (1974) has shown. (He insists that, in the strict sense in which I want to use the term—as an arouser of erotic excitement—fetishism "is a male sexual perversion" [p. 193], a position to which this chapter provides a corrective footnote, as have previous reports of nontransvestic fetishism in women.) To reduce a bit the clinical confusion that results from such blurring, I have suggested (Stoller 1968, p. 176) that "transvestism" be restricted to fetishistic cross-dressing, that is, erotic excitement induced by garments of the opposite sex. This definition helps us distinguish a behavior with a different clinical appearance and dynamics from others, some of which may share with it not much more than the cross-dressing.

Second, though it is common enough for authors to say that fetishistic cross-dressing is rare in women, they do not cite cases; "rare" may have been a safer way for them to say "unknown" or "never."

How rare, then, is this condition? I have of course not read every case of sexual aberration ever published. But since, in the modern literature, I have found a report of only one such person, I feel comfortable with the impression that this behavior is extremely rare. This fits the finding that all fetishism is rarer in women than men. (Rember: there have been plenty of writings on "transvestism" in women but with no mention of sexual excitement sparked by the clothes.)

1. For example, Allen 1969; Barahal 1953; Benjamin 1966; H. Ellis 1942; Fenichel 1930; Krafft-Ebing 1906; Kubie 1978, pp. 196, 198; Lukianowicz 1959; Redmount 1953; Rubinstein 1964; Zavitzianos 1972.

2. Fenichel 1945; Greenacre 1960; Sperling 1963; Spiegel 1967; Winnicott 1953.

CASE MATERIAL

Since the condition has not been reported before, the subjects are allowed to appear here in detail so that readers are less at the mercy of their own or my imagination. For the same reason, it is safer to use direct quotes than to present an abridged, paraphrased version.

The one study known to me is by Gutheil (1930). The following are excerpts from that report, arranged to exemplify pertinent categories present in the three cases described here.

Case 1

This thirty-four-year-old, unmarried, middle-European woman was seen some time in the 1920s.

1. *Normal Female Anatomy and Physiology.* Gutheil reports: "primary and secondary sexual characteristics of normal appearance. Menses regular, onset about 13 years of age" (p. 281).

2. *The Erotic Fetishism.* " 'As regards clothing, I may say that simply putting on men's clothing gives me pleasure. The whole procedure is comparable to that tense anticipation of pleasure which subsides in relief and gratification as soon as the transvestiture is complete. I even experience lustful satisfaction in dreams of this act . . . [p. 284]. It affords me downright sexual pleasure. Simply putting on my suit can provoke an orgasm. . . . The transvestiture has a far greater pleasure-value in my eyes than any intercourse, and I could easily forgo the latter in favor of the former. . . . I can also remember that up to the time I was eight or nine, I differentiated between the sexes only according to the difference in clothing. In my mind it was only the clothing that made the difference between guys and girls . . . [p. 289]. The beginning of my transvestitism also occurred at this time (between fourteen and fifteen), and I experienced my first orgasm in a suit belonging to my brother Edward. We had all put on costumes for a ball, and when I looked at myself in the mirror, I found that I resembled my father remarkably' " (pp. 305–06).

3. *Marked Masculinity*. Gutheil reports: "Claims to be able to undertake the hardest of work even during her period. Self-possessed appearance, male type of walk with long steps. . . . She urinates in a standing position" (p. 281).

" 'During the war, I was often stopped on the street because I was taken for a man, but even to-day, it is unpleasant enough for me to walk in public . . . [p. 282]. In my phantasies, I often see myself as the father of a family, caring for a wife and children . . . [p. 284]. My masturbatory activity used to be performed by my lying prone on my abdomen and making the movements of a male in coitus' " (p. 287).

4. *Masculine Impulses since Childhood*. " 'I had a distinct dislike of girls' toys as far back as I can recall. I played only with boys' things, e.g., sabers, guns, soldiers, etc. My favorite toy was a large rocking horse. A doll which I received for Christmas once was destined to destruction at my hands, and a box of knitting goods was thrown into the fire. I also recall a winter coat of dark blue cloth which I once had. It had ties instead of buttons and I cherished it very much. It is possible that the resemblance between this coat and the uniform coats of the hussars was what influenced my taste; to such an extent, indeed, that I insisted on wearing the coat even in the spring and summer. . . . As the years passed, the question of clothing became a serious dilemma. To go out dressed in airy skirts and hats with ribbons and lace made me feel like a dressed-up monkey. Following promenades or visits in such clothing, I would be overcome with a deep depression and was glad when I reached home again and could tear the stuff from my body. Even then I felt just as dissatisfied with such clothing as I do to-day. Every new dress was the signal for a bitter struggle, and if I did submit to the necessity of putting it on, I felt rather like hiding myself away in a corner than being seen among people in it' " (pp. 281–82).

5. *Similar to But Not the Same as Transsexualism* The differences are:

- Some femininity. " 'When I was between five and seven, we children played 'father and mother.' I often played the part of the mother, and dolls and playmates were my children. I also had a 'husband who went to work' while I stayed home and cooked. In my phantasies I had identified myself with my mother, and even tried to fix my hair in the same way that she wore it . . . [p. 289]. Until I was about twelve or thirteen, I wore earrings and girls' clothes. It was about that time that my desire for men's clothes first appeared' " (p. 294).
- No effort to pass permanently as a male. But " 'I would beg you, dear doctor, to help me gain permission to wear men's clothing and thus enable me to live a more human and happy life' " (p. 283).
- No effort to change sex. "Sex change" surgery was not available then.
- Homosexual relations acceptable. " 'In my thirteenth or fourteenth year I had my first affair with a girl named Marie' " (p. 289). About another woman, the patient says: " 'One day she suddenly suggested that we perform mutual cunnilingus. I was agreeable and from that day on we satisfied ourselves frequently in this manner' " (p. 299). Transsexual women, in my experience, do not let their genitals be touched, for that act unbearably emphasizes that they are not males.

Case 2

This is an American woman, unmarried, in her thirties, whom I have never met. The quotations are extracts from letters she sent me.

1. *Normal Female Anatomy and Physiology.* She raises no suspicion of biologic abnormality; she mentions her breasts, vagina, and clitoris.

2. *The Erotic Fetishism.* "I am particularly interested in your position on female transvestism: 'In summary, it can be said that there are male transvestites and male transsexuals; among

women there are female transsexuals but no female transvestites.' Apparently, the view is a common one; I have read it
before. I believe that perhaps there *are* female transvestites,
and I feel myself to be one. My discovery of this proclivity
occurred almost accidentally. A couple of years ago, I purchased a moustache, feeling my intent to be merely a lark.
However, I became fairly obsessed with the idea of wearing
this accoutrement in the streets. The compulsion, while short
of orgiastic, was definitely erotic. I bought some unequivocally
male clothes. Donned in this garb, I felt great excitement in
parading about the streets, driving through downtown, going
to a movie or to a bar. I took to going into men's departments
at the larger stores; my feeling amidst these clothes was one of
fetishism. My enjoyment when out on my usually solitary
transvestic missions was that of the narcissist and exhibitionist.
The excitement was such that I could barely avoid shaking; the
excitement enhanced when I would pass a bystander in the
streets. . . . I do not engage in this practice too often, but when
I do, it is always satisfying. . . . When practicing TV, as I call
it, my goal is not to pick up another man or woman for purposes of sex. My activity is something in itself."

3. *Marked Masculinity.* "Today my sex life is mostly satisfied by
masturbation, with transvestite episodes occasionally providing a pleasant stimulus to masturbation. I've dressed as a man,
replete with moustache, and had my partner call me by a
man's name. I take pleasure in being called by a man's name.
Dressed as a man, I've sucked my partner's penis. I felt myself,
during experience, to be a gay male."

4. *Masculine Impulses since Childhood.* "I played with the boys
next door. This was preschool. We played cowboys, each of us
assuming the role of a favorite male star. I always had plenty of
toy guns. My mother remarked that it did not seem right for a
little girl to have all those toy guns. At age eight I got a full-
blown cowboy suit for Christmas. With the boys I also played
baseball, catch and other hardball games. One day one of the
boys urinated outside, and I first became aware of an important difference between boys and girls. I was curious about the

difference but not traumatized. Once I tried to go to the bathroom standing up, in imitation. My grandmother said that this was not 'nice' so I didn't do it again."

5. *Similar to But Not the Same as Transsexualism.* The differences are:

- Some femininity. "I live and work as a woman. My luck falls down in the area of transvestism. It took me a while to face the fact that my facial features do not sustain this proclivity. No matter how mannishly I dress, sans moustache, I always get; 'Yes, Miss?' Each failure cuts into me anew. . . . A five-year-old child of one girlfriend—the child had not seen me for a year—recognized me instantly. That hurt. Sometimes I flatten my breasts, using a corset, dress in men's clothing, but don't use the moustache. Still taken for a woman, men once or twice tried to pick me up. I told them cooly that I was a male. I received satisfaction from this (?) deception."
- No effort to pass permanently as a male. "I do not want to be a man (except if I could be born over again and have the choice—men have more freedom in this society, and no one could willingly choose to be a member of the oppressed sex. . . . One perversity, perhaps, is that I like the idea of looking like a rather feminine male."
- No effort to change sex. "I do not desire a penis, but I do wish that my anatomy was a bit less curvy so that I could more successfully practice TV."
- Homosexual relations acceptable. "I consider myself bisexual."

Case 3

I have known this thrice-divorced American woman in her forties—reported on extensively elsewhere (Stoller 1968, 1973, 1975) in regard to other gender issues—for over twenty-five years, during several of which I treated her. Many data are available on her, and they may be—because she was studied so extensively—more reliable than those of the first two cases. I therefore quote her at greater length.

1. *Normal Female Anatomy and Physiology.* Numerous physical exams revealed no anatomic or physiologic abnormalities, despite her belief (hallucination), for over thirty years, that she had a penis.[3]

2. *The Erotic Fetishism.* In response to my request, the patient wrote the history of her fetishism: "I've experienced special feelings while dressed in Levi's since I was very young—possibly prior to attending school. I do remember feeling definitely sexually excited around eleven years old, and being fully aware that my Levi's were a contributing factor. The neat part is that those same feelings are still available to me now, many years later. It was during this time that I also discovered that wearing boots intensified those feelings.

"When I put on a pair of blue denim Levi's—and not any other male clothing has this effect—I feel much more than just masculine. The excitement begins immediately—as I begin to pull them over my feet and up, towards my thighs. There is no sensation comparable, and that is probably because the peak of this sensation involves a large range of feelings, including impossible-to-repress sexual excitement. I feel emotionally strengthened, assertive, confident, and totally unafraid. When I put on a pair of Levi's it's as though I shed the neurotic crap that plagues me constantly, all of that stuff that makes me hate being a female, or, all of that stuff that keeps me afraid of being feminine. When I'm dressed casually, in pants other than Levi's, and I see a girl that I would like to be intimate with, I feel unsure of myself. I'm embarrassed to make an overture, and I feel frustrated, while being fully aware of feeling completely alone. I usually turn to a man when this happens, but it never occurs when I'm dressed in Levi's. Sexual excitement is available when I don't wear Levi's, but the possibility of my becoming sexually involved with a female is very remote. The sexual excitement I feel when wearing Levi's is a more pro-

3. Compare Greenacre 1953, p. 95: "The one female fetishist [nontransvestic] whom I have encountered was a woman with a well-developed bisexual body identification and an almost delusional penis" (Hug-Hellmuth's case, reported in Greenacre 1953 and in Balint 1960).

nounced, much stronger, and much more pleasant sensation than what is available at other times.

"I wear boots almost exclusively now, and in the acceptable fashion of today, and they continue to fit my moods, and to make me feel secure within myself, but don't cause any sexual excitement. My Levi's are the single exception. Women's Levi's are available now, and I own several pair. I have never become sexually aroused while wearing women's pants, even when the pants have a 'fly' and appear to be men's pants. No other men's pants excite me. Only the blue denim Levi's.

"It isn't important what I wear on top; it's as though I deny myself the opportunity to put on the Levi's until I actually ache. I feel the need in my breasts, my gut, and my genitals. I'm seduced by the damn things. I'm not sure, at all, what the exact sensation is: it's anxiety and pleasure being provoked while I'm holding those Levi's like I would be holding someone close. When they touch my skin I become intensely sensitive, and I hold them very tightly. It's like nothing else in my sensuality, or other sexual contacts. I don't mean that I have a sexual encounter with my Levi's. I just become very aroused by them, and it goes beyond arousal when I choose—that still isn't exactly right—when I put my feet into them it's as if someone were caressing my skin: as I pull them up over my ankles, legs, and thighs they do caress my skin. I feel a surge of something like strength, or power, along with the sexual desire. When I put on the Levi's, I strut; I feel I can take what I want, sexually [women].

"When putting on the Levi's, I feel very excited immediately. I feel the texture, the roughness of the material, as I pull them over my feet, over the calves of my legs, into my thighs, and somewhere inside as well as in my clitoris. It's a marvelous sensation but becomes close to painful if I'm unable to relieve the sexual tension. My sexual fantasies, when wearing the Levi's, always involve a female.

"I first became totally aware of the connection between the Levi's and my sexual excitement just prior to my first pregnancy. Probably about twelve years old. Teenage girls had just begun wearing blue jeans, bobbi-sox, and loose fitting skirts. I was upset with my mother because she had purchased me a pair of pants that were not Levi's. *I had to have Levi's.* I yelled and screamed obscenities, and threatened. I rarely behaved this way with my mother because quiet, subtle attacks were much more effective. Her response to my yelling was to ignore me and my request completely. This was also the first time that I ever did anything that was blatantly illegal. I forged a check of my mother's, cashed it at the local pharmacy, and purchased my beloved Levi's. The following sensations, as I began to pull my Levi's on, were magnificent. I remember them vividly, because that exact same experience was never available to me again. I was triumphant. I won. The 'trophy' was the Levi's. I was breathless with excitement, not so much sexual at that point. I ran to my girl friend's home to meet with her and 'our gang.' I was high with excitement, and I wanted to share it. I grabbed my friend affectionately and hugged her tightly, experiencing a marvelous orgasm that made her laugh and tease me.

"I remember the events that led up to my desire to wear blue denim Levi's and how I acquired the pair that were the first that created sexual excitement. There was to be a school Halloween carnival. My gang, girls, were to wear a man's white dress shirt with tails out, saddle shoes, and real Levi's (not other brands, like Sears, Montgomery Ward's, Penney's). The proof they were real was the tag—with the name "Levi" visible—attached to the right hip pocket. I tried to tell my mother how extremely important it was for me to have the Levi's and to have that tag on my butt. She couldn't understand why I couldn't wear a pair of my 'good' blue jeans. I couldn't understand her stupidity: if those blue jeans had been acceptable we wouldn't be having a discussion. I screamed, begged, and made wild promises about attending school. She would not budge. She would only say that she had troubles enough with my dad gone, and a new baby to care for, and her midnight to 8 A.M. job. I was not sympathetic; I wanted Levi's, and nothing else was acceptable. I was the only 'gang' member whose mother worked.

"So I stole a pair of Levi's and hid them in the bushes by the school. My mother gave me a white shirt that had been my dad's, I had the required shoes, and I put on a pair of my old blue jeans. I almost ran all the way to school. I could hardly wait to wear my new Levi's. It was early, but dark. There were a lot of kids on the street. It was Halloween. I saw one of the girls, in my gang, standing and waiting for the rest of us. I slipped into the bushes as quickly and quietly as I could and undressed. It was exciting from the start. I was out of breath from hurrying, and I got pleasure, I was sexually excited, by removing my old blue jeans. I'm not really clear where the excitement began. I took off my panties and, although I was afraid of being seen, I needed to grab my genitals. I wasn't masturbating, but I had my hand between my legs, holding the excitement and shivering, but I wasn't cold. I'm not sure how long I stood there, only semi-aware of the kids on the other side of the bushes I was hiding in. I was really caught up in a fantasy. In the fantasy I was standing there without my panties, and a girl that attended the same school was with me. I knew that my mother was not only aware of my sexual excitement but was watching, somehow, knowing I wanted the girl, encouraging me, and was equally sexually aroused. The girl watched me step into the legs of the Levi's and came closer. I took my hands from between my legs and touched her face. Then, holding her next to me, I reached down to pull my Levi's up. I could feel the rough, starched material against the skin of my legs, and my excitement increased. I pulled them up slowly because it felt so damned good, and I knew I was going to have a super orgasm. I was teasing myself, and my mother, at the same time. I finally pulled the Levi's over my crotch and up to my hips. I let go of the material I was holding to pull them up, and put one hand to my mouth to stop any sound I might have made, and the other between my legs as I was experiencing one of the most profound orgasms.

"My legs quit. I sat down in the dirt and remained there until my breathing could return to normal, but I was in no hurry. I could see my mother, like I was dreaming, and she was smiling and looking happy. I didn't go to the Halloween parade. I stayed in the bushes until my friends left and wandered around town, killing time so I could get home after my mom had gone to work. When I did go home, I hid my new Levi's. I put off wearing them even though I had plenty of opportunities. It was like saving the frosting till last—after eating the cake. I would be anticipating the moment the Levi's would begin their journey up my legs, but I would deny myself access to them and those marvelous sexual feelings, until I had done something that I could reward myself for. If I attended school for one entire week, but my mother's head was still stuck on the previous week, and whatever discipline she had chosen was still in effect at the end of a good week, I would reward myself with my Levi's. This ritual didn't last long. Nothing in my life lasted very long during the years between ages nine and fifteen. However, the Levi's never lost either their appeal or their ability to arouse me sexually. As I began my teen years, along with my first pregnancy, and the constant shift between my mother's home and my grandparent's home, the effect of the Levi's changed. The changes were subtle, but clear-cut in my head. I felt strong, powerful, unafraid, assertive, less vulnerable. I'm fairly sure that these changes in my personality, when dressed in Levi's, were obvious to my mother, but she never insisted that I change my dressing habits. I picked fights with neighborhood boys twice my size, until there were none left who would become involved in any confrontation with me.

"I would wait, if necessary, until I was alone in the house before I would dress in my Levi's. A lot of the excitement, at this point, came from anticipating that moment when I would pull the Levi's up to my hips and achieve orgasm. Those feelings of assertiveness, strength, etc. came after I had experienced the orgasm, and had left the house dressed in the Levi's.

"It isn't, and wasn't, necessary for me to touch any part of myself to achieve orgasm. It wasn't really necessary for me to fantasize a sexual partner, but it was nice, and I enjoyed it. I would fantasize a nice, soft looking, young girl who was sad and lonely. I would hold her, reassuring her that she was safe with me. She would then hug and kiss me, and [in reality] I would pull my Levi's up. I would be sexually excited, feeling it in my gut, feeling my vagina straining towards orgasm, and that fabulous moment when the in-seam in the crotch collided with my pubic area and I would have an orgasm. I've always felt that my mother knew and approved this behavior. I don't know how I came to believe that. She would probably go into cardiac arrest if I suggested such a thing, and I've had to control the urge to drop it in her lap. There was no sexual interaction with the girl in my fantasies. The holding was sufficient, and remains the best part of any homosexual encounter today.

"My Levi's are just as effective, sexually, as they were when I was young. I don't rely on them for sex but do wear them if I'm feeling particularly sad or vulnerable. I discovered that wearing boots further enhanced those feelings of strength: if I'm dressed in Levi's and boots there isn't a man alive who could threaten me on any level at all. This is true today."

3. *Marked Masculinity.* "I've recognized, more recently, that when I'm dressed in Levi's, I also feel quite superior to any male in the immediate vicinity. Maybe that's because I never fail to seduce the female of my choice. And they are almost never homosexual. They are usually young, pretty, and have long dark hair. They look clean and un-used. They look as though they have neither been sexually involved with a male, nor have they mothered a child. . . . It gives me a feeling of power to own them. I'm not sure what I mean by 'power' but that's the only way I know to describe the sensation. I think if I were in fact a man I would be powerful.

"No other clothing provides any sexual excitement. However, if I wear any men's pants and *boots*, I feel strong, confident, and capable of taking whatever, or whomever, I want sexually. I do not wear boots exclusively, because of the aggressive feelings and the effect on my attitude. I do have to get along with men, for survival's sake, if for no other reason."

4. *Masculine Impulses since Childhood.* "My first pair of boots were 'engineer boots.' They were black leather with a strap across the instep that buckled on the outer side of the boot. My first pair of boots were purchased to wear while riding a horse, and for working around horses. I was consistently truant after

the fifth year of school, and spent the majority of my time riding horseback, and swimming in the ocean. I was very small and underweight prior to my first pregnancy. Yet when I wore my Levi's and was able to complete my costume with the boots, I knew that no one, or nothing, could frighten or harm me. Girls in those days didn't wear pants very often, and they definitely weren't worn to school. My sexual encounters with females were limited to mutual masturbation with other members of my 'gang.'

"Girls did *not* wear pants to school when I was little, but I did, and so was sent home repeatedly. I was thin and I protruded in the front, as though I had a penis. . . . Even when I wore a straight skirt (rather than a gathered full skirt) there would be a swelling, or my pubic area protruded."

5. *Similar to But Not the Same as Transsexualism.* The differences are:

- Some femininity. "A few times I've succeeded in minimizing my femaleness, but I've never been able to satisfy my requirements for the all-male look."
- No effort to pass permanently as a male. "I have always wanted to be a female. I am not a male. I have never tried to live as a man."
- No effort to change sex. "That's absurd. Why would I want to change my sex? I'm a woman."
- Homosexual relations acceptable. See above quotations.

DIFFERENTIAL DIAGNOSIS

On the basis of these three cases, the syndrome (is it a syndrome, or a disorder, a problem, a condition, a symptom, or just a habit, a state, or a behavior?) of transvestism in women can be described as follows. An anatomically normal woman, who has sensed a strong masculinity in herself since early childhood, discovers (in two cases) near or after puberty (and in the third case in her late twenties) that a particular piece of male apparel is erotically exciting. Despite her markedly masculine appearance, behavior, and fantasies, she also has manifest egosyntonic feminine qualities. She is therefore not impelled to change her sex; is not convinced that, anatomy to the contrary, she is nonetheless a male; and though fascinated and excited—not just erotically—by dressing somewhat as males do, she does not try to pass unnoticed as a male in order to live as one. (Perhaps today case 1 would try for "sex change.") She has overt homoerotic desires, but she may (two out of these three cases) also willingly indulge in sexual intercourse with men. Though having dreamed of having a penis since childhood, she is not appalled by her female genitals and does not try to hide her femaleness from her sexual partners, male or female.

In this description is buried a differential diagnosis. First let us compare and contrast the transvestite woman to women with related disorders. (The differences are more clear-cut in the describing than in clinical reality; the transvestite women share features with those in the other categories. That is true of so much in psychiatry: the boundaries of the conditions listed in our classifications are vague. Most of our "diagnoses" are better described as means that segment continua.) Then let us look at the situation with male tranvestites.

1. *Intersexuality.* The only condition to which we need attend now is the fetal androgenization syndrome in girls (the result of such conditions as hyperadrenalism or progestin treatment given their pregnant mothers to prevent abortion). These girls, modified genitally in utero in a malelike direction, are more active, rough-and-tumble, and interested in boys' games and dress than a control group of girls. Though some may in time have homoerotic interests, none is reported to be fetishistic with males' apparel (see Money and Ehrhardt 1972, Reinisch 1981).

2. *Transsexualism.* Unlike the women in this report (certainly cases 2 and 3), transsexual females wish to live permanently as men, which accordingly includes always wearing men's clothes; making every effort—social and legal—to pass successfully as males; trying to be rid of their hated genitals and to get their bodies converted to male; believing, while recognizing they are

anatomically and physiologically female, that they are none-theless—somehow—male; being uneasy when associating with homosexual women lest they be categorized as the same (and, in such categorizing, be therefore included in the class; female); being discomfited at the thought of sexual relations with women who recognize them to be females; and not feeling themselves to be nor having the appearance of being feminine from earliest childhood to the present (Stoller 1968, 1975b).

3. *"Butch" Homosexuality.* The butch homosexual woman is not erotically excited by the men's clothes she may wear, does not deny she is a female, knows she is a homosexual, does not wish for sex change, and does not try to pass as a man.

4. *Mothers of Primary Transsexual Males.* These are women with some overt femininity, manifestly heterosexual and married, who, for several years in childhood—until the anatomic and physiologic changes of puberty—want to be males and behave as do female transsexuals. These women do not cross-dress after mid-adolescence, are not fetishistic, and do not seek "sex change" (Stoller 1968, 1975b).

5. *Women with "Penises."* These biologically intact women feel and openly state that they are anatomically equipped with an intraabdominal or intravaginal penis, truly physically present. Our case 3 is an example (reported elsewhere [Stoller 1973]); I have known two others, neither of whom was aroused by the men's clothes she wore (Stoller 1973).

In brief, transvestite women have transsexual tendencies but are not transsexuals. They seem, rather, to be bisexual women who, in their fetishistic episodes, are aroused by a male-signi-fying fetish.

And how does transvestism in women compare with that in men? The most obvious difference is that the behavior is so rare in women but not in men.

Second (though this opinion is based on the kinds of limited observations already reported), the two behaviors "feel" differ-ent clinically. The fetishism is less demanding in the women. It

is not the necessary, main, or preferred means of erotic gratification, whereas the typical transvestite man is dominated by his
perversion. It is the central feature of his life. At its most intense, from puberty on for—let us say—thirty or so years, he
cannot get enough of handling females' garments, putting them
against his body, buying or stealing them, reading about them,
enjoying transvestite pornography, planning and executing his
masturbatory transports, churning with guilt over his pleasures,
devising ways to end the transvestism and excuses to revive it,
trying to decipher its nature by reading professional journals
and books or by introspection, hiding the behavior and yet
dreaming of exhibiting himself cross-dressed, performing for
himself before a mirror in what he defines as hyperfeminine
poses and movements, photographing himself cross-dressed,
searching in fantasy or reality for accomplices (an understanding wife or girlfriend, other transvestite men), studying clothes
catalogs, looking at women's clothes in shops and department
stores, and spending large amounts of money on women's
clothes. In other words, the typical transvestite man in his peak
years is consumed by his fetishism. The women in this report
experience no such bewitchment.[4]

Whatever their heterosexual impulses, the women are clear
that they have homosexual desires powerfully present. But by
far the greatest number of transvestite males are overtly heterosexual; they are excited by female, not male, bodies, and most

---

4. And what about the atypicals? I know men and have heard of more who
tell of rare—a total of a dozen or less—episodes of erotic cross-dressing over
ten, twenty, or more years, usually in adolescence or young adulthood. In
some there was no other visible gender disorder; in others the urge to cross-
dress in time moved the man to crave to change sex. Then there are those who
do not fully cross-dress but get their excitement from a single type of garment
(such as shoes), unchanging as the decades pass. But note the vagueness of
this report. I do not say how many men I myself have examined, under what
circumstances (for example, evaluation, long-term treatment), or who told
me—and how—about others (for example, a sentence in a published paper, a
patient described by a resident in supervision). This uncontrolled reporting,
which deserves an essay of its own, is common in the psychiatric and psychoanalytic literature. Sometimes we cannot avoid the vagueness, and sometimes
we can. At any rate, it reflects how little we still know about sexual behavior.

of them marry (Fenichel 1930, Prince and Bentler 1972). Bisexuality (in the form of conscious, accepted erotic need for both sexes) is rare in the men. Except when in the throes of his excitement, the typical male transvestite is unremarkably masculine in appearance, demeanor, professional life, and other role manifestations of identity. On the other hand, the appearance and behavior of these three transvestite women are at all times shot through with heavily masculine elements mixed in with some feminine elements.

The women, when into their transvestism, act more in the way with which we are familiar from reports of most women's erotism in other regards. They do not search for endless numbers of objects—in this case, garments; they want an infinity neither in quantity nor in variation within the preferred category. But with few exceptions, male transvestites in their most tumescent period act as if they can never get enough, with their erotic interest augmented by the aesthetics of the fetishes—styles, textures, colors, fit, and so on.

QUESTIONS AND SPECULATIONS

This description is a first approximation of an extremely rare erotic pattern. It may call forth reports of more cases from others, but even these will not confront us with a major clinical challenge. Its value for us is more in important questions hidden in the behavior: what are the links between these women's fetishism and their masculinity; what are femininity and masculinity and what are their sources; why is fetishism rare in women; why are perversions found less in women than in men; what are the inherent (biologic) erotic differences between men and women and how can they be extracted for study from the mass of nonbiologically induced desires; why and how does an inanimate object elicit desire; and how does *anything*, including another person, lead to sexual excitement?

What about a learning theory model for the etiology of fetishism: that hard, free-floating erotic arousal is, the first time it is experienced, fortuitously joined to an object—the fetish-to-be—that happens to be present? Putting aside other arguments and data that oppose this model (for example, why the far greater prevalence in men than in women?), I shall note only that none of these women gives a history to fit that conditioning hypothesis. I also disregard for now psychodynamic explanations such as castration anxiety, attempted identification with "the good breast," separation anxiety, or the maternal phallus. Despite their acceptance in analytic circles (and, in part and at times, by me), they are at best nonspecific factors that do not show why fetishism, rather than some other behavior, occurred. And I find biologic theories just as flabby ("global") in dealing with the living details of erotic life; for example, "the typical differences between men and women in sexual feelings can be explained more parsimoniously as resulting from the extraordinarily different reproductive opportunities and constraints males and females normally encountered during the course of evolutionary history" (Symons 1980, p. 171). Yes, but . . .

Clarifying the nonsomatic aspects of these problems will come, I believe, from the kinds of detailed and reliable data that are released in a trust-filled, insight-seeking treatment. For instance, in that circumstance we could expand the observation (first made during the treatment of case 3) that these three women (as is common with other very masculine women [Stoller 1973]) felt they suffered from their frozen, uncaring mothers since infancy. The following quotes represent comments of the sort all three women made:

> My mother's an old woman who wants me to die, and I hate her guts. She never said, "I wish you were dead." She always said "I think you'd be better off dead." She really said that. I felt like I should go home and take fifty sleeping pills. Only one time I went to her. And I told her, "Look at me. Look at me, I'm crazy. Help me!" She didn't know what to do, so she turned the television on. I never talked to my mother. My mother never had the time. (Case 3)

Or my suspicion might be firmed up that the terrible mother-daughter relationship experienced by many very masculine women is a motive in a lifelong daydream with the theme that if she were a man rather than a woman, she could undo the past and find a loving mother inside a feminine erotic partner:

> I used to phantasy another mother to myself who, I was sure, would not refuse children this necessary attachment [a mother's love]. For example, I would imagine such a woman lovingly slipping her hands down about my head and face, or over my cheeks; or she would press me close to her, etc. As I grew older, I came to feel these phantasies so intensively that I could almost sense them physically and a shudder of delight would run through me. (Case 1 [Gutheil 1930, p. 287])

Or more cases may in time confirm the finding in these three women that they did not have a functioning father:

> I was born into a fatherless household containing three women: My mother, maternal grandmother and maternal great-grandmother. Each of these women had displayed a singular lack of success with their men. . . . the relationship to my father [when she was born] was a casual one and he was gone from the picture by the time I arrived. Mother made occasional rare trips to see him for the next several years. Once when I was seven or eight, he sent me a dress. Mother wanted me to take good care of it but it fell apart. I don't remember my father at all. (Case 2)

Some day, with more details, we may be able to connect this loss of father with the development of masculinity in these women and their search for an ideal mother.

But hints such as these, even if they turn out to be pertinent, touch only on the masculinity, not the fetishism; we do not know why *this* masculinity in females, as different from all the other instances of females' masculinity, occurs with fetishism.

Perhaps a clue to the dynamics in the women can be found in the males: as the years pass, some male transvestites develop a new, more diffuse feeling for women's garments. The fetishism becomes less absolute (related to a decrease in libido?) and is increasingly mingled with a sense of femininity—a move in a transexual direction. The change in style is, in itself, nonerotic, though the erotic cross-dressing continues. Now the man more and more cross-dresses to feel feminine and to release "the woman within." This new behavior serves to produce tranquility and to relieve anxiety, depression, or other less precisely experienced forms of misery. In some cases (perhaps those with a weaker fetishistic need from the start), this desire to feel like a woman replaces the fetishism. The point here is that, with the decrease in phallic intensity, male transvestism can begin to resemble more the transvestism of the women reported here, in that the festishism seems more nearly embedded in the sense of cross-sex identity and less to be an isolated, overwhelmingly erotic break with one's habitual sense of identity. In the male, cross-dressing typically started as an apparently unmotivated irruption of erotic desire into consciousness; but in the women, from the start, the fetishism is consciously related to an identity issue, a sense of being manly. Later, for the men, when, over the years, their erotic intensity has cooled, the dressing is done more and more for reasons equivalent to those in the women: to manifest an otherwise hidden part of oneself.

I suspect that this latter identity aspect is present but unconscious in the men during those earlier, intensely fetishistic years and only gradually becomes conscious. (Note: the shift from being unconscious to conscious is crucial; we should not equate an unconscious with a conscious mental element. When a thought, feeling, or affect is unconscious, it is in a different dynamic state than if it is conscious. That is, the distribution of resistances—and resistances present themselves as reasons, meanings, attitudes—is very different. Fenichel [1930] disagrees.)

I have a hunch about the dynamics of erotic fetishes, which, as data accumulate, is moving toward becoming a testable hypothesis: an object (inanimate thing, animal, or body part) becomes a fetish when it stands for—condenses in itself—meanings that are, wholly or in crucial parts of the text, unconscious: a fetish is a story masquerading as an object. We should not be fooled, because the conscious experience is of instantaneous arousal, into thinking that the process is therefore simple, obvious, reflexive, unmotivated. Rapid arousal without a formed daydream only indicates a highly efficient dynamic, not the absence of a dynamic. A second hypothesis:

if the text becomes conscious, the fetish no longer in itself causes excitement, is no longer a fetish. Instead it now serves as a prop in a consciously enacted erotic drama; the whole scene must be played if excitement is to occur.

CONCLUSION

The more I have learned clinically—that is, from people rather than from theory—about cross-dressing, the more questions have emerged from former answers. Beyond presenting a fragment of new information, then, this chapter is meant to illustrate how such data let us glimpse uncertainty. We all know that it helps to make explicit what we do *not* know.

CHAPTER 8
Erotic Vomiting

Having found no literature on erotic vomiting, I want to report the following cases. We never know what clues may help solve puzzles of behavior, a truism that fits erotic life, so much of which is still unexplored. There is value, then—beyond the impulse to capture rare specimens for humanity's zoo—in searching out oddities that can spotlight forces too muffled to be perceived in ordinary conduct.

All three of the following cases are women, two of them reported on in the last chapter, and all have a clear-cut bisexual element. Are these two findings significant or coincidental? The quality of the observations is too low for a useful answer. I have studied only case 1 (the case 3 of the last chapter). Case 2 is an acquaintance of case 1; the case material is pure hearsay. Case 3 (the case 2 of the last chapter) is known to me only through letters she wrote me, sent mainly to tell of her erotic cross-dressing. Nonetheless, the impulse to publish these findings manifests a belief: even behavior as rare or bizarre as erotic vomiting can have its reasons, is somehow motivated, is not random, and is ultimately, though not yet, explicable.

CASE 1

This woman, now in her forties, markedly bisexual in her erotic choices, and encompassing within herself at one time or another all too many of the diagnoses in *DSM-III,* was in treatment with me for several years. She has been a vomiter since infancy. Labeling her a "vomiter" implies that she feels the symptom is part of her identity, not just an occasional experience. It has always been a primitive form of communication for her, emerging out of a raging, murderous intimacy between her and her mother. This form of her vomiting is not under control but has always been precipitous and projectile. A puny, premature baby, she had feeding problems from the start, which in time settled into two habitual intermittencies: skinniness/obesity periods (no anorexia) plus the quirk of vomiting (no bulimia). "I was a difficult baby," she said. "The biggest difficulty seemed to be in getting me to eat and to retain what I had been fed. During the crawling period it's been said that I ate strange things like soap and dirt and vomited milk and baby food." She recalls that, from the time memory begins (around age four) onward, she could vomit with ease—it may be voluntary or involuntary—when disgusted, angry, frightened, or threatened. For instance: "When I think something's bad [that is, dangerous], I vomit and I get scared and I feel shaky inside. When something makes me crazy, my stomach is one of the things that is affected the worst. And I can prove that by vomiting."

One of her first memories is of being abandoned by her mother, expelled from the household (before age five), and transported by car to a cold and powerful grandmother; the resulting vomiting episode in the car, according to the patient, flooded that environment, particularly those transporting her, and was thereafter a famous family story. Other volcanic vomitings: the one time when, while drunk, she attempted fellatio; the rare occasions when, following homoerotic intercourse, she discovered her partner was a mother, not nulliparous; and when, in intercourse with a man, he introduces an unexpected, frightening erotic element. In this category of vomiting, which is nonerotic, one thread in the experience, she knows, is rage; she is getting revenge by pouring these awful, poisonous contents on others.

At any rate, as with hysterical vomiters and those with anorexia nervosa, the sluices are less tightly shut than with more ordinary folk. "If I was whole, I would be just like other people: I could do things I wanted to do without vomiting."

A second form of vomiting for her is that which, as with anyone who is simply sick (though more easily with her), can accompany physical illness. At these times, it is an unpleasant experience not meant as interpersonal communication and with no erotic tinge.

I asked her to write a summary of her third category, erotic vomiting.

"It is extremely difficult to verbalize the sensations derived from vomiting except in slang expressions used by people who use drugs. For instance, to 'dump' means to vomit, but it's a different kind of vomiting than what you do, say, if you had the flu. When I begin to vomit I get a 'rush.' My thought about a 'rush' is a flood of good feelings throughout my entire body. Usually when you inject a narcotic in the vein you experience a rush and then you dump, which is often pleasurable. I don't put needles in my arm because I get those sensations and much more from simple vomiting. I am almost convinced that that is one of the big reasons I never became an addict.

"Anyway, I enjoy vomiting. It's something I've done all of my life, but it didn't really become pleasurable until after I had my first baby [age thirteen].

"I always vomited prior to going to bed after a stealing session if I'd gone out alone. [She was a burglar for several years.] I always slept beautifully after I had stolen something. The relief from the buildup and tightness in my gut was so immense that I would sleep like a newborn.

"Vomiting for me is like sex or an orgasm in that I'm tensed, I feel the rush or intense flood of good feelings almost continually throughout the vomiting and experience relief and quiet warmth in my body when I'm finished. It is not identical to an orgasm. I do not feel it intensely in my genitals alone, but I do feel it there as well as the rest of my body and feel pleasure in my mouth. It does not excite me to think about vomiting. I do not have fantasies about vomiting. It doesn't excite me to see other people vomit. Yet, I make myself vomit often and at other times I'm not aware of causing myself to vomit."

CASE 2

Case 1 writes of a woman she has known casually: "She says she began to actively masturbate at about age 11 years. She was caught by her stepfather, who placed her across his lap and spanked her very hard. She said she could feel his penis against her stomach (erect?) and began to vomit. She claims that experience was *the best*. The accompanying orgasm, during the vomiting episode, was the most intense sensation she had, or has ever experienced.

"She began to have sick spells, especially in the presence of dominant males—teachers, principal, stepfather, uncle—and twice during encounters with the police over minor traffic violations. She has had upper/lower G.I. series done on various occasions with negative results. She has never felt sick prior to or after a vomiting attack resulting in orgasm. She does not have orgasms when actually ill with the flu or during various childhood illnesses.

"She says that she doesn't get any pleasure from regular sex, but does enjoy giving head, yet says she rarely has an orgasm—with the exception of manual masturbation or a vomiting episode. During masturbation her fantasy primarily consists of being an executioner in a men's prison and vomits when the prisoner is twitching in death. They are usually prisoners who are being hung for the rape and death of a small child. She occasionally fantasizes the crime, and it seems to make little difference whether the child is male or female. She has also vomited with an accompanying orgasm, during the actual crime [rape] fantasy, at the moment of penetration [of the child] by the criminal.

"Men make her sick with their superior position in this world and she would like to see them all hung.

"She appears to be strict, or rigid, in her attitudes and manner, with the exception of discussing her sexual behavior. She also claims to have an almost uncontrollable urge to steal. She would not tell me the type of thing that she steals. She has never been arrested or had a psychiatric hospitalization or exam. She doesn't think she's unusual because of the vomiting/orgasm behavior and has promised to introduce me to several 'weird' friends.

"This girl does not behave in what I consider a masculine manner. She wears more feminine attire than most of the young girls her age, yet I always have a feeling, during our conversations, that either there is something totally lacking in her personality that would make her 100% female, or that she is somewhat like a caricature of a female—like a male drag queen or transvestite who doesn't quite make the grade. She doesn't attract me, sexually, in any way, but I'm fascinated because of the impression I have that I'm really talking to a penis dressed and behaving like a female."

CASE 3

The following quotes are from letters written to me: "The vomiting syndrome exists today. I can reach a sure orgasm by imagining someone vomiting in a hard, humiliating fashion. The someone can be myself or someone else, since I am so quick to identify with those for whom I have erotic feelings. I think I was 4; I was wearing overalls, as I often did for play. My grandmother balanced me on one knee and held me while I vomited. Perhaps I received vaginal stimulation from the way she was holding me; this I conjectured later. My earliest memories were those of being ill, although I was never seriously ill and was generally a healthy child. When I was ill, the whole household was awry. My mother was overexcitable, overconcerned. I felt embarrassed by her concern. My grandmother was also very, very concerned. I would be lying in the bedroom in the semidarkness. A dim light would be burning during the night. I thought of this light as the 'vomit light,' knowing that it burned for just such an emergency.

"Once (age 4 or 5), my mother came home from work with a virus and she vomited with great difficulty and much crying. I was embarrassed. Later I had trouble telling my mother and grandmother when I felt sick. I feel humiliated by sickness. (Then, in my fantasies, I am obviously humiliating myself.) My two cousins also seemed to have a vomit hang-up; the three of us would often get together and make unseemly noises.

"At age 6 I went to school. One of the nuns I saw as particularly mean. She had apprehended me unjustly and yelled at me unfairly. I hated this nun. She became the first fantasy character on the sex-track. These fantasies I have before I drift off to sleep, usually. The nun is the first that I can remember. I would see the nun's face before my eyes while drifting off to sleep. I believe that I imagined the nun vomiting, or otherwise in distress.

"There was a child in my first grade, a small girl with a puckered face like a kitten. I felt attracted to her. Much to my surprise—I was shy and did not make friends easily—she and I became good school friends. I had occasion for erotic excitement when, one Friday afternoon in class, 10 minutes before the final bell, she vomited.

"When I was 11 or 12, I got erotic satisfaction from watching wrestling matches on T.V. or live. My favorite wrestler wore long black tights and cast himself in the villain's role. I fantasied about him consistently for a year. I identified with him. His ultimately being pinned to the mat was the zenith of the fantasy."

"Patsy had a 4-year-old sister named Barbara. This 4-year-old also possessed a tough, husky voice. I felt erotically, sadistically attracted to the child, the only occasion where I can ever remember indulging in mental pederasty. I actually bumped into the little girl once or twice, and was erotically excited by her crying. I also fantasied her vomiting, of course."

TRUISMS AND CONCLUSIONS

1. It may seem regressive to return to publishing the specifics of erotic behavior à la Krafft-Ebing, Havelock Ellis, et al. To do so could, however, help us. In the details (which, I suspect, are almost never reported by patients in treatment and are not found in the literature—only in pornography, where they are more mythic than true to life) are clues to what goes on in the experience—how it felt, what it meant, why it was done—with the complexity and layering of the elements united into what seems on the surface a spontaneous simple act.

2. Concentrating on exact, naturalistic data collecting would show us how much we do not know. That insight has been submerged by the theories that have proliferated over the years

(and not just in psychoanalytic circles). Facts are searchlights that reveal the cosmetic intent of theory.

3. Erotic impulses are a never-ending source of ingenious, even wondrous constructions.

4. Almost any object or body function can be erotized.

5. We still have a lot to learn regarding erotic life.

Which brings us to certain problems in using psychoanalysis—its technique, findings, and theory—for research. My aim in the following part is not to attempt a definitive discussion of how to do research on psychodynamic issues or how to use psychodynamic treatments for doing research. Rather, as usual, I am mostly interested in brush clearing, reminding myself and colleagues to watch for weaknesses in argument, rhetoric that papers over ignorance, demonstrably untestable pronouncements, ungraceful defensiveness, unverifiable observations, and other baggage unnecessary for the psychoanalytic journey.

Most analysts—all who are physicians—were once trained to appreciate the power of scientific method in testing hypotheses. Somewhere within our scruffy consciences we recognize when we are off the mark in our reports, and as we reveal when we gossip about colleagues' work, we have no trouble seeing weaknesses in data collecting, data arranging, methods of reporting, and theory building in others.

In this and other books, I have sometimes marked the tricks we analysts use: where my biases shape ideas, where writing style—aesthetics—is applied to influence your thinking, where observations are incomplete, how one is tempted to fill a gap by dumping in reference to authorities, how grandiose and mystifying jargon covers ignorance, where my personality shaped patients' responses ("the observations"), where grand conclusions follow meager findings, where enthusiasm or impatience led to premature confidence, and how hidden fear of humiliation can be covered by declamatory propaganda. This performance, as we sometimes see also in theologic discourse and philosophic debate, is the result of great thoughts unsupported by scientific method. Once recognized, it does not make for pleasant reading.

Perhaps some day psychoanalysis can become a science in the restricted sense of that term, a discipline built on scientific method. Until then, I wish we were content with what we can well be: the best of all naturalistic observers of human behavior. It would be so easy for us to mend our ways; we need neither new technology nor new theory. We need only be as clear as possible (which, of course, includes clearly stating where we are unclear). That is why the commonest phrases I use are "It is obvious" and "Everyone knows." For it is dangerous to deny that something is obvious when it is obvious that it is obvious.

Though it may be a while before we analysts can present testable hypotheses, we can, starting now, renovate two sectors of our work: our rhetoric and the reliability of our observations. The last chapters discuss that pleasing prospect, drawing on three of the activities—observing, treating, and writing—that analytic scholars use for doing that most satisfying experience, psychoanalytic thinking.

PART II
Observing the Erotic Imagination

CHAPTER 9

Psychoanalytic "Research" on Homosexuality: The Rules of the Game

In this chapter, I shall use homosexuality to exemplify how the way we analysts write our reports not only can serve to distort our observations but also shapes our theories and conclusions, with resulting ethical, moral, political, and other social consequences.

Expecting to lose friends in the process, I nonetheless want to write an essay drained of visible theory and data, built out of problems that allow only one reckoning: we—psychoanalysts and everyone else, professional or otherwise—do not understand homosexuality. Our ignorance includes not knowing what is to be called homosexuality; what its dynamics, etiology, epidemiology, life course, and prognosis are; and how it is best treated, how we apply research techniques to compare our treatment—our techniques and our results—with another or with none; and what the long-term effects of treatment are. The rules of the game have not yet been established.

I do not deny that anyone's findings, theories, conclusions, or recommendations about homosexuality are correct but only insist that *we cannot know when anyone is correct*. My questioning of the authorities comes less from poor training, weak scholarship, modesty, discretion, passivity, or cowardice than from the megalomanic idea that I can detect ignorance beneath the appearance of knowledge and can get others to agree. The claims underlying my argument are two: that none of us has done the work that yet warrants formal acclamation, and that we cover our lack of demonstrable, reliable observations by manipulating words, not variables.[1] I offer no new ideas or theories.

This chapter would fare better were it offered during a conversation over drinks rather than as a formal piece of writing to readers expecting a formal piece of writing. Each circumstance has its rules. I remind you now of those for the presentation game.

I. RULES FOR PRESENTING AND PUBLISHING

1. Use the rhetoric of science, a formal, not a conversational, writing style:
   a. Good scholarship—proper citations and intelligent review of the literature.
   b. Heavy use of technical language (*cathexis, deneutralization, projective identification, narcissism*), for which we have less agreement on definitions than we admit publicly or to ourselves.
   c. Ponderous tone ("a function of the narcissistic libido which is amalgamated with the object cathexes").
   d. Replacing modest truths such as "I think" or "I guess" with prouder statements such as "I submit" or "The

---

1. Home (1966) speaks for many of us:
The stimulus to write this paper has come from attending the scientific meetings of psychoanalysts for many years. From the first I was overwhelmingly struck by the essential incomprehensibility of the clinical papers couched in what is often called "technical language" and by what seemed to me the philosophical naivete of the theoretical papers. Although part of my difficulty sprang from lack of experience in the clinical situation, ten years of clinical work has only served to strengthen my initial impression that, although all the authors I heard undoubtedly meant something by what they said, and although I have learned from experience to interpret what they say to some extent, yet a great part of what was said did not in fact, in a strict sense, mean anything. The formal meetings stood in contrast to clinical discussion in informal seminars where meanings were readily communicated in more ordinary language. Part of a sentence from a paper by Sandler "On the Concept of Superego" (1960) may serve to illustrate the point. He writes: "The two techniques of restoring a feeling of being loved (of increasing the level of libidinal cathexis of the self). . . ." The first part of this sentence seems to me completely comprehensible, the second part is, I believe, meaningless. (p. 42)

analysis of a number of cases reveals the likelihood that it is substantially true, as Hartmann has conclusively shown, that . . ."

e. Using pseudoquantifying words to bring science to one's declaration (*extreme, overwhelming, normal, archaic, healthy, borderline;* "in a *considerable number* of cases I have found that . . ."; "the patient was *obviously extremely* narcissistic, *almost* psychotic"; "the fixation *points* of the *central* psychopathology of these cases are *located* at *a rather early* portion of the time axis of psychic development").

f. Granting ourselves authority by declaring that we are discoverers. ("It was established beyond all doubt that . . ." and "the analysis revealed beyond all shadow of doubt that . . .," says Freud twice on one page. He lays it on even thicker: "The position of affairs which I shall now proceed to lay bare is not a product of my inventive powers; it is based on such trustworthy analytic evidence that I can claim objective validity for it"[1920, p. 156].)

g. Acknowledging publicly and repeating (*reiterating* is the grander word) endlessly that our work is scientific and that we are scientists.

2. Take the position, and review the literature to show, that we analysts share a corpus of knowledge ("our science").

3. Offer as data—as acceptable observations—anecdotes a few paragraphs long in which the audience can experience none of that went on in the office.

4. Pretend to take on good faith one another's reports while at the same time either not believing them, if we dislike the authors, or witlessly swallowing the words of our heroes.

5. Find a quote from Freud that agrees with our position or note that, had Freud lived, he would have come to see what we discovered.

6. Shape our argument in adherence to our present school.

7. To support our disagreeing with a colleague's interpretations, style of practice, line of argument, or conclusions, be convinced that, unlike us, he or she was not practicing analysis ("it is only psychoanalytic psychotherapy") or is not an analyst. And ignore that there are no criteria yet for

deciding who is "really" practicing analysis or who is "really" an analyst.

8. Handle ignorance gingerly; admitting a bit is charming, but admitting a lot invites the audience to feel we have nothing to say.

II. RULES FOR DISCUSSING HOMOSEXUALITY

Here I shall take a different tack from that of the first section and, rather than list the rules, shall only remind you how wobbly argument, rhetoric, and failures of definition are inflicted on and accepted by the uncomplaining toilers in the analytic fields. Let us start with my claim that we do not understand homosexuality. When we see or hear the words *homosexuality* and *homosexual,* we do not question their meaning. We should, for though we agree each refers to the conscious erotic desire for same-sexed people, this is only the beginning of their meanings. Yet in analytic writings, they are not defined.

Why no definitions? I guess because of what at first seems good reason: "everyone knows" that homosexuality refers to the desire for or the practice of erotic relations with a person of the same sex. What could be simpler; it goes without saying. But such a definition seems unsophisticated. It does not even hint at the complications that arise when we look below the surface to find dynamics and origins, when we contrast conscious and unconscious states, and when we see how the homosexual impulse can be turned to emerge in other forms than manifest desire for same-sex people. But once we recognize these factors, the chance for definition slips away. As with so much else in analysis, we must contend with the hidden, the silent, the obscure, the presence of the missing.

There are further problems. We also know that *homosexual* may label gender disorder (as in the idea that the homosexual defensively identifies with the opposite-sexed parent), and *homosexual* then can appear in the sentence without the author's making clear whether the reference is to erotic or gender impulses or both. Though a great insight, extending the meaning of homosexuality into these unconscious and defensive dimensions has its price: an adjective may become a noun, with the owner of a homosexual *impulse* now called *a* homosexual. What had been just one impulse among others has been changed, by the magic of words, into an identity, a condition, disorder, disease, perversion. And then we find careless writers (sometimes, I think, not just careless but accusatory) saying that "homosexuality"—not quite the same thing as "homosexual impulses"—is at the root of countless pathologies: psychoses and lesser forms of paranoidness, alcoholism, addictions, all of what are now called gender disorders, fetishism, masochism, sadism, in fact all perversions (even the lesser ones—for example, "the homosexually tinged desire to put it [fire] out with a stream of urine" [Freud 1932, p. 187]), heterosexual excesses such as promiscuity, depression, jealousy, friendship, tenderness, hatred, even "all neurotics" (Freud 1905, p. 166)—that is, everyone.

But if it is there in us all, then what test will tell us when it is etiologic? (First repeat: I am not saying that homosexual impulses do not cause defenses, only that we have no accepted rules of demonstration.) How shall we measure when homosexuality (or bisexuality when we want to connote the heterosexual side as well) is not just an aspect of humanness but a pathologic process? Obviously, when it is stronger than normal, opposed by less effective defenses, or qualitatively different, for example, "narcissistic."[2]

When, in the last paragraph, I said "if *it* is there in us all" and "what test will tell us when *it* is etiologic," my *it*, if not modified, implies that we know what it—homosexuality—is. But we do not. Let me state, therefore, a position not often expressed in the analytic literature on homosexuality (not expressed, I think, because not agreed with): there is no such thing as homosexuality, and therefore there cannot be a unitary theory for the etiology, dynamics, or treatment. There are *the* homosexu-

---

2. By the way, what are the dimensions of a normal amount of homosexuality or of normal defenses? And can you show me—in a human, not in a jargon-loaded sentence—how I can detect qualitatively normal homosexuality (you know, the kind found in normals) from the pathologic kind (for example, "narcissistic," primitive," "archaic," "near psychotic")?

alities (see, for example, Bell and Weinberg 1978), and they are as varied in etiology, dynamics, and appearance as the heterosexualities.[3] Do we not also know that there is no such thing as heterosexuality but rather that there are the heterosexualities? I shall glance at that later.

I am not arguing here whether a homosexual impulse can play a part in manifest behaviors; I am only joining with others who warn against confusing a dynamic (which may be present only as a whisper, not as a roar) with a permanent structural state—the difference between saying "It is a homosexual impulse" and "He is a homosexual."

III. RULES FOR RESEARCHING HOMOSEXUALITY (OR ANYTHING ELSE) PSYCHOANALYTICALLY

What, then, are the rules of the game for measuring the strength of an impulse and for tracing its connections with other impulses and structures, for making analytic observations, and for reporting them, and who is the arbiter—the well-calibrated instrument—whose measurement can be trusted? If a colleague reports, for instance, that he finds it true and an essential factor that the homosexual is extremely narcissistic, he tells us that the homosexual is far more narcissistic than someone (the heterosexual?) who is simply normally narcissistic. So how are we to differentiate "extremely" narcissistic from "markedly" from "very" from "quite" from "rather" from "somewhat" from "a bit" from "not very" from "normally" from "narcissistic-with-no-modifier"? And then there is the problem that since none of us agrees with the rest on what behavior in a particular person (not just in general) we shall say is narcissistic, much less on what is narcissism, we have no

---

3. This business of definition has its consequences. As Marmor has said, "The issue of psychiatric classification of homosexuals is by no means a harmless or theoretical one" (1980, p. 392).

small problem in telling an extremely narcissistic impulse or act from one that is less so or one that has in it no narcissism at all.[4]

If a fundamental difference between a homosexual and a nonhomosexual man[5] is that the former has "archaically cathected objects," what shape will the archaically cathected objects take in the real world where we are to observe them and their effects, so that we shall know the archaic ones from the nonarchaic ones?[6] And if, as Freud said, we all have a bisexual constitution and latent homosexual impulses, how shall we differentiate the heterosexual's archaically cathected objects from those of the homosexual? By the homosexual's "weak ego structure based on narcissistic and prenarcissistic dispositions"? By the fact that "the boundaries of the homosexual ego lack fixity"?

The answer to these questions is that there are, say I, no rules to the research game played when analyzing our patients, since, for reasons of confidentiality, we can never let anyone else watch us collect our data (and even transcripts or tape recordings, though helpful, also have insuperable problems). No one, not even ourselves, can report exactly what happened.

We have, then, no definitions of such key words as homosexuality, narcissism, or archaically cathected objects. So we have no standard from which to measure difference. Let us look more closely at that problem.

---

4. My problem is even bigger, for I am one of those who do not believe there is any such *thing* as narcissism, or any such *thing* as beauty or happiness or time or normality or libido or cathexis or ego or psychic energy or neutralization or mind or self.

5. I pretend here that there are such simple things as a homosexual man and a nonhomosexual man.

6. Question: how old should something be to be archaic? Answer: quite, perhaps even very. Is its age what makes something archaic? Not age, but primitiveness. How do we recognize primitiveness? By how extreme is the narcissism. What is narcissism? The cathexis of the self. What is cathexis? The most primitive form of narcissism. Question: and what is self? Answer: how lucky we are to have metapsychology.

IV. RULES FOR ESTABLISHING BASELINES

We cannot have the abnormal without implying the normal, illness without health, aberrance without the fixed point from which we measure the deviance. How can we say "extremely," "weak," "decisive," or "powerful" without a scale that gives us the baseline? For instance, let us together look at a person— a particular one, here, now. George. He is very angry. Does his anger contain narcissism? (The popular terms used to be "orality" or "oral libidinal cathexes" or "preoedipal cathexes.") How much? We cannot measure the anger, much less the narcissism, by ergs of tooth grinding, rise in diastolic pressure, or degradation of acetylcholinesterase but only by looking, listening, feeling: we interpret what we see as meaning that he is very angry. (And were we careful, as Schafer recommends, we would know we could never measure anger, since there is no such thing, but only George being angry: *we have to measure George.*) Suppose George has learned how to keep from feeling angry, so that instead of being openly angry he grows more quiet. How do we distinguish (measure) his quiet-quiet from his angry-quiet, except by interpreting what we observe? When is he justifiably angry—"normally," "appropriately," "nonnarcissistically," "realistically"—and when is he pathologic? Suppose that George, when angry, is always openly angry. Is he so because he is insightful, frank, and trustworthy—that is, "normal"—or is he impulsive and narcissistically fixated at a symbiotically fused self-object stage? You say it is the latter; I say the first. On whom can we rely to tell us who is right?

We forget, as we read the journals and attend the panels, that our beliefs (formally labeled theory, hypotheses, concepts, principles, or findings) come from our direct observation of people; that we are fallible observers; that those who criticize our observations can never see what we saw (not that *we* ever saw what we saw), for the living moment never returns, not even on tapes; that we do not have the consensual validation we claim but only our belief, the belief of those who choose to believe us, and argumentation to make the audience share our belief and think we have more to give than belief.

Suppose a colleague claims that in the homosexual—*the* homosexual, not "some" or "a few" or "most" or "most I know" or "53.9 percent"—

> the archaic, narcissistic ego structure makes the ego vulnerable to the impact of libidinal stimulation, and renunciation of primitive gratification becomes difficult if not impossible. In his repetition compulsion the homosexual dramatizes a repeatedly unsuccessful attempt by the ego to achieve mastery of the libidinal and aggressive impulses and of the archaically cathected objects. In place of object cathexis, the ego seeks gratification in a short circuit act between the self and pseudo-objects, for example, between various substitutes for the ego and for parental images. (Socarides 1978, pp. 159–60)

Can you see how the words assume precise-enough measurement, as if there are techniques to do the measuring, so that the rest of us—skeptic or believer, Kohutian or Rosicrucian—can test the statement? Take just the first sentence, much less the rest of the words in that quote: *archaic, narcissistic, ego, structure, the ego, vulnerable, impact, libidinal, stimulation, renunciation, primitive, difficult, impossible.* (The false self of psychoanalysis is our jargonized theory.)

It is obvious that none of those words can be measured. But let us pretent they could. And now I claim to have a cousin, George again, who has an archaic, narcissistic ego structure that makes the ego (as a scientist I must not say "him," not even "his ego") vulnerable to the impact of libidinal stimulation, and so on. But I also claim that George is not a homosexual. He is a heterosexual. At least he says so, as does his wife, girlfriend, daydreams and choices in pornography, sexual history, and hunger for women's anatomy. I suppose—because I know that he is rather boastful about his erotic prowess, inclined to drink too much when socially ill at ease, given to telling jokes about queers, smokes big cigars, regularly plays poker with his male friends, and wastes weekends watching football on TV—that we can now claim he is a latent homosexual. Fair enough, since, by the rules of the libido-theory-game, everyone is.

Therefore, we need a usable definition of the heterosexual, since the heterosexual has been the baseline of normality against which the homosexual is measured. We cannot use people such as George. He has too many flaws; his homosexuality just oozes out of him. (You might almost say it is what makes him heterosexual.) Worse than that, he is downright pre-Oedipal. But if we look in the analytic literature for examples of bona fide heterosexuals, those—male or female—not contaminated by conscious or unconscious latent homosexuality, we find in the thousands of cases reported that none fits; the closest we come are those personae of the Oedipal complex, "the father" and "the mother" (and they are only our patients' imaginary, shifting versions of real people). Nor do we find a definition of the state. Rather, the definition is assumed, since "the heterosexual" is made to by synonymous with "the normal."

The following represents this rationalization, so helpful to analytic researchers. "In normal heterosexual development the masculine needs of the male become to a great extent ego invested, that is, the ego feels the need to discharge personally and directly his masculine tension" (Socarides 1978, p. 113). "Weiss . . . has stressed that children of both sexes identify in varying degrees with both father and mother. In normal sexual maturation, however, only the introjected parent of the same sex is maintained while that of the parent of the opposite sex is externalized in a modified form (ego passage [?])" (p. 114). "Beneath an apparent willingness to get well, the real intent of some patients may be to prove that homosexuality is as rational as heterosexuality" (pp. 418–19). "With therapy the patient ultimately moves in the opposite direction; first he prefers homosexual fantasy instead of acting out the irresistible impulse, next he attempts heterosexual fantasy, and ultimately he achieves heterosexual reality" (p. 419).

Here, in males, are some of the heterosexual realities with which clinicians are familiar: sadism, masochism, voyeurism, exhibitionism, satyriasis, preference for prostitutes, rape, frottage, masturbation with pornography as more exciting than using live females, incest, necrophilia, pedophilia with girls, infantilism (the diapers pinned on by a female), coprophilia, urophilia, klismaphilia (the stimulus delivered by a female), telephone scatologia, amelotatistism with heightened SAK preference, preference for women in jodhpurs, excitement with other men's wives but not one's own, and preference for fat women, thin women, tall women, short women, blonde women, red-headed women, steatopygous women, big-busted women, small-busted women, black women, white women, Italian women, Jewish women, Gabonese women, Thai women, women with a cute little penis (a.k.a. clitoris), ladies, actresses, policewomen, poetesses, and women who are jet copilots.

Where is our paragon? What did you say was the definition of the heterosexual?

We read that the essential ingredient of homosexuality is "the unconscious and imperative need to pursue and experience sexual pleasure and orgastic relief with individuals of the same sex," an act that "expresses, in a distorted way, repressed forbidden impulses and most often brings temporary relief, either partial or complete, from warring intrapsychic forces." Does that "essential ingredient" not also hold—except that one's object is of the opposite sex—for "the heterosexual"? How many happy heterosexuals do you know? How many of them are untainted by archaic and primitive narcissistic cathexes? Those of you with extensive experience in treating the heterosexual may disagree that the following insights are confined to the homosexual:

> In essence we are confronted by a condition which baffled clinical investigators attempting to determine its etiology. Of all the symptoms of emotional origin which serve simultaneously as defenses, homosexuality is unique in its capacity to use profound psychic conflicts and struggles to attain, for limited intervals, a pseudoadequate equilibrium and pleasure reward (orgasm), often permitting the individual to function, however marginally and erratically.
>
> This neutralization of conflict allows the growth of certain ego-adaptive elements of the personality, and the homosexual may therefore have appeared not ill at all to others except for the masquerade in his sexual life. (Socarides 1978, pp. 3–4)

> In clinical experience, nevertheless [i.e., in opposition to the report of other workers], the connection between homosexuality and both paranoid schizophrenia and paranoia is striking in a great number of patients and it occurs with considerable regular-

ity. Although this material may not be on the surface and therefore cannot be garnered by statistical methods, paranoid content may appear during the therapy of any homosexual. It is clear that the homosexual fears persecution and attack on many levels. Some of these, social censure, for example, seem realistic, but others involve threatened castration at the hands of either parent or both. He fears anal attack; he fears the use of feces as a destructive, powerful weapon against him; and he fears poisoning due to intense, oral-sadistic incorporative drives. The presence of archaic mechanisms suggest [sic] the primitive introjective-projective dilemmas which beset him. (pp. 60–61)

"Every homosexual remains strongly fixated to his mother." Suppose I say, "As the result of extensive experience with full analysis of many men, I can assert that every heterosexual remains strongly fixated to his mother"? Does such an announcement appeal to your scientific sensibilities? (Imagine a paper entitled "The Psychoanalysis of a Heterosexual." How mystifying that would be.)

Second repeat. I am not saying that the homosexual is not—to quote some of the juicier phrases in print—an archaic narcissistic—maybe even prenarcissistic—anal erotic, orally enraged, intractable, borderline, overwhelmed, profoundly regressed, passive, masochistic pervert, catastrophically threatened with annihilation of the self in psychoticlike reactions, his lifelong intolerable anxiety masked by pseudoadequate equilibrium, neutralization of conflict, and growth of certain ego-adaptive elements of the personality so that he may therefore have appeared not ill at all to others. (One does not say "sinner" in analytic circles. And we "cure," we do not "save.") I am only saying that these words do not really describe, measure, or define and that we cannot pick out in the real world those who fit the description and those who escape. I am not offering new findings to refute old, only trying to show how technique of argument can be the weapon of analytic research more than is data collecting.

V. RULES FOR WRITING A REPORT ON HOMOSEXUALITY

In a science such as physics, one can describe what one observed without needing a subtle vocabulary and an articulate if not artful writing style. The report does not create or even shape the findings. But in reporting an analytic observation, there cannot be even a sentence that is not the writer's interpretation—that is, modification, editing, translating—of each observation. Let me show what I mean by opening a journal, finding each paper's section on what went on with a patient, and choosing a sentence at random from each: "I think we have here a type of projective identification in which despair is so effectively loaded into the analyst that he seems crushed by it and can see no way out"; "The silences had a sad, depressive quality but they did not suggest anger"; "We discovered that they had infantilized Arthur and alternately projectively identified him with these grandiose fantasies and then exploited his helpless, dependent, depressed inept aspects"; "Alice's dreams of love and yearning for John reveal what she must repress, because to face the loss of a much-loved man would cause too much pain"; "During the course of his analysis, the dynamic interplay between this ego pathology and the traumatic-depressive nature of his nuclear family milieu—dominated by a narcissistic and brutalizing mother and a largely absent and idealized father—became the core element in his emerging transference neurosis"; "Doubtlessly for a young boy of 6 or 7 such a situation inevitably must be experienced as a severe narcissistic humiliation, must give him the feeling of being 'impotent' *vis à vis* his mother"; "At times the distinction between his father and the analyst was not maintained, and his expectations of criticism and belittlement from the analyst were identical to those he had experienced from his father"; "Thus her sexual fantasy could be understood as a wish that her mother, represented by the repulsive woman in the fantasy, was still in control of her body because sexual excitement for her was identified with uncontrollable violence against her mother's babies"; "My patient is a presentable, attractive Englishman."

These are the words the writers chose for conveying what they felt was happening. Read each sentence carefully. Suppose you needed to know, say, as in a courtroom or in a piece of scientific research, just what had happened. Could you? And has there ever been a paper that could tell us what to do next with our patient at this moment? Take what is perhaps the simplest, least theoretic of any descriptive word in these sentences: *sad*. Its meaning should be clear enough. What more do we need from the author? (The answer is in chapter 12.)

You know that these judgments form an endless stream (and are far more than one affect thick at any moment) from beginning to end of each hour.

If I say my patient was sad, why should you believe my report? Because I have been analyzed, because I am an analyst, because you like me, because I am/am not a Kleinian, am/am not in private practice, am/am not a man, was/was not analyzed by Freud, am/am not a necrophiliac or frotteur or homosexual or heterosexual, am/am not a good therapist, do/do not honor my father and my mother, am/am not a vegetarian or Type A personality, am/am not a training analyst, am/am not Hungarian, have/do not have tropical fish in the office?

We are, then, in a field that relies on accurately evaluating minute, primarily subliminal behaviors and that needs data, such as fantasies, memories, and affects, that are, sadly, impossible to measure. And these microscopic observations and immeasurable measurements must be made with a rampantly fallible instrument, the analyst. Should we not therefore make our claims with more humility?

VI. RULES OF THE GAME FOR PRESENTING CLINICAL MATERIAL

What conclusion regarding the nature of homosexuality can we draw from a case presentation, spoken or written, formal or informal? I wish we could agree that no matter how authoritative a speaker or writer, no matter how well formed the report, no matter how aroused we get on one side or another of an issue, a case presentation cannot tell us what happened in the reality of any moment of treatment. To write a narrative description of a clinical moment—of *any* moment between two people—is like presenting a piece of music by describing it only in words. Even when we have an exact transcript, we do not know: think of the innumerable interpretations possible for a great drama or of how differently two orchestras play the same score.

This does not mean that we cannot teach by means of clinical anecdotes, only that we cannot reach scientific conclusions thereby; for the latter we need data, while to teach, for example, clinical skills, we work via impressions, beliefs, imagery—from our convictions rather than from facts. Yet we analysts are forever coming to conclusions and insisting that we do so from reality. And, unwilling to display uncertainty, we try to create validity from persuasive sentences. We coerce.

Having struggled for years to give clear clinical descriptions, I have no illusions that in anyone's presentation what is said is what happened. We give impressions only, and our purpose should be to create impressions, not Truth. On the other hand, though it does not have the trappings of science, one-to-one discussion, as in supervision, has a better (but perhaps still not very good) chance of approximating clinical realities. Therein, depending on the quality of the relationship between the participants and the amount of time they have, misapprehensions can be cleared up, and in the benign atmosphere of the supervision—so different from that of the formal meeting or published paper or book—people can better understand each other. In a formal presentation, however, ambience and personal style play too great a part. Scientific issues—and this does not happen just in psychoanalysis—are battered by politics, charisma (that is, seductive paranoia), and our techniques as entertainers. But we should not forget that there need be no relationship between a presentation that teaches, that stimulates, that even gives us something new and important and the question of whether that presentation reflects "what actually happens."

VII. CONCLUDING RULES, ALL OBVIOUS, NONE NEW

The foregoing remarks allow me to pinpoint my argument. Rule 1: anyone can assert anything. Rule 2: no one can show anyone is wrong, since no one can check anyone's observations (including his or her own). What is left, then, but bombast, scientific or otherwise?

The passing years, with their burden of more clinical knowledge, have, I fear, shown that we analysts have not done well in trying to understand homosexuality. In fact, we have been as inept as we were before correcting the matter in our theories of the development of females and femininity (*JAPA* 1976). The way toward better understanding, then, begins with our understanding how little we understand. Rule 3: ignorance can be wisdom.

Dynamics, we sometimes know, are not necessarily explanations. Dynamics found in everyone cannot be used to explain particular states. To understand a psychic event, what counts is not the presence of a dynamic but its quality, form, intensity, timing, underlying biologic pressures, and the nature of the defenses surrounding it. Because dynamics are not palpable but must be inferred from behavior, we can decide on their significance only by what we observe in the clinical situation. But there is no way the clinical situation can be shared with an objective observer. Even worse, there are no objective observers, not the patient, the analyst, or anyone farther removed. Rule 4: use dynamics warily.

On admitting the dangers in dynamic explanations, we can dispense with grandiose, overinclusive answers and turn to the joy of the admitted question. Rule 5: ease up; forswear rhetoric; love clarity; relax.

Our clinical descriptions, boggy with their load of proclaimed but undemonstrated unconscious dynamics, leave out the person and the moment. Rule 6: describe people as we see, hear, or otherwise sense them, carefully and in detail. Do not use the metapsychology language in the midst of clinical description sentences.

We ask theory to explain so much. Rule 7: when it comes to deneutralized narcissistic projective identifications of the self object, less is more.

Is it improper to suggest that some analysts' problems in understanding homosexuality have—to put it delicately—psychodynamic roots? That would tell me, as the more rational explanations do not, why we have by-laws against accepting homosexuals as candidates, members of the faculty, or supervising and training analysts. The justification for such regulations is our "knowing" that these people must, by definition, be as alleged: fatally flawed psychoticlike creatures in states of near-annihilation of the self (covered over, of course, by normal-appearing behavior). If we mindlessly judge people that way—"everyone knows it"—then we are very cruel. How many grossly, overtly heterosexual candidates have been accepted and been graduated who—as their analyses demonstrated and their later behavior confirmed—have severe character defects? We have transformed diagnosis into accusation, covering our behavior with jargon. But though it hides hatred, it promotes cruelty; jargon is judgment. It serves hidden agendas. We should tighten our logic and loosen our by-laws. Rule 8: stop picking on homosexuals, whether patients or colleagues.

My last potshot is aimed at analytic colleagues. Nothing here is new, remarkable, subtle, hard to confirm, or beyond belief. At least half of you believe at least half of it. Yet hardly a twitch of recognition surfaces in the literature. Rule 9: let us then, regarding homosexuality, start afresh.

Final note. You recognize, of course, that this is not really a report on homosexuality but, rather, one that uses homosexuality as an example of the failure of psychoanalysis, so far, as science.[7]

7. The dictionary (*Webster's* 1961) gives definitions of *science* broad enough to include psychoanalysis. To quote a few: "possession of knowledge as distinguished from ignorance or misunderstanding"; "knowledge possessed or attained through study or practice"; "a branch or department of systematized knowledge that is or can be made a specific object of study"; "studies mainly in the works of ancient and modern philosophers"; "accumulated and accepted knowledge that has been systematized and formulated with reference to the discovery of general truths or the operation of general laws"; "comprehensive, profound, or philosophical knowledge." Some of the examples used are "The basic tool sciences of reading, writing, and ciphering; . . . theology ("The queen of the sciences"]; . . . sport; . . . the science of evading work; . . . cards; . . . fencing; . . . boxing; . . . works . . . formally taught . . . at Oxford University; . . . subjects taught in one of the departments of natural science." Add library science, mortuary science, Christian Science, and Scientology.

CHAPTER 10

One Homosexual Woman

In the last chapter, I said that we still do not know much about male homosexuality. First, there is no one entity—homosexuality—but rather there are *the* homosexualities, for which a single etiology should not be propounded. Homosexuality, like heterosexuality, is a mix of desires, not a symptom, not a diagnosis. Second, since psychoanalytic reports are unreliable, we cannot accept one another's descriptions of our patients or of what went on in the treatment to produce our clinical descriptions. That is hardly a viewpoint embraced by most analysts, for it puts in doubt the usefulness of many reports, not just those on homosexuality.

I suppose, though, that colleagues will be less irritated if I say the same about female homosexuality. First, less has been published—less theory, few case reports. Second, we have the now notorious fact that, in holy writs and the law, little is made of women's erotism. Third, our explanations were created mostly by men. Last, in classical analytic theory women were seen as no more than failed men. At any rate, no one's territory is invaded this time when I say we know little about homosexuality in women.

Unacknowledged ignorance being, you will agree, a heavy baggage in analysis, I bore down in the last chapter on the cost. But the situation is different with women's homosexuality. The sparse literature reflects our willingness to admit ignorance. So I need not show in detail that interpretations about *the* homosexual ("the" means "all" in this parlance) can be, despite a rhetoric of science, more insult than objectivity. (One example is enough: ". . . a weak ego structure based on narcissistic and prenarcissistic dispositions. The archaic, narcissistic ego structure makes the ego vulnerable to the impact of libidinal stimulation, and renunciation of primitive gratification becomes difficult if not impossible. In his repetition compulsion the homosexual dramatizes a repeatedly unsuccessful attempt by the ego to achieve mastery of libidinal aggressive impulses and of the archaically cathected objects." Were we forbidden to talk this way, would we say less?)

I can, instead, focus on the other idea in the last chapter: that, as in males, no single clinical picture, with common underlying dynamics and etiology, holds for all homosexual women. Only when we deluge our paragraphs with undefined and unmeasurable words like *archaic, narcissistic, prenarcissistic, primitive, incorporation and projection anxieties,* and the like does the blur of verbiage give the illusion of homogeneity. For the present, until we have more complete and well-described observations, let us simply be naturalists. After that, we can look for common factors. (We need not feel embarrassed to say we do not yet know. Better late than never with such modesty.)

To represent that position, I shall use one homosexual woman, and because it is impossible to present an analysis in the confines of a chapter—impossible in a whole book or in ten volumes—I shall make do with discussing a single theme that played a part in her homosexuality. Should I succeed in showing you how this theme influenced her, then you can judge whether it is present in all homosexual women. If, as I think, it is not, even such thin argument may suggest to you that each case is different. (One cannot prove, confirm, validate a psychoanalytic idea by means of a clinical report. We only suggest, and when the audience is receptive, convince.) I have tried to make the following description accurate and believe it is so. If you are sensible, however, you will take it (and all other analytic reports) as a fiction that nonetheless stands for sensible and useful premises, as good fiction also does. (In picking one theme from the unending complexity that is psychoanalysis, I can also minimize distortions imposed for the sake of confidentiality.)

CLINICAL FRAGMENTS

The patient, Lisa, a white, single woman in her late twenties when analysis started, was beginning, years later than she should have and in a desultory, delayed, exhausted, ineffective way, her education as a student in one of the biologic sciences. She came for treatment primarily to be relieved of a lifelong, though fluctuating, sense of oppressive, dark, imprisoning deadness exacerbated when her previous therapist—not an analyst—died. She had seen him for years, starting in her mid-teens, because she felt that her creativity—her capacity to write, paint, learn, be generous, and love—was present but trapped in her. The treatment had gone well to the degree that he had functioned as her mentor, spending the hours with her showing her how to write and paint and by praising her. Unfortunately, she was creative only with him beside her; the impulse never became self-generating. In addition, she came to see me in the hope that an also-present sense of heterosexual desire might be mobilized into a gratifyingly heterosexual life.

In her early twenties, she had her first homoerotic relationship and was shocked and desperate on experiencing its power. In the next months, though struggling against it, she was swept up by her homosexuality, to her therapist's despair. He told her she must turn from it or be destroyed, and though she agreed, she could not. (He did not judge it as I came to: as the completed form of a frenzied effort begun in childhood to save herself—to save her self.) So he reduced their appointments and could no longer encourage her. Then he became ill and soon died. With his rejecting her, the blackness settled in more heavily. She had pretty much lost her capacity to feel. When, for instance, in analysis, tears ran down her cheeks— "tears are coming out of my face"—logic alone told her she was crying.

On meeting me, she—child of her times—was displeased with my couch, that symbol of constricted intellect and oppression of patients. She also found me, as the several hours of evaluation progressed, too distant, too cool—it was later to be "cold"—too quiet, not supportive, but, on the positive side, curious, attentive, and firm. And I found her too resistant, too venomous about psychoanalysis, and too affectively blighted. On the positive side, I thought I dimly sensed an intact person—more precisely, woman—within the walls.

I did not suit her. So I sent her to other therapists she might choose. She returned in a few weeks because she felt I was reliable, not burdened by depression when I did talk, and prone to say what I thought. At this point, let me remind you of an issue noted but not openly reported in our literature: what we are—more accurately, what we believe we are— regardless of our patients' projections. (I put aside the problem that our labeling a patient's opinion as projection may be our projection.) Yet, as everyone knows and few deny, our demeanor and presence—our identity—are as absolute factors as are the patient's. In brief, both her reluctance to work with me and her deciding nonetheless to do so were based on deep, indivisible convictions she had of my personality. For this homosexual woman, my form of masculinity fevered her resistance.

She was passionately hungry for women—for their bodies and for their companionship. She had never had an erotically satisfying relationship with a man and in all her life had had only one man to whom she was an affectionate friend. She— unwilling racist—was distressed by men's bearing and dismayed by their maleness—hair, muscles. She was put off by me, by my body and the way I inhabit it. My selfhood— which one does not eradicate, no matter how quietly one sits or how firmly one clings to the notion that the real relationship is a myth in analysis—is not a mirror on which the patient reflects only fantasies. Two strong reality factors, then, shaped the analysis, one cultural (the scorn she and her peers felt toward analysts), the other idiosyncratic (my maleness and my personality).

The theme I emphasize in this chapter is "I am crazy," which after several years of analysis became "who is crazy?" to transform finally into "they are crazy." This issue, you will see, is one of separation-individuation.

In keeping with my belief that each homosexual is different from others—not just the humanistic plea that we respect individuality—with this case I offer two cautions. First, a child's sense that he or she must take responsibility for being crazy—wrong, bad, evil—or lose mother and father is found in many people. But it leads to many other consequences than homosexuality. So it does not serve us here as a universal cause of homosexuality. Nor do I know if it is significant in other homosexual women. Second, to find separation-individuation issues at the bottom of homosexuality is also not a sure clue. In whom are they not present? We must also show their precise form and precisely how they influence development. That, to repeat, requires good description, not just "archaic, narcissistic, self-object cathexis." In other words, even when they are present, we must, we know, treat each instance—each person in whom these themes exist—as having his or her own unique version of them.

In regard to the great issue in this patient, her struggle between wanting to separate from her mother and wanting to avoid that dangerous temptation, there was a story repeatedly told the child. Once there was a mother who lived in the sea with her daughter, Minnie the Mermaid. Minnie would swim toward shore. Sometimes she even got to shallow water where she touched bottom. She once went on shore to play with friends, walked up a hill toward them to have lunch, and then, choking and panicked, fled back to the sea. Each time mother told the story, something terrible threatened Minnie, who thereupon returned to the deep water and mother's protection. The message was obvious: Lisa must not leave mother, not swim off on her own, not get to solid land, not become an independent woman. As a child she could never sleep at friends' homes; a couple of attempts led to humiliating panic that returned her to her own bed the same evening. The only period when she left her parents was when she went to college in another city. At first she was exhilarated by the freedom, but the effort collapsed and she had to return home. (Even vacations were spent with her parents.) After that, trying again to become adult, she moved a few miles away but still visited her parents regularly and talked on the phone with her mother once a day or more.

Though it will be obvious to you, and though I sensed the

following, it took years before I fully integrated this next awareness. The first time Lisa told me the story of Minnie the Mermaid, she said she did not know where it came from. She pre-
sumed her mother had made it up, for she had never heard of or
read such a tale anywhere. I let it go at that; the name "Minnie"
simply floated in me without resolution (I think because it was
not ready for resolution in her) until one day when, for the
thousandth time, we were working on the problem of her
struggle for and against independence. She was preparing a
piece of creative work that, like a rite of passage, would shift her
status in the world to that of a successful adult. She had described her effort to complete this task as "superhuman" and
"incredible." I interrupted her to disagree, telling her that the
hyperbole—an issue discussed before—made the project even
harder and in that way made her progress out of the water less
sure. (In addition, it served to get the attention of a mother who
was rarely focused on her child unless the girl was ill or otherwise suffering, at which point mother always came through
with love incarnate—good food.) During the previous week, I
had been struggling to dissect out an attribute so much a part of
her that I thought she could never see its defensive nature. (It
was so egosyntonic that egosyntonic is the wrong word.) That
attribute was her believing herself to be physically too weak and
tiny to defend herself. Along with this she knew that she was
less resistant to illness and to psychologic stress than normal
people. She was, in identity, a dyed-in-the-wool neurotic
(another form of the too-smallness that tied her to her mother),
never questioning that she should spend days on end in bed if
she was unhappy, tired, ill, or under pressure.

At this point, I, referring to the story, say, "Minnie Mouse."
She does not correct me, but as I go on, I hear what I have said
and repeat the slip.[1] I tell her what had been subliminal—not
unconscious—since I first heard "Minnie the Mermaid." The
only association I can image for someone in our country (un-

1. I always use my slips, explaining them to patients as soon as I understand
what caused them; when they occur in an analysis, they tell me what I should
have been talking about and was avoiding. I can then say not only what I was
thinking but also what the patient was doing to me and I to the patient by not
having spoken sooner. The slip forces me—properly—to speak up.

less he or she had an aunt half a century ago named Minnie and except Minnie the Moocher) is Minnie Mouse, with its connotation of smallness. (She later discovered a song from her mother's childhood: Minnie the Mermaid. The lyrics did not contain the separation issues her mother used.) So I extend the earlier interpretations of the parable standing for a mother's need not to let her child free and bring the seemingly unanalyzable subject of the patient's sense of physical weakness into our understanding. "Your mother needed you to be puny, to believe you were inadequate to leave the water and stand on you own feet." (Her being crazy, to be looked at shortly, was another form of this theme.)

She responds by saying that, of course, Minnie means small, as in minimal. Though of normal height and build now, she was a very small child, "two feet shorter than all my friends." She then tells how the preceding night she had another of the unending series of fights that are an essence of her relationships with all her lovers. The present woman had asked for help with an assignment in college, and Lisa had done it for her easily and well. (By this point in treatment, she could, for periods, reclaim her mind.) Her girlfriend became enraged and stormed out of the house, because "since I could do this better than she could, she felt I was independent of her. If I do something good, with them I'm bad. First they figure that I will leave them and second they take it as an accusation that they have failed their lives." In the "them" she included her mother.

I can trace Minnie's presence through three generations. Lisa's mother's parents, especially her beloved maternal grandmother, kept constantly present a belief that became, as happens in families, one of Lisa's identity themes (Lichtenstein 1961). It was a universal truth: bad follows good; happiness brings catastrophe. All joyous moments evoked the story of how grandmother and grandfather, after a brilliant life in Europe, had their wealth and social status destroyed by the Nazis. Their precipitous escape and the success they then created here counted for nothing in the tale of no-hope that shaped first Lisa's mother and then Lisa.

Lisa's mother was a woman of high but blighted intelligence

and talent. Just as Lisa's childhood was filled with her grand-parents' version of reality, so she was witness to her mother's fearfulness and failure. I am not surprised that Lisa' mother invented Minnie, the mermaid who must not leave her mother and stand on solid ground.

And so, though Lisa's mother recognized, confirmed, and identified with Lisa's creative abilities, she could not allow them to flourish lest she lose her daughter. Because mother dared not be free—to be free is to drop one's guard, which, said the family myth, brings disaster—she could not free her daughter, flesh of her flesh. Lisa was ordained to be mother's cure, and, as also happens with some very feminine boys, the two must be forever linked or mother suffers desolation. In such a situation, a child is treated more as mother's thing than as a person. A person is an individual; an individual is a free agent. The Minnie story, then, contains mother's terrors wished onto Lisa so that she will not abandon mother. The love between Lisa and her mother was obscured by, and they were connected more by fear, coercion, trauma, and conflict than by love. The damning—damnable—part is that every woman she ever loved used the same techniques on her and was powered by the same dynamics as her mother.

THE "CRAZY" THEME

The theme "I am crazy" ran through her relationship with her parents, her homosexual relationships, and the transference. Its meaning was that someone had said, and she agreed, that her perception of a situation was wrong. By the time she came to me, this belief had so demoralized her that she was almost immobilized. She did not attend school or support herself, did no creative work, and often spent whole days alone on her bed.

Relationship with Parents

To compact years of work into a few sentences, "I am crazy" was a survival theme she invented in early childhood. It con-cretized her denial of her true self and her accepting her parents' accusation—"you're crazy"—as the price for their not abandoning her. She dared not let herself know she was right, for that meant they were wrong. Since they denied they were wrong, she could either become enraged at them, which they would not stand for, or repress that knowledge and, taking the blame, hate herself. If she was to keep them, she had to automatize this process, deflect the rage away from her mother and father and into the environment and herself.

Each parent delivered the message differently. Her father did so with rage, often so barely controlled that she felt, though he never struck her, in mortal danger. (Recall her conviction that she was puny.) Her mother, on the other hand, never seemed physically dangerous; rather, she simply disconnected. Even when mother was in contact, Lisa knew that the contact was rarely the result of their relationship mostly a random connection mother made or withdrew as a result of mother's internal status.

Relationships with Lovers

The "crazy" theme was, most precisely, essential for her to feel she loved a woman. In its absence, if she liked a woman, it was friendship, an experience to which she then could bring qualities she valued in herself. But for her lovers she could only create that miracle of Hell, self-destructive behavior.

Her first homoerotic experience occurred in her early twenties. Until that night, she had convinced herself that she was not homosexual. In fact, though her relations with men were not "good or consistent," she could experience keen erotic need and pleasure with them. She had had crushes on pretty, feminine women her own age. These, however, had not been accompanied by conscious erotic desire, nor had she had homoerotic daydreams.

She was entangled with a woman whose great potentials were overwhelmed by a suicidally intense sense of worthlessness. Not able to explain to herself why she was with this failed, not even physically attractive person, Lisa nonetheless spent most of her time only with her. They often slept in the same room, though in separate beds. Lisa knew this woman had strong homosexual desires. Finally, one night, "to prove I was not a lesbian," she went to her companion's bed. The power of Lisa's response—far beyond any previous erotic experience—appalled her. She felt condemned, that she had somehow committed suicide. From then on she had homosexual affairs. They were all serious, never experimental, never casual, never promiscuous. In each case, the woman gave off tantalizing signals of loving availability that either were withdrawn when Lisa responded or were emitted unrelated to anything Lisa did. When she discussed this with them, each told her she was crazy, misperceiving. Then, terrified that their anger would lead to their leaving her—they regularly stormed out to their own apartments—she would frantically phone. Since that did not placate them, she would rush to them at any hour of the night and, with screaming and panicked crying, make them relent. We came to see that the black emptiness seizing her after these episodes was, in part, the surface awareness that she would accept any amount of humiliation rather than be abandoned. "My craziness is picking crazy people and then going crazy from it."

As the analytic process made headway, she began connecting these dramas to her mother: mother's unprovoked, frozen withdrawals that could be stopped only by Lisa's abject apologies (mother never gave in but waited silently, for days if Lisa held out that long, till the child's resistance collapsed); waiting in the hall, unable to sleep, every night her parents went out and then, on their return, creeping, ashamed, to bed without letting them know; unrelieved, vast hopelessness when they went on vacation. (Even the Minnie story contained a touch of mother's unpredictability that had to be denied: who, other than a crazy person or a mermaid, would say that dry land was dangerous and deep water safe?) She wondered how she could commit herself to such chaos but was nonetheless compelled to repeat.

What was the essential element in her choosing these women? The one, of course, that had dominated her relationship with her parents and me (until it was understood): the accusation, "you're crazy." Once she was in analysis and I witnessed the onset of a few affairs, she could see what had previously been unconscious, that she selected the women (and they her), that it was not chance that had brought them together. And at the heart of the selection was her sensing, in the moment of meeting, that these women could never be possessed by her, that when they focused on her it happened not because of her but because of unfathomable movements deep within them. "Always, at the end, is leaving." They were unreachable, thus irresistible.

During lovemaking, Lisa often felt ignored. This happened only after her partner was familiar with her needs—go slowly and tenderly—and had at other times given her a bit of that goodness. So she would freeze. The partners did not notice. If they later expressed delight with the experience, she would rage that they had not perceived her. To which they replied, "You're crazy." If she agreed, all was calm. If she resisted, hell broke loose, fading only when she showed remorse. "But I know they know how to listen. What drives me crazy is that I know they listen. They turn off *because*, somewhere, they're listening."

One of my oddest experiences was to hear Lisa talk for months, sometimes years, about a woman and never learn the woman's last name, occupation, where she lived, where she was from, or anything else about her history, present status, or appearance. Nothing but body surface from which femininity and loving care could seem to emanate. For the rest, I learned only of rare moments when eyes met (the women's eyes were, in almost all encounters, unfathomable, glazed, or enraged),[2] of wild fights, frozen rage, misunderstandings—long, long descriptions with no other content than affects.

---

2. The most horrifying movie she ever saw was something about body snatchers, aliens who took ordinary people, withdrew their soul, and then returned to society the unchanged but now evil-possessed body. In the crazed eyes of these former humans one could see the subtle, and therefore even more awful, transformation. I think the appeal of these tales draws on some of the same dynamics that link them to such seemingly disparate states as erotic excitement and other excitements such as art, risk-taking sports, humor, and neurosis. (A neurosis, as good analytic treatment reveals, is a joke whose point its owner cannot yet see.)

What then locked the connection—the love—in place was her discovering that the women treated her keenest perceptions—her capacity to pick up what was going on in other people (a capacity *invariably* correct in her relationship with me)—as dead wrong: "You're crazy." Which confronted her with the same dilemma she suffered with her mother.

To survive she taught herself that her perception had been wrong. She *was* crazy, not they. And Lisa having broken herself, the woman returned, restoring Lisa from desolation to a calmness worth even her knowing that it was transient and that she had once more snuffed herself out. She died to live.

As the analysis progressed, each new woman was less disturbed and less homosexual. Lisa was now some months into an affair with A., an often warm, cuddly, feminine, loving woman. A. was becoming erotically alive though anorgasmic. One night, giving way to Lisa's tense curiosity, A. most reluctantly confessed that she had never in her life had an orgasm. At that instant, something shifted within and soon after their lovemaking forever stopped, though the relationship continued, monogamously and rage-filled. They still slept in the same bed most nights, no longer holding each other, not even touching. What had happened?

Each felt abandoned. A. had somehow known that Lisa would take the anorgasmia as a bad portent—a promise of unending rejection—and so had kept it secret (further rejection). Lisa, devastated, made A. feel abandoned, completing the mutual expectation of rejection and guaranteeing just the result each awaited in all relationships.

Months later, something shifted. Though they continued with each other in this alienated state, Lisa began remarking to me over several weeks' time that, while deeply asleep, A. had lain with a hand touching her, then an arm, and now with the arm around her. Why? Lisa felt she had done nothing to encourage A. Then I got the answer.

During these weeks, Lisa had been preoccupied with an arduous project that made her anxious and upset her growing self-esteem. Her manifest distress signaled to A. that, for a time, Lisa was her old, troubled self. Now Lisa understood. As with her mother and all the earlier lovers, as long as she was sick, she was—they were assured—too weak to own herself, to be free. She would not leave them for dry land. (She makes a slip of the tongue—"leave" for "love," a microdot of her erotic and affectionate life.)

I omit the evidence—obvious to me, unbearable for Lisa (till resolved)—that her lovers and her mother suffered the same fears of abandonment and of freedom that she did. She saw their behavior the way a child would, as being willful, mysterious—they have the ability to comfort but withold it—vindictive, planned, inevitable, nonnegotiable. The women, mother included, were, however, also different from Lisa. She always knew, and in time became conscious of the fact, that though they, like she, somewhere hungered for the truth, at the end they turned from it and she to it. This yearning, above all, saved the analysis, whatever else threatened.

A second factor made her, though similar, different from them: "I can act crazy [be enraged, for example], but I know I am not really out of control. They do that too, but at a certain point they lose control and really go crazy. When I throw something, it misses by a mile. A. threw a glass at me. It almost hit me; she was out of control and so could easily have hit me."

I cannot, within the confines of a brief chapter, describe the hidden self we eventually found or even the process of discovery. Let us for now leave it at this: the "crazy" theme progressed from "I am crazy" to "they say I am crazy" to "it is not clear who is crazy" to "I am crazy for not admitting they are crazy" to "they are crazy, and I am not."

Transference Relationship

As we know, a fine way to validate a reconstruction about early childhood is to find that theme dominating the transference. And that was the case with Lisa and me. The unremitting theme for years was her expectation that I would not listen because I considered her crazy. Examples: For years, she was astonished whenever I remembered a detail she had mentioned in the past, for she could not believe either that I listened or that, should I listen, I would concentrate or, should I listen and concentrate, that I would care enough to remember.

With all patients, whenever I do not hear a word, I ask them to repeat (the first time or two explaining that I shall always do this when unable to hear). For years she took my asking for a repeat to be, rather, a condemnation.

The same was true for interpretations. I quickly learned to give them with the lightest touch, for any that bit deeper were also accusations, at bottom "You're crazy. What do you know? *I* shall tell you what is your truth and shall ignore your version." And for years, the most benign response she had, when all was well between us and I was accurate, was, "Yes, but . . . "

For years she insisted she worked with me in spite of my being an analyst. Her fear was that my interpretations would simply be the rote remarks all analysts make, emerging from theory and commitment to one's training, not from understanding one's patient. For this reason, it was almost impossible to use her dreams, for dreams epitomized, more than any other element of technique, her belief that analysts would not listen to their patients' subjectivity but only—like her mother—to what interested or preoccupied *them*.

So, for the first years, she gave me almost nothing. (Fortunately, what little she gave was enough, but sometimes she cut close to the bone. What preserved me was that in doing so she was being true to herself at rock-bottom, however willing she was to bear my becoming hopeless rather than try, with falseness, to be a good patient.) She also tried to do to me what she reported doing successfully to lovers. In revenge for feeling driven crazy by our failure to listen truly, she tried to drive us crazy: "To not tell you is to do to you what they do to me." It was only when I gradually absorbed this insight that I could let her know what she was doing, with the result, of course, that it died away, to be revived only in moments of despair.

You can imagine, then, how intense was Lisa's struggle between not changing—staying forever with mother—and moving on in life. *Every* improvement, *every* insight, *every* release of the neurosis for years was followed the next day by a rivet of anxiety driven down the pole of her body.

This "negative therapeutic reaction" took, toward the end, a form comparable to that seen in some manic patients who refuse lithium because it modulates the marvelous part of mania. Lisa saw freedom as a beautiful calmness but feared that, with the "crazy" theme removed, she would lose the high passion—the profound yearning—that made the good moments glorious.

What experience can match the analytic process for seeming to remind patients they are crazy? The fundamental belief in analysis is that we humans are more than our conscious subjectivity, that what we perceive in ourself can be contradicted by what lies below. The analyst is forever skeptical. So, for Lisa, the transference relationship could not have more closely matched the past. (But is that not so in every true analysis?)

REPETITION COMPULSION

Why did she keep up this destructive behavior? I do not follow Freud when he considers activity such as Lisa's to be a repetition compulsion—that is, a biologic imperative, a drive he ultimately named Death Instinct. The repeating is better considered a maneuver, a matter of scripts we must decipher, rather than a mysterious function of cellular chemistry. Scripts as explanations are, however, less romantic than the mythic Thanatos and thus less appealing to the psychoanalytic identity.

Though there are biologic repetition compulsions—for example, various forms of conditioning; inherited and other, induced, brain functions such as drug addiction—Lisa, I think, is different. As I have speculated elsewhere (Stoller 1979), I believe that much of erotic choice has a mental mechanism, undoing, at its core, the effort to change trauma to triumph, to make bearable the unbearable experiences of infancy and childhood and finally—this time, every time—to make them work out well. The success is in such contrast to the original bad experiences that, as in true addiction, one is offered precipitous but fleeting cure at highest intensity. Such relief and pleasure were what Lisa earned at moments from her mother and her lovers. If those moments could extend permanently, who would not swallow the bitterness?[3]

---

3. A second nonbiologic factor in the compulsion to repeat is the uneasy belief that the present situation, because familiar, is better than change—the unknown. A third, close to undoing: if I do the painful thing before someone

CONCLUSIONS

Let me be sure that what I have done here is visible.

1. No jargon, that is, no theory bootlegged in on a "scientific" vocabulary. (The chapter is, however, as you must have noted, all theory.) Instead, I relied on narrative, on subjectivity, on themes, on scripts (characters interpreted as acting from described motives). The argument is laid out in ordinary language. My motive is to reveal, not obscure (as if that is not the wish of us all). You are not forced to judge—without having been either in the room with us or a witness to Lisa's childhood—the presence, degree, or mix of such fine-sounding but to me noncommunicating elements as "quantities of excitation" or "excessive libidinal cathexes." If the bottom line of an etiologic explanation is "self-damaging tendencies masked by a pseudoaggressive facade" or "repressed emotions centered around oral deprivation," then I think we have no explanation. Nor do I trust an argument that completely depends on alleged measurable differences between homosexuals and others, when the "things" to be measured are "narcissism," "cathexis," "orality," and "aggression," with the measurements made not by any usable scale but by rhetoric alone: "deepest" regression, "profound" sense of guilt, "utterly," "excessively," "totally," "completely," "extremely."

2. The fragments torn from the analysis depict events that, like all events, never happened before and never will again. If they had etiologic force for Lisa, they are nonetheless idiosyn-

---

else or fate does it to me, I control it; it cannot catch me unaware and thereby traumatize me. Fourth: pleasure reinforces; it encourages repeating. This is the case for the *physical* sensations of pleasure but also, more complex, for *psychic* satisfaction. The latter can even, because it is built of meaning, make pain a pleasure (for example, with marathon runners, medical students, and masochists; see Freud [1920, pp. 16, 17]). Fifth: the processes we gloss with the term *identification*, the frictionless, built-in mechanisms that capture—forever repeat—aspects of earlier relationships. And in some patients a sixth: the megalomanic ideas that one's suffering is monumental; one's failure beyond prediction, beyond belief; one's masochism unbearable to others; or one's hidden cry for help so piteous that the world will finally hear and apologize. But let us put these aside now.

cratic and, unlike Koch's postulates, have only slight general application. In that way I argue against a common etiologic constellation to account for homosexual behavior or a common clinical picture labeled "homosexuality."

3. I tried to show that Lisa's story comes out of her needs (wishes, desires, drives, conflicts, and so on) played out on two stages: the remembered, reported interpersonal events of the past (history) and the analytic relationship wherein the story is buried in present living (transference).

4. Though dwelling here on Lisa's unreachable mother, I do not believe that that anguish was the only causative factor in her homosexuality. Her relationship with her pre-Oedipal father, her Oedipal father, and mother-and-father-as-a-unit contributed heavily, as did essential reinforcing from siblings.

5. Caution: remember, I reported only Lisa's version. In all analyses, we hear only from the victim. What the baby feels to be highly motivated, consciously willed parental brutality may not be so by anyone else's standards. In that unfinished and vulnerable brain, with its psychic consequences, small motions have great effects. (I believe infants are almost as vulnerable to their environment as the gosling to Lorenz.) Children make the mistake of judging the strength (that is, the motivations) of what their parents do to them by the strength of their response to their parents: "how much more important parents are to children than children to parents" (Simmons 1976, p. 42).

6. I restricted myself to one idea: we do not have a unified theory to explain homosexuality in women. Painful though it is for me to leave out so much, I used observations on only one theme—and sketchy material at that—for the argument. But I hope that, by sticking close to clinical experience, I made Lisa's case sound like those we have for years comfortably thought of as neurotic constructions. You might, then, be interested in the idea that her homosexuality is an erotic neurosis, not, as most analysts believe regarding aberrant erotic practices, a different species of behavior (Mitchell 1981). If so, we have here simply another example of these propositions: first, much of erotism is energized by variations on themes of hostility; second, all erotic behavior is aberrant.

CHAPTER 11
Judging Insight Therapy

When young, I thought inexperience—that is, not knowing what others know—prevented me from understanding how to do insight therapy[1] well and from understanding why it helped; I had no doubt that it did help. Now, thirty-six years later, I still do not know the answers, and though I now have the courage to be conscious of the questions and the knowledge to know how to ask them, I am still terribly unsure of the facts needed for the answers. Yet I practice such psychotherapy, especially that form which is analysis, much better as time passes: now I hear my patients and myself in ways that were impossible before and often can make clear to them and me what we are both saying. I cannot prove that today's patients like my treatment more than those in the past, but I like better their reasons for liking it.

These remarks, typical of the aging therapist, reveal the raw bias at the bottom of the excursions that follow. My point is that reports *about* the effects of insight therapy cannot be believed because reports of the details of what occurred in the treatment are all fictions. Let me expand on this proposition, obvious but unacceptable to most.

Years ago, when youth kept me from daring to believe what I knew, I worked with a colleague, Dr. Robert Geertsma, to prepare an examination that would validly test medical students' ability to evaluate a patient for psychotherapy by making decisions on diagnosis, prognosis, psychodynamics, theory, psychopathology, what was directly observed, what was observed via empathy-intuition, and treatment (Stoller and

---

1. For the purposes of this chapter, insight psychotherapy also covers analytic psychotherapy and psychoanalysis.

Geertsma 1963). That complex evaluation was one of the crucial skills our faculty tried to teach during the year's clerkship these students finished just before taking the exam. The technique we used aimed to avoid a common problem in exams: that factors unrelated to the exam's intent (for example, students' handwriting neatness, spelling, adroitness in essay writing versus multiple-choice performance or in oral versus written exams; multiple examiners; examining by using live patients so that students do not observe the same patient at the same time from the same position in the room) can prejudice the grader. Instead, we found a patient—not an actor—and filmed the actual initial evaluative interview. This meant that everyone taking the exam would see the same patient in the same circumstances.

When the film was ready, it was shown to members of the faculty—twenty-seven professors, all practitioners of psychotherapy—who actually did the teaching (in this way controlling for differences that might show up in established therapists from one geographic area or medical school as compared to another). After seeing the film, the professors were given the preliminary form of the examination—565 items ranging from concrete observations to theoretic conjecture (for example, from "At this point the patient is not elated" to "The patient would benefit from supportive psychotherapy" on to "The need to exhibit herself serves as a denial of infantile castration fears"). Each item was rated from 0—not at all characteristic of this patient—to 5—highly characteristic—with the midpoint indicating that one was not sure how the item applied to the patient. The film, a half-hour in length, was stopped seven times, and the teachers rated the patient on these items at this moment in the interview. Our plan was to discard all items on which the instructors did not agree strongly, the residue being the students' exam. How close each student came to the composite score of the faculty on all the retained items determined the student's grade. We asked the teachers to identify themselves not by name but by years of experience, whether they were psychoanalysts, and so on, and found no group agreement based on such criteria.

We had done a lot of work; we had not set out to fail. But we did fail, for there was only 1 item of the 565 on which 90 percent or more of these professors agreed (on each of the seven trials, they all felt she was not elated), and on 85 percent of the items there was poor agreement.

Such a study confirms what we all have noted in countless private and public discussions of insight therapy—that experts disagree on their interpretations of what is happening at the moment, what has been happening during the course of the therapy, what happened in the patient's life that contributed to the problems, and what should be said and done from moment to moment in such a therapy in order for us to do our best work. They disagree on diagnosis, prognosis, etiology, psychodynamics, what the patient is feeling consciously at any moment, and what can be inferred as to unconscious thoughts and affects. In mentioning these obvious points, I am not arguing that insight therapy does not work but rather that we (in private or public) do not agree about what goes on. So judgments we make are not likely to have a scientific basis. Don't you suspect that we keep inventing new psychotherapies, keep talking about new directions in analysis, because we are aware of this?

The recent excitement over Lacan is another example. What intuition guided him when he decided it was, as a general principle, therapeutic to end hours after different periods of time had passed? What intuition at the moment in a particular hour made him decide it was time to end? What evidence did he present, and his followers after him, that this technique worked for him and—a different question—for them? If it did work, what is the evidence that his effects were not the result of suggestion, his charisma? How does one objectively judge Lacan's decisions? And what about mine, my—at least with analytic patients—metronomic fifty minutes?

What is the definition of a good result, how is it measured, and who is in a position to measure it?

The form of therapy that I now practice almost exclusively is psychoanalysis. When I say "I am a psychoanalyst" or "I practice psychoanalysis," what have I told you? What do you know? Can you picture anything of what goes on in my office or my mind? Can you predict how I will act, including what I shall say at any moment? What are the chances that you, at that moment, would have done what I did?

Suppose I want to report to you what I did; can I? Were any reports ever given that told—precisely, accurately—what happened, not just over the course of the treatment, but at any particular instant? If by some miracle or experiment you could observe me at work, would your report of any particular moment be more accurate than mine?

Once upon a time Franz Alexander received what in those days was a huge grant in order to study the process of psychoanalysis. He gathered together a group of seasoned colleagues who were to review filmed interviews of each hour of an analysis. They had so much to say about the first hour—as many opinions as there were analysts (and far more opinions than that, since each analyst has mixed and layered attitudes about every moment in analysis)—that the project died.

Once upon a time, a sociologist at UCLA, a congenital nonbeliever in psychotherapy, ran a project that, masquerading as a clinic to advise students with problems, really aimed at showing the power of suggestion. The student entered a booth, behind a wall of which sat the therapist, invisible. The student could ask advice about anything, knowing that the answers would be only yes or no. The therapist behind the wall was actually a graduate student who had before him a randomized list of yesses and nos. As you have guessed, the students found the answers wise, correct, and therapeutic.

Dahl (1974) and Gill (1982) have recently advocated a scientific approach to measurement in psychoanalytic practice. They work from typed transcripts of treatment sessions. Having also used transcripts for years, I can vehemently state that the richness and realness of two people in a room together are hardly conveyed on a typed page. For instance, when listening to my tapes once time has passed, I cannot fill in all the silences with a description of what I experienced, much less of what the patient felt and thought. And even if the research effort is strengthened by using audiovisual recordings, we still inevitably run into the impossibilities exemplified in the example of the psychotherapy evaluation exam and the Alexander study.

Freud once remarked on "the intellectual working-over of carefully scrutinized observations." The unending discourses on what Freud really meant and really did are evidence enough that his reports are no more trustworthy than those of the rest of us.

To overcome these problems, teachers of short-term dynamic psychotherapy have videotaped all the treatment sessions of selected patients, with the powerful research bonus that outside observers can also judge what happened. (For reasons of logistics and confidentiality, this can hardly be done with other kinds of psychotherapy, especially analysis.) Though this technique, despite the small number of sessions as compared to an analysis, may be as interminably complex a research method as the failed Alexander project, it hints that our search for a competent research methodology may not be hopeless.

Knowing these grave uncertainties and yet refusing to admit to their consequences in clinical reports has made fools of analysts. Let me here remind you of the rhetorical tricks so ubiquitous in the analytic literature that readers do not even notice what is being done to them and what the readers do to their own capacity to think. Each of the excerpted phrases below was used by its author in referring to psychoanalytic data, but in *none* of these examples did the accompanying text give the data. When these quotes appear in our literature, the reader is asked to believe that the data were there and that he or she would agree that they were observations true enough to support—confirm—the discovery announced in the rest of the sentence and the paragraph, paper, or book that followed. You know that phrases like these appear dozens of times in dozens of papers read at meetings and published each year.

Psychological considerations of a deeper kind justify the assertion that . . .
In individual cases direct observation has also enabled us to show that . . .
Analysis revealed that . . .
Analysis unmistakably showed that . . .
It became evident in analysis that . . .
My experience as a psychoanalyst has convinced me that . . .

There cannot be the faintest doubt that . . .
The psychoanalysis of men and women of all ages, all coun-
tries, and every social class shows that . . .

Here is an exercise in reading the psychoanalytic literature. I
pick a sentence, for generations typical of what we read daily:
"Clinical experience shows, for example, that unusually strong
oral strivings are often found in the children of addicts, alco-
holics, or manic-depressives." "Clinical experience": whose, of
what sort, how described, how checked for accuracy, how
many cases? "Shows": what actually occurs, in the clinical situation, that is condensed in "shows"; what are the processes
in the observer's head while observing, later while remember-
ing, and finally while revealing via report to others? "Unusually": what is the baseline of "usualness"; what is the manner
of measurement that pushes the usual into the range of unusual? "Strong": the same issues as with "unusually." "Oral
strivings": what are oral strivings; describe the scientific
method that detects and then quantifies oral striving; how can
we be sure that a piece of behavior is an oral striving; give
examples of striving that has no oral component; give examples
of nonoral strivings that do not contain oral strivings; differentiate pseudo-oral strivings (oral strivings in someone you admire) from truly oral strivings. "Often": how often is something found before it is often? "Found": by whom; when is a
manifest finding a symbol for, a disguise for, a defense against,
a primary process rendering of a finding, and when is it not
related to the thing for which you say it stands? When is an
interpretation of an observation correct: for you, for your
friends, for enemies?

A colleague at one of our recent meetings stated that he had
successfully treated a psychotic patient "without using parameters" (Eissler's meaning of *parameter* as a deviation from proper
analytic technique). As you sit in the audience and hear that
declaration, what evidence do you have and what evidence do
you need in order to know if the patient was psychotic, had
what kind of psychosis, was successfully treated? What behavior is a parameter, and what is not? Would it not be a parame-

ter never to use parameters? In other words, do you have the faintest idea on what this claim is based?

The question then (certainly for psychoanalysts, probably for most insight therapists) is: do we understand each other? When one of us presents clinical material, the discussion by our colleagues is as variable as responses to a Rorschach card. We do not agree on the definitions of key words. We cannot agree on what is a psychoanalysis. Why are we not embarrassed? Why are we not more modest? Why do we not publish the evidence for the failure of the old ways of treating patients with psychotherapy as we search for the new psychotherapies?

Perhaps by again using myself for the example, I can defend these contentions. Despite deep uneasiness about *research* on psychotherapy—uneasiness about experts' declarations of how it should be practiced and about the results of different practices—I note at this point that psychotherapy, mostly in that form called psychoanalysis, is essentially the only clinical work I have done in over thirty years. I practice it not because it is personally congenial or because it is an unrivaled technique for studying psychologic development, function, and pathology— these alone would not be ethical reasons for treating patients— but because it works. "It works"—short, simple words that, were this a research report, would require precise description of the "it" and precise demonstration, beyond rhetoric or other coercion, that it works.

Note again that in no way have I claimed that these therapies do not work; my point has been only that we can never know, from anyone's report, that they do work, what he or she did, or why they work. Even when we supervise colleagues' efforts and, as the months pass, they get to know us and accept the clinical vignettes and clarifications that illustrate our technique, who can be sure if our reports, though convincing, tell what happened?

Skepticism such as mine is, at bottom, more optimistic than the avowed optimism created by all the favorable reports on and new directions in psychotherapy/analysis that have emerged since Freud began the process (and note, by recalling "Analysis Terminable and Interminable" [1973], the price in despair he paid by the end for his years, especially the first decades, of promises of success). Are not the writers of these reports trying to talk themselves out of their uncertainty? And does not the way they use their words to construct their sentences—as in the examples above—show their subliminal awareness that they are fooling themselves? (Rangell [1974] calls this process "compromise of integrity.") For when we really value something—know that its fundamental substance is worthy—we are not frightened of its weaknesses or incompleteness and do not hide our doubts in defensive enthusiasms.

Why say this out loud? It is hard enough to practice our art without being told that its rules are not backed by acceptable evidence. Are we not uncertain enough of our skill, and if we carry in us this burden of skepticism, will we not be even less convincing with our patients? Why not leave well enough alone?

Because our "well enough" is not good enough. We would do better—though it will be painful at first—to admit our problems clearly rather than avoid them diffusely. Perhaps, once that admission is out, you will find the same pleasure and relief that should always come when we recognize the scope of our ignorance. It is worth trying. Maybe informed ignorance can be the latest new direction in the insight therapies.

CHAPTER 12

Psychiatry's Mind-Brain Dialectic, or The Mona Lisa Has No Eyebrows

Since psychoanalysis is my home, I feel free not to treat it politely. It needs constant upkeep and can always use renewal. On the other hand, inseparable from the weaknesses on which I have concentrated—most of all the problem for researchers that our observations, the fundament of analysis, cannot be validated—is our great innovation. We study the mind, that is, people, at depths and from perspectives other disciplines ignore. These days, with analysis so little admired, our contribution has been submerged. So let me now lay out this reminder to those who would discard the analyst's clinical strength.

We psychiatrists pay a high and unacknowledged price these days for our great advances: more and more, we ignore the clinical skills that detect, at all levels of awareness, what another person feels. The shift is clearly marked in our practice, research, teaching, literature, and ideal for professional identity: brain replaces mind, miraculously erasing the great philosophic problem.

The reasons for this swing of the pendulum ("dialectic" is a more accurate metaphor—we do progress—but you cannot shove a dialectic) are not mysterious. First, the empathy/insight therapies, pride of American psychiatrists in the 1950s, produced a literature so dense with explanations that most of us finally reacted against systems that explained everything but did not often produce the expected results. Second, as we struggled with these realities, other techniques appeared that, whatever their indifference to insight or character change, could move behavior and reduce or eliminate painful syndromes. These treatments, especially the pharmacologic and behavioristic ones, demand no high interpersonal awareness in us (though they may work better when the doctor-patient relationship is good).

So, except in certain enclaves such as analytic practice, the clinician is out of date whose touch has the daintiness of a safecracker's fingers. Sensitivity to proper drug levels—no small art—has pushed aside sensitivity to emotional nuances. As psychiatry has turned back to the rest of medicine—has finally been equipped to turn back—we may believe that we need be no more receptive than is a good internist or pediatrician. And in many situations, that is correct; even a psychiatrist with a tin ear, helped by the recent discoveries, can sometimes assuage, sometimes remit, and sometimes cure mental illnesses. But without slowing this progress, can we not promote high clinical sensitivity? An awful suspicion: many psychiatrists cannot decipher the subtle, pervasive, nonverbal communications that are the way humans express their interior. These colleagues were not trained to do so, were not in their training exposed to teachers who could, and do not feel that doing so is important. They don't know what they are missing. Are such skills too nonscientific, too nonmedical, too removed from brains or synapses or molecules or reflexes or cognitive dissonances or contiguous associations or evoked responses; even grimmer, are they statistically unmanageable?

Let us imagine that we are with a patient who we sense is sad. You cannot deny that there are circumstances when the patient's welfare and what we do next depend on our distinguishing whether he is sad, very sad, regretfully sad, agonizingly sad, tragically sad, deeply sad, sad/dreary, sad/dull, sad/troubled, sad/strong, bitter/sad, bittersweet/sad, sad/wretched, sad/rueful, genuinely sad, exhibiting sadness for masochistic effect, sad as the character structure remnant of a way of manipulating mother, glad to be sad, sad without grief, inexplicably sad, bravely sad, shallowly sad, noisily sad, gravely sad, choked-up sad, tearfully sad, lachrymosely sad, whiningly sad, voluptuously sad, sad after a heterosexual loss, sad after a heterosexual loss mitigated by unconscious homosexual relief, sad for a moment, sad for two days, sad/anxious, sad/guilty, sad-as-the-mood-to-be-in-that-always-leads-to-erotic-excitement, sad as a transference reaction, sad with a sad smile, sad yet amused, sad from an old memory, sad from a trashy song, elegiac, nostalgic, sober, pitiful, miserable, bathetic, pathetic, glum, brokenhearted, forlorn, desolated, lugubrious, dolorous, woeful, despairing, dampened, crestfallen, blue, melancholic, gloomy, depressed rather than sad. If you were the patient— even if a back-ward schizophrenic—wouldn't you hope your doctor could tell the difference?

Remember Clever Hans, the wonderful horse that seemed able to read, spell, and do arithmetic? It turned out, you recall, that its responses were determined by cues clear enough to the animal but subliminal for humans around him. Surely our performance in the clinic (or in personal relationships) should be no less fine-tuned than a horse's, but can our registering of the subliminal be brought to consciousness, become reliable, be taught? What a shame if we did all that work to create, test, and implement our new diagnostic system—*DSM-III*—and then its users were not competent to observe and weigh the signs and symptoms that are the basis of our classification. *DSM-III* is the product of a great effort to improve, from the clinical side, research on etiology and treatment. Perhaps we do not need much skill to diagnose the grosser schizophrenias or affective disorders, but are not our arguments over "borderline" or "narcissistic personality" built from interpretations of observations? And how much do our labors in the diagnostic swamps known as "the neuroses" and "the character disorders" depend on each psychiatrist's sense of the clinical moment? Another example. Your experience is like mine: we judge prognosis—each of the prognoses that, in algebraic sum, are *the* prognosis—not on the diagnosis but on subtleties, resonances set up in us by the patient, often quite independent of the diagnosis.

Let me give you a vignette, typical, in illustrating empathy, of the daily experience of any analyst or other dynamic therapist, to remind you that awareness of our patients' feelings improves our work. This account is taken from a treatment session that began minutes after the last paragraph was written.

The patient, a young man, exhibits, among other severe erotic disorders, pedophilia. I am trying to invent a treatment for him because he is pretty hopeless after repeated failed insight and noninsight individual and group therapies and several bouts of behavior therapy. He is, by nature and circumstances, not (yet?) suitable for analysis. He had seen me months ago for a few weeks but had left because I told him I had never treated a man like him before, could neither get him better quickly nor even promise ever to do so, had little understanding beyond the surfaces of his illness, and was treating him partly for my effort to understand erotic behavior, though the primary, ever-present motive would be his treatment. He was back because another course of treatment elsewhere had failed. He was desperate. He feared he was losing the battle, fought with the aid of pornography, against using real children and gave me another try because, he said, he had no place better left to go.

The invention is this. He is to bring in his favored pornography, pictures of more or less pubescent boys or girls, and together we shall look at the photographs he finds the most exciting. In the first session, I had him tell me what he saw and then do it again, this time attending to every detail—background and foreground, obvious and subtle—with the idea that we would go from the surface, the manifest images, to the scripts he brought to the pictures. This review might then lead to our finding subliminal scripts that were nonetheless necessary for the aesthetic appreciation. In time, we might move, via his associations, to unconscious scripts and memories that would help explain why these scripts—conscious, preconscious, and unconscious—were created. (The royal road to unconscious processes via dreams is full of potholes, detours, faulty directional signs, crazy drivers, and soft spots where unwary travelers sink without a trace. Daydreams, such as pornography, are a less romantic route with less psychedelic views, but you'd be surprised how effectively they can get you there.)

The tactic had some effect. He came in next time saying that he had been upset—depressed, mostly—to have described so accurately (the photographs do not encourage vagueness) to another person the terrible pleasures destroying him. In that first session, he had pointed to the predominant theme in his excitement—that the children are being humiliated. The photograph we had spent the most time on showed a crouching prepubescent boy, nude, urinating with one leg in the air, as a dog would. Around his neck was a collar to which was attached a leash, held by a man visible only from the thighs down. The boy had (to me) a tormented smile.

In earlier years, the patient had seen therapists with psychodynamic interests (not analysts), and so, during our first attempt months before, he told me what he had told them: his uncle had made him masturbate the older man, first when the boy was five or six and then when he was pubescent. (That sort of incest is often suffered by pedophiles. Abused children become child abusers, as we also know about battering, the nonerotic form of incest.) So he already knew, before we began looking at the pictures, that humiliation was in his erotic core. And now, having to lay out for another person his degrading desires, he was again, though this time not so pleasurably, humiliated. Nonetheless, he felt better feeling worse: at least treatment had touched him a bit. (Humiliation will be a big part of the transference.)

We continued our search for fantasies in the second hour, and I, encouraged, enthusiastically went for more details. The enthusiasm undid him. As the hour progressed, he responded to my enjoyment by feeling used. But I was too busy to realize that. (As I learned in the next hour, he did not believe I could enjoy poking around for etiology and theory so much and still be focused primarily on the treatment, a reasonable though incorrect judgment.)

I begin the next hour like the last, by returning him to the photographs and, as interested as ever, ask my questions. He looks unchanged as he sits in the chair, and the voice I experience sounds no different from his of other days. Yet I start to be irritated. We are still dealing with the photographs, but I now listen to my insides and know I am angry at him "for no reason." In an instant, I scan the past few minutes—make them more conscious—and so sense that his mood does not match mine; he is a bit distant. "Distant," I now perceive, had led me subliminally to slip, faster than time, from being uneasy, to troubled, to tense, to irritated. (Later I will tell him accurately that right then—though I was still not consciously aware of it—he had been "a big sullen bear." But no one reviewing the tape could detect any of this; it is not there in the words, the voices, or the silences.) Now I know that the irritation can help us. It is my resonance with him.

I tell myself, "He is angry; I don't know why; I know he is because I know now that *my* anger is not really mine." I must shift from enthusiasm-inexplicably-turned-to-anger to a new mode: sensitivity to why he is angry. So I ask him if he is angry. "Yes." I suggest that he put the pictures down for now, saying that nothing is as important as our dealing with the anger. (Mine, of course, is gone the moment I get to work on the problem.) He talks of his anger that fate has cursed him with erotic needs that are destroying him and anger that, though he understands the problems, the treatment does not help and may never. I tell him I believe he is angry at *me*, not only at fate or the treatment.

His insides loosen; he expresses several angers he feels toward me. Now I am relieved, interested, lively, in touch with him and myself, curious, hopeful. Also calmer: the emergency has been dealt with. He will not walk out as I feared he would when the silent anger was the most intense.

As he begins to talk now of being interested in our experiment, I feel—only a hunch—that he wants to make sense of his behavior, to learn why, not just to be done with it. So I ask him to tell me again about his uncle.

Pt: He'd tell me not to tell my aunt. I told my parents about it. I remember their reaction was, "If it happens again, tell your aunt," which he told me not to do. I loved him. So I didn't tell anyone else. But I did tell my parents. My parents never gave me any help when I started my collection of pornography at the age of fifteen or sixteen. They never even said, "Why are you reading books of little children instead of books of women?" which would be more normal at that age.

S: How did you feel, that they didn't——

Pt: Hurt. I remember thinking when I was five years old and told my parents about it that it wasn't right that they didn't want to talk to my uncle. I remember that very clearly and of course now there's a lot of anger about that, a lot of anger [but not in his voice and demeanor at this moment] that they didn't try to help me. When I was fifteen years old, I went on my own to a therapist to the Free Clinic. On my own. I got on my bike, went to the Free Clinic and said, "I never even had sex with a woman."

S: *They* never thought of sending you.

Pt: Let me finish. That's the whole thing. You're right. That's the whole thing: they would never think of it. I went on my own and I said to the lady at the Free Clinic, "Something is wrong with me. I like boys." Fifteen years old! "I like men and I don't like women." I went twice, and then I stopped going. Then I got arrested at fifteen for masturbating in a park. What I was actually doing was engaging in a homosexual thing with another man. I was real glad they arrested me because finally—"Okay. Fine. My parents have to deal with it now." I was happy [after the arrest]. I wasn't scared. [But] my parents wouldn't help me. "I'm mixed up; I need help." I even told the officers that arrested me that I had gone for therapy, that I needed help.

And so on.

You can see that he is sure his parents throughout his life abused him by choosing not to help him when they could have. As he speaks the words transcribed above, I *feel* a sense of poignancy and I *think* that, were he fully conscious, he would be—to say the least—angry at them. My *feeling* and my *thinking* become one, and I then interpret to him that I now understand his anger toward me earlier in the hour. (I shall find another time for telling him that though he could be angry with me he could not be with them.) I remind him of the start of this hour, when he felt I was not interested in his treatment—in him—but only in my studies and then ask if that attitude would not make me similar to his parents: I had abused him. "Of course!" he says. And now the hour has been emptied of his hopeless, scarcely admitted rage and my resonating to it. He relaxes, softens, eyes moist. He has had a glimpse of the use of insight and is no longer about to abandon the treatment. He knows he is ready. The next hour is packed with feelings, facts, insights, revelations.

There is no magic in intuition or in the process of making it conscious. Something of the sort occurred in all of us when, with experience, we transformed what had been senseless noises in the stethoscope into three-dimensional awareness of the state of the heart. When I get to know him better, just as when all of us get to know someone, subliminal vibration, in that form of identification called empathy, will have moved to full consciousness. Why not embrace this old-fashioned, powerful, comfortable art as psychiatry lays down sound scientific foundations?

Why not? Because, despite my sensible argument so far in its favor, empathy is not reliable. Anecdotes that report its successes are not data others can examine but are simply the author's version of a therapeutic event (as is mine above). As I was complaining in the last chapter, who is the final arbiter we can trust to tell us which version of an observation on behavior is correct? In reading a report, can you know the author's clinical ability? Do we have techniques to measure who is empathic and who is not, whose interpretation of a patient's behavior is accurate and whose not?

With my anecdote, you have only the words printed above. You cannot know if, as I suppose is true of some case reports, its essence is manufactured. And if my version of the events is pretty accurate, we still cannot say that interpretations that warm both of us will bring the patient what he wants. And surely we do not know, for all the earlier treatment failures, that some other treatment than mine may not work. We might, for instance, give him depo-Provera to cancel his androgens and stop making self-control via mind (insight-free will-conscious responsibility) a higher moral state than other-administered control via brain (hormones or conditioned reflexes): the theologic issue at the heart of Burgess's *A Clockwork Orange*. Will we ever outgrow the prejudices MacIver and Redlich (1959) described that rule A-P (analytic and psychologic orientation) versus D-O (direct and organic orientation) patterns of psychiatric practice?

My argument (that is, my bias) runs like this so far: (1) psychiatry is wrong to depreciate empathy, for there are treatment and research problems that can be resolved only if we can

detect what the patient feels; (2) but even if empathy sometimes is effective, it is, to date, unreliable, unmeasurable, and
unteachable.

So that is the problem. A hint at the solution is in Clever
Hans: within the limits of our personalities—some of us are
more observant than others, more observant with some people
than others, and more observant at some moments than at
others—we can be taught to observe better, just as we were
taught how better to do a physical examination, to become so
skilled that we finally could hear and feel beyond what we
thought we heard and felt. This chapter is the result of my
having refereed a paper (Nakdimen 1984) on the pseudocom-
munications to which we respond in others' surface anatomy—
physiognomy, bearing, secondary sex characteristics, and so
on. The paper points out that part of the effect we get from the
Mona Lisa comes from her eyebrows. The *Mona Lisa* has no
eyebrows! Who'd have thought it! (Who notices?)

The author discusses subliminal clues in nonpathologic sexuality, a pretty esoteric concern to psychiatrists who are beginning, via truly scientific methods, to understand the devastat-
ing mental illnesses. Even more precious, his subject is erotic
attractiveness. Being interested in how sex works, I am perhaps unduly drawn to his findings, but I find inherent in his
report the larger perspective on which my essay dwells: we do
better as our clinical vision grows keener. We need, then, a
naturalistic science of observation, so that, if we attend closely,
we shall observe more, and more accurately.

Fortunately, we already have that science—ethology; and it
does not study only nonhumans. From Darwin to Birdwhistell
to Lorenz and Eibl-Eibesfeldt to Ekman and McGuire and other
distinguished workers in addition, its methods of research and
products of that research lie close at hand for us clinicians to
pick up and use. It can make naturalists of clinicians and scientists of naturalists.

Research in human ethology (including infant observation)
has grown greatly in the last twenty years. Into one corner of
it—we are not here concerned with ethology's larger and more
controversial interest in the origins and mechanisms of behav-

ior—fits the work on signals, subliminal or fully attended. It is no huge task for psychiatry to acknowledge the many pieces available for a science of human observation and to ready them for our use. (We shall need a textbook.) Then this new/old basic skill can be in the curriculum of medical students, psychiatric residents, and psychoanalytic candidates and a part of each psychiatrist's work.

Our technology and our science are not so advanced that we can throw away art, and our art is not so delicate that it would collapse from a whiff of science. Maybe now that psychiatric research has confirmed its strength, we need not fear that the impreciseness and unreliability of empathy will harm our reputation and corrupt our professional identity. The change would be exhilarating.

REFERENCES

Adams, R. M. 1977. *Bad Mouth.* Berkeley: University of California Press.

Allen, C. 1969. *A Textbook of Psychosexual Disorders.* 2d ed. London: Oxford University Press.

Bak, R. C. 1974. Distortions of the Concept of Fetishism. *Psychoanal. Study Child* 29:191–214.

Balint, M. 1960. A Contribution on Fetishism. *Internat. J. Psycho-anal.* 16:481–82.

Bandura, A. 1969. *Principles of Behavior Modification.* New York: Holt, Rinehart & Winston.

Barahal, H. S. 1953. Female Transvestism and Homosexuality. *Psychiat. Quart.* 27:390–438.

Basch, M. F. 1976. The Concept of Affect: A Re-examination. *JAPA* 24:759–77.

Bell, A. P., and M. S. Weinberg. 1978. *Homosexualities: A Study of Diversity among Men and Women.* New York: Simon & Schuster.

Benjamin, H. 1966. *The Transsexual Phenomenon.* New York: Julian Press.

Buruma, Ian. 1984. *Behind the Mask.* New York: Pantheon.

Collingwood, R. G. 1958. *The Principles of Art.* London: Oxford University Press.

Dahl, H. 1974. The Measurement of Meaning in Psychoanalysis by Computer Analysis of Verbal Context. *JAPA* 22:37–57.

Devereux, G. 1967. *From Anxiety to Method in the Behavioral Sciences.* The Hague and Paris: Mouton.

Dooley, L. 1934. A Note on Humor. *Psychoanal. Rev.* 21:49–58.

Ellis, H. 1942. *Studies in the Psychology of Sex.* New York: Modern Library.

Feldman, M. P., and N. J. MacCulloch. 1971. *Homosexual Behavior: Theory and Assessment.* Oxford: Pergamon.

Fenichel, O. 1930. The Psychology of Transvestitism. *Internat. J. Psycho-anal.* 11:211–27.

219

———. 1945. *The Psychoanalytic Theory of Neurosis.* New York: W. W. Norton.

Freud, A. 1965. *Normality and Pathology in Childhood.* New York: International Universities Press.

Freud, S. (1905) 1953. *Three Essays on the Theory of Sexuality. Standard Edition* (hereafter *S.E.*) 7:130–243. London: Hogarth.

———. (1919) 1955. A Child Is Being Beaten. *S.E.* 17:179–204. London: Hogarth.

———. (1920) 1955. Beyond the Pleasure Principle. *S.E.* 18:7–64. London: Hogarth.

———. (1920) 1955. The Psychogenesis of a Case of Homosexuality in a Woman. *S.E.* 18: 147–72. London: Hogarth.

———. (1905) 1960. *Jokes and Their Relation to the Unconscious. S.E.* 8:9–238. London: Hogarth.

———. (1932) 1964. The Acquisition and Control of Fire. *S.E.* 22:187–93. London: Hogarth.

———. (1937) 1964. Analysis Terminable and Interminable. *S.E.* 23:216–53. London: Hogarth.

Gagnon, J. H., and W. Simon. *Sexual Conduct.* Chicago: Aldine.

Gagnon, J. 1981. Book Review. *New York Times Book Review*, 12 December pp. 10, 37.

Genet, J., 1964. *The Thief's Journal.* New York: Grove Press.

Gill, M. M., and I. Z. Hoffman. 1982. *Analysis of Transference.* Vol. 2. Psychol. Issues 54.

Gillespie, W. H. 1956. The General Theory of Sexual Perversion. *Internat. J. Psycho-anal.* 37:396–403.

Gombrich, E. H. 1956. *The Story of Art.* New York: Phaidon.

Greenacre, P. 1953. Certain Relationships between Fetishism and Faulty Development of the Body Image. *Psychoanal. Study Child* 8:79–98.

———. 1960. Further Notes on Fetishism. *Psychoanal. Study Child* 15:191–207.

Grotjahn, M. 1958. *Beyond Laughter.* New York: McGraw Hill.

Grover, S. 1980. The Bodice Busters. *Wall Street Journal*, 5 November, pp. 1, 14.

Gutheil, E. 1930. Analysis of a Case of Transvestitism. In W. Stekel, *Sexual Aberrations.* New York: Liverwright.

Heiman, J. R. 1980. Female Sexual Response Patterns. *Arch. Gen. Psychiat.* 37:1311–16.

Herdt, G. H. 1981a. *Guardians of the Flutes.* New York: McGraw Hill.

———. 1981b. Semen Depletion and the Sense of Maleness. *Ethnopsychiatrica* 3:79–116.

————. Ed., *Ritualized Homosexuality in Melanesia.* Berkeley and Los Angeles: University of California Press.

Home, H. J. 1966. The Concept of Mind. *Internat. J. Psycho-anal.* 47:42–49.

Khan, M. M. R. 1979. *Alienation in Perversions.* London: Hogarth.

Kohut, H. 1957. Observations on the Psychological Function of Music. *JAPA* 5:389–401.

Krafft-Ebing, R. v. (1906) 1932. *Psychopathia Sexualis.* Brooklyn: Physicians & Surgeons Book Co.

Kris, E. 1952. *Psychoanalytic Explorations in Art.* New York: International Universities Press.

Kubie, L. S. 1978. The Drive to Become Both Sexes. In H. J. Schlesinger, ed., *Symbol and Neurosis. Psychol. Issues,* 44.

La Barre, W. 1980. *Culture in Context.* Durham: Duke University Press.

Lichtenstein, H. 1961. Identity and Sexuality. *JAPA* 9:179–260.

Lukianowicz, N. 1959. Survey of Various Aspects of Transvestism in the Light of Our Present Knowledge. *JNMD* 128:36–64.

MacIver, J., and F. C. Redlich. 1959. Patterns of Psychiatric Practice. *Amer. J. Psychiat.* 115:692–97.

Marks, I. M., S. Rachman, and M. G. Gelder. 1965. Methods for Assessment of Aversion Treatment in Fetishism and Masochism. *Behav. Res. Ther.* 3:253–58.

Marmor, J. 1980. Ed., *Homosexual Behavior.* New York: Basic Books.

McGuire, R. J., J. M. Carlisle, and B. C. Young. 1965. Sexual Deviations as Conditioned Behavior: A Hypothesis. *Behav. Res. Ther.* 2:185–90.

Mitchell, S. A. 1981. The Psychoanalytic Treatment of Homosexuality: Some Technical Considerations. *Internat. Rev. Psycho-anal.* 8:63–80.

Money, J., and A. A. Ehrhardt. 1972. *Man & Woman Boy & Girl.* Baltimore: Johns Hopkins University Press.

Nakdimen, K. A. 1984. The Physiognomic Basis of Sexual Stereotyping. *Amer. J. Psychiat.* 141:499–503.

Nin, A. 1966. *The Diary of Anaïs Nin.* Vol. 1. New York: Swallow Press.

Ovesey, L. 1969. *Homosexuality and Pseudohomosexuality.* New York: Science House.

Prince, V., and P. M. Bentler. 1972. Survey of 504 Cases of Transvestism. *Psychol. Reports* 31:903–17.

Rachman, S. 1966. Sexual Fetishism: An Experimental Analogue. *Psychol. Rec.* 16:293–98.

Rangell, L. 1974. A Psychoanalytic Perspective Leading Currently to the Syndrome of the Compromise of Integrity. *Internat. J. Psychoanal.* 55:3–12.

Read, K. E. 1965. *The High Valley.* London: Allen & Unwin.

Redmount. R. S. 1953. A Case of a Female Transvestite with Marital and Criminal Complications. *J. Clin. and Exper. Psychopath.* 14:95–111.

Reinisch, J. M. 1981. Prenatal Exposure to Synthetic Progestins Increase Potential for Aggression in Humans. *Science* 211:1171–73.

Rekers, G. A. 1978. Sexual Problems: Behavior Modification. In B. B. Wolman, J. Egan, and A. O. Ross, eds., *Handbook of Treatment of Mental Disorders in Childhood and Adolescence.* Englewood Cliffs, N.J.: Prentice-Hall.

Rose, G. J. 1980. Some Aspects of Aesthetics in the Light of the Rapprochement Subphase. In R. F. Lax, S. Bach, and J. A. Burland, eds., *Rapprochement.* New York: Jason Aronson.

Rubinstein. L. H. 1964. The Role of Identification in Homosexuality and Transvestism in Men and Women. In I. Rosen, ed., *The Pathology and Treatment of Sexual Deviation.* London and New York: Oxford University Press.

Sante, L. 1985. Scientist of the Fantastic. *New York Review of Books,* 31 January, pp. 14–17.

Simmons, C. 1976. *Wrinkles.* New York: Farrar, Straus & Giroux.

Simon, W., and J. H. Gagnon. 1984. Sexual Scripts. *Society* 22:53–60.

Socarides, C. W. 1978. *Homosexuality.* New York: Jason Aronson.

Sperling, M. 1963. Fetishism in Children. *Psychoanal. Quart.* 32:374–92.

Spiegel, N. 1967. An Infantile Fetish and Its Persistence into Young Womanhood. *Psychoanal. Study Child* 22:402–25.

Stoller, R. J. 1968. *Sex and Gender.* Vol. I. New York: Science House.

———. 1973. *Splitting.* New York: Quadrangle.

———. 1975a. *Perversion.* New York: Pantheon.

———. 1975b. *Sex and Gender.* Vol. 2. London: Hogarth.

———. 1979. *Sexual Excitement.* New York: Pantheon.

Stoller, R. J., and R. H. Geertsma. 1963. The Consistency of Psychiatrists' Clinical Judgments. *JNMD* 137:58–66.

Storms, M. D. 1981. A Theory of Erotic Orientation Development. *Psychol. Rev.* 88:340–53.

Supplement. Female Psychology. 1976. *JAPA* 24.

Symons, D. 1980. Précis of the Evolution of Human Sexuality. *Behav. and Brain Sci.* 3:171–214.

The TV Pornography Boom. 1981. *New York Times Magazine,* 13 September.

Van Baal, J. 1966. *Dema.* The Hague: Martinous Nijhoff.

———. 1984. The Dialectics of Sex in Marind-anim Culture. In G. H. Herdt, ed., *Ritualized Homosexuality in Melanesia.* Berkeley and Los Angeles: University of California Press.

Webster's Third New International Dictionary. 1961. Springfield, Mass.: G. & C. Merriam.

Winnicott, D. W. 1953. Transitional Objects and Transitional Phenomena. *Internat. J. Psycho-anal.* 34:89–95.

Zavitzianos, G. 1972. Homeovestism: Perverse Form of Behaviour Involving Wearing Clothes of the Same Sex. *Internat. J. Psycho-anal.* 53:471–77.

Zuger, B. 1980. Homosexuality and Parental Guilt. *Brit. J. Psychiat.* 137:55–57.

INDEX